COOKING TIME TABLES

ROASTING TIME FOR

Kind	Oven Temp.	Minutes Per Lb.	Kind	Oven Temp.	Per Lb.
Beef, Roast	300 F		Capon	325 F	22–30
Rare		16–20	Chicken	300 F	30–45
Medium		22–25	Duck, domestic	325 F	20–30
Well Done		27–30	Duck, wild	325 F	25–35
Pork (fresh)	350 F		Duck, wild, rare	325 F	10–12
Loin		30–35	Goose	350 F	20–25
Shoulder		30–35	Goose, wild	350 F	15–24
Ham		30–35	Guinea hen	325 F	18–25
Ham (cured)	300 F		Partridge	350 F	25–35 total
10 to 12 lbs.		25–30	Pheasant	350 F	15–20
Half ham		22–28	Rabbit	300 F	25–35
Lamb	300 F	30–35	Squab	325 F	40–55 total
Veal	300 F	25–35	Turkey	300 F	20–30

PRESSURE COOKING TIMES

Vegetables

Kind	Amount of Water	Cooking Time Minutes	Kind	Amount of Water	Cooking Time Minutes
Artichokes	½ cup	10	Corn on the cob	½ cup	3–5
Asparagus	½ cup	1–2	Onions, whole med.	½ cup	5–7
Beans, Wax, Green	½ cup	3–4	Peas	½ cup	1–2
Beans, Lima	½ cup	2–3	Potatoes, small, whole		
Beets, whole	½ cup	10–18	large, halved	½ cup	10
Broccoli	½ cup	2–3	baking, large, whole	½ cup	15
Brussels Sprouts	½ cup	3	Sweet Potatoes, Balls	½ cup	8
			Sweet Potatoes, whole	½ cup	10
Cabbage, quartered	½ cup	3–4	Spinach, other greens	½ cup	1
Carrots, sliced	½ cup	3	Hubbard Squash, cut	½ cup	10–12
whole	½ cup	4–8	Summer Squash, halved	½ cup	8–10
Cauliflower, Flowerettes,	½ cup	2	Tomatoes	½ cup	1
whole	½ cup	5	Turnips, cubed	½ cup	3–5
Celery	½ cup	2–3	halved	½ cup	8–12

Fruits

	Fresh				Dried	
Kind	Amount of Water	Cooking Time Minutes		Kind	Amount of Water	Cooking Time Minutes
Apples	½ cup *	1		Apples	2 cups	3–5
Apple Sauce	½ cup	1		Apricots	1 cup	3–5
Apricots	1 cup	0		Figs	2 cups	15
Peaches	½ cup *	5		Peaches	2 cups	3–5
Pears	½ cup *	5		Pears	1 cup	3–5
Plums	2 cups	0		Prunes	2 cups	3–5
				Raisins	1 cup	3–5

* For 6-qt. Cooker use 1 cup   ** Per lb. of fruit

The NEW CRUISING COOKBOOK

Russell K. Jones & C. McKim Norton

The NEW CRUISING COOKBOOK

Easy-to-cook meals on a two-burner stove

W · W · NORTON & COMPANY · INC · *New York*

SBN 393 03151 9

Library of Congress Catalog Card No. 60-8950

PRINTED IN THE UNITED STATES OF AMERICA
FOR THE PUBLISHERS BY THE VAIL-BALLOU PRESS.

7 8 9

Contents

CONTENTS

Part Two
TWO-BURNER RECIPES

Foreword

ONE OF US is a cook who was called upon to perform at sea. The other is a sailor who, without any cooking training, has spent many hours in the galley. Our aim has been to set down the basic rules and recipes for cooking in small craft, recognizing both the laws of good eating and the conditions and limitations of small-boat living.

This book has not been written without some fairly fierce arguments between us, raised by the requirements of the experienced cook and the sailor's instinctive impatience with the whole art of cooking. The results must speak for themselves, but we believe that while no culinary standards have been lowered, the sailor-cook will find this book thoroughly practical.

We have written in terms that we think the average small-boat sailor can understand. For example, even though ten generations of cookbook authors may turn in their graves, we have used the American word "fry" when the process described step by step in the recipe is clearly to "sauté."

We know that the sailor who cooks on a small boat usually wants to spend a minimum amount of time in the galley. For this reason many complete meals are included which take less than thirty minutes. Most of the recipes call for less than an hour's cooking time from the moment the stove is lit. We have omitted all deep frying because of danger of fire and accident. Baking and roasting recipes are limited because we recognize that many small boats do not carry ovens.

On the other hand, this book is not for those who believe that bad food is a necessary evil on a small boat. The pseudo-rugged life typified by eating cold beans or tuna fish right out of the can is not for us. Our philosophy is maximum comfort within the limits of that essential simplicity without which life on a small boat becomes a round of chores. We have even had the temerity to include a few dishes which take over an hour to prepare for harbor-bound days. Then the galley stove, working away all afternoon on the dinner to come, keeps your boat dry and warm. Time passes quickly for the cook. The praise you receive for your mighty effort makes you realize that cooking is fun as well as part of the day's work.

Finally, we realize that all recipes are subject to the correction of whatever spark of creative cooking genius the reader may have. The best seagoing cook we ever knew, as a matter of fact, couldn't read.

Revised Edition

THANK YOU, dear galley slaves, for your support of this work. You have kept us in light sails. You have written many fine letters. So many brides say they like us, we may sell the boat and move to Salt Lake City. One wife even wrote us we had changed her religious life. Since her husband bought this book, he has cooked Sunday dinner while she goes to church. Alas, we aim to set men free, not to enslave them.

What we have learned in the past decade is now between these covers. Mostly it is to value simplicity at sea. A boat should never be regarded as a house; even a house boat is not a boat house. A boat is a means of transport, not just from one harbor to another, but from one way of life into another. When you enter the galley, leave the kitchen ashore. This book shows you how.

Finally, thanks are due to many people, especially for help in revisions to Ham deFontaine of *Yachting* magazine and to Lee Metcalfe and Mary Ranney of the staff of our publishers. Also a deep bow to our wives for timing, testing and tasting, indexing, proofreading, and washing up the dishes.

RUSSELL K. JONES
C. McKIM NORTON

Manhattan Island

How to Use This Book

ALL RECIPES in this book serve four persons. To serve more, increase the quantities of the ingredients proportionately (except in the cooked hot bread recipes).

Every item of information in the recipes from soup to nuts is listed in alphabetical order in the *General Index* at the back of the book. Consult this index often. It has been prepared with great care and is, we believe, complete in every detail.

The cooking time for each recipe is indicated above the recipe. Cooking time includes the few minutes generally necessary to get pans hot, water boiling, foods cut up, eggs beaten and so forth. If more than a few minutes are needed before cooking can begin, such as time required to soak smoked meats or certain fresh vegetables, or to scrub shellfish, this period is indicated as preparation time and is listed above each recipe in addition to cooking time.

A summary *list of cooking times* and preparation time (if any) of all recipes is given so that the cook can determine easily from the longest dish he has to prepare the minimum time required to produce a given meal.

To keep this cookbook short we have included a number of "omnibus recipes." Crab meat à la king, for example, also applies to a similar dish made with canned clams, lobster, frogs' legs, mussels, oysters, salmon, or tuna. Each of these latter dishes has its separate listing in the index.

The chapters on "The Galley," "Stoves and Fuels," "Fire

in the Galley," "Cooking Gear," "Cleanup Gear," "Table Gear," and "Stowage" contain valuable information for newcomers to the cruising fraternity and possibly some advice of value to the seasoned skipper or sea cook. In general these chapters should be read before you put to sea.

Ideas on "Food Planning" are included and should be consulted before you stock your boat. The "Suggested Menus for a Two Weeks' Coastal Cruise" have been planned with considerable care to provide a balanced diet of high-energy foods as well as interesting food combinations. The suggested "Rough-Weather Menus" are found to be really practical from our actual experience. They are very easy to prepare, and they seem to minimize seasickness. "Food for a Two Weeks' Coastal Cruise" and "Food for an Ocean Race" are included in the chapter on "Food Planning." Use them as they stand or as a check against your own provisioning list. As a further convenience for your food planning, "Check Lists of Basic Provisions, Condiments, Basic Ingredients, Frills and Garnishes" are also included.

For those who lack cooking experience, we have included "Hints and Short Cuts" which will minimize galley chores and help to produce well-cooked meals.

Part One

The GALLEY, GEAR, and SUPPLIES

THE GALLEY
LAYOUT

Our first galley was a three-sided box into which a Primus single-burner kerosene stove was secured. Normally stowed forward of the mast of a 17-foot knockabout, the "galley" came aft at mealtime, usually secured in battens on a cabin transom seat, sometimes in hot weather carried into the cockpit. This device served us very well for cruises lasting two and three weeks. A fixed galley area, however, for which space is almost always found even in the stubbiest tabloid cruiser, is standard practice today.

A galley aft, occupying four to five feet of floor space just forward of the companionway steps, is the usual location in most powerboats and auxiliary sailboats. Advantages of this position are maximum cabin headroom (often under the companion slide), least motion, nearness to the helmsman, coolest location with hatch open, and maximum warming and drying effect with hatch closed, since the cabin draft in most boats is from aft forward. With the galley in this position, the amateur cook keeps in contact with what is going on in the cockpit and is not surprised by unannounced maneuvers such as tacking ship.

On sailboats of 35 feet and over water line, where a party of four is usual, and especially if a paid hand is contemplated, there is much to be said for a galley forward of the main cabin. The off watch can cook and smoke without annoying the helmsman on night runs. The space alongside the cockpit can be devoted more readily to quarter berths. Though subject to more motion, the forward galley is drier in bad weather and need not be too hot if fitted with a skylight and a set of baffle-box ventilators. A paid hand can work there while the afterguard sleeps.

There are cooks who like to be able to sit down while working. A folding seat secured to a bulkhead is good for this purpose; or a drawer can be rigged to pull out as a seat.

"For the reason that galley stoves are liable to promiscuous, unskilled or ignorant operation more than any other piece of boat's gear involving fire risk, it is important that such equipment should be selected and installed with a view to minimizing both the personal and physical hazards." So reads the opening paragraph on galley arrangement of *Fire Protection Standards for Motor Craft*, published by the National Fire Protection Association. Three of the basic recommendations of these standards may be paraphrased in the following words of wisdom: (1) Don't locate stoves in the same compartment with machinery or gasoline tanks. (2) Protect woodwork within one foot of bottom and sides and two feet over top of stove with ⅛ inch asbestos board covered with sheet metal and a dead air space of ¼ inch left between the protecting asbestos and the woodwork. (3) Stoves should be permanently secured in place; portable stoves are not recommended.

If your stove is hung in gimbals, it should run fore and aft so that it may swing to compensate for rolling and heeling. A coal- or wood-burning stove may be set across-ships to gain galley space and to minimize the danger of accident or fire from a carelessly closed oven or firebox door. Plan working space carefully. A rule of thumb is that it should be at least twice the area of your stove top. A shallow Monel or stainless steel tray which fits over all or a part of your working space is most useful, not only while you work below, but also as a tray to serve meals on deck.

REFRIGERATION

The blue-water cruiser may have little use for an icebox except as a locker in which to stow canned or dry goods. Experienced coastwise cruisers in cold-water areas often do without refrigeration, and more and more we agree with the philosophy which rejects the notion that a boat should be a mechanized house afloat. Cruising should be a return to a more independent way of life. The "need" for ice has lost many a fair tide and makes some cruises little more than runs between the standard ports. If you are willing to cool your milk and butter in a mesh bag floating astern and to drink your whiskey without ice, you will find yourself in many more interesting anchorages. Of course, each man must decide where his pleasure lies. All we say is, don't become a slave to your refrigeration. With this introduction, let us admit that we cruise with an icebox—even though it's not always filled with ice.

A top-opening icebox is best. It has two advantages over ones with front-opening doors. It does not waste a boxful of cold air every time the door is opened and, more important, it cannot dump its contents out in a seaway. A well-insulated box of this type can hold ice up to a week. The drainpipe should be fitted with a water seal for the purpose of not losing cold air, and it should drain into a sump tank rather than into the open bilge. A sump tank can either be connected with a pump or can be emptied by merely lifting the tank out of the bilge and dumping the water overboard. A properly installed icebox should have an air space all round it, particularly on the side next to the hull. Iceboxes can be lined with stainless steel, Monel or fiberglas. A rule-of-thumb capacity for iceboxes is 1 to 1½ cubic feet per berth, according to Philip Rhodes.

There are now many boat-size electric refrigerators on

the market. Though they are fairly expensive, ones with a capacity of 2 cubic feet are advertised to make 4 pounds of ice in two hours. Some of these electric refrigerators are portable and can be used ashore and then packed and carried to the boat for cruising. Conversion units for iceboxes are also available, complete with ice-cube trays. These are fitted into your existing icebox. Conversion units and the ready-made refrigerators use as little as 2½ amps. and can operate off both a 110-volt AC current on shore or a 12-volt DC supply on board.

Electric/kerosene convertible refrigerators are also marketed now as well as gas refrigerators, combination refrigerator-freezers, and ice-making units which operate off the main engine.

The literature on all this equipment may be beguiling to you. To us, it looks like a lot of maintenance for small potential gain for the cruising man. For week-end sailors and marine-based craft, however, electric refrigeration may win its way. As for our comments on gas appliances of any kind, see the later section on gas stoves.

GALLEY SINK

The galley sink need not be too large—and seldom is there space enough to overindulge on this point. For the real offshore job, a rather deep sink is preferable. For the ordinary cruising boat a sink 6 to 7 inches deep is adequate and easier to work in. Don't install a check valve in the waste line, because these valves invariably foul up with grease. On smaller boats it is seldom that a sink is high enough to drain overboard. For this reason it is customary to lead them to a sump tank or to have them directly connected overboard through a rotary pump. Neither of these systems appeals to us. If your boat is too small to have the bottom of the sink above the water line, the chances are

your galley is but a short step into the cockpit and a reach
overboard. A dishpan or double bucket made of plastic
makes a safe and satisfactory sink. We cruised for years with
a "disappearing" dishpan sink worked out as follows: at a
convenient height under a drawer top (ours was under the
top the stove was secured to), install a flat pull-out slide
similar to the type found in office desks. Cut a hole in this
slide so that a standard white dishpan can be fitted into it.

A salt-water sink pump is useful, especially since detergents are reasonably effective in salt water. A board which
fits over the top of your sink helps to increase working space.
Sinks should be made of stainless steel, Monel, or fiberglas,
not plastic. Incidentally, one of the easiest ways to ruin a
sink is to make a hole in it when chipping ice with an icepick.

GALLEY LIGHTING

Galley lighting is important and rarely good enough.
Kerosene- and candle-lit galleys are always badly lighted,
since the lights cannot be overhead, where they belong.
Electric lights should illuminate the stove and work areas
without shining in either the cook's or the helmsman's eyes.
Dome lights are the usual solution and can be improved by
shielding. Flashlights held in brackets or ones with magnets
on the handles are available today, but be sure the bulkhead
you tack them on is not near your compass.

WATER SUPPLY

As regards water supply, it is difficult to get too much.
Availability of space within the hull, when the tanks are
placed low in the vessel as they should be, is more often
than not the limiting factor. However, current practice would
indicate that for boats with a 20- to 25-foot water line, the
fresh-water capacity is approximately 10 gallons per berth,

in boats with 25- to 35-foot water line, the capacity is 15 gallons per berth, and for boats from 35- to 45-foot water line, the capacity is a little upwards of 20 gallons per berth.

For coastwise cruising there are real advantages in rigging your water supply so that it runs by gravity flow and does not require a pump in the galley. This means a relatively low spigot with consequent bending every time you use it, but it eliminates the foibles and irritations of small galley pumps. For offshore cruises a gravity flow system is not recommended, since carelessness or the failure of a valve might result in draining your tank.

Water tanks should be made of tin-lined copper or Monel. Galvanized iron tanks corrode. If your tank is corroded or if your boat is equipped with a water tank susceptible to corrosion, Aqua-clear, manufactured by Sudbury Laboratory, South Sudbury, Mass., may be the answer to your problem.

If you are able to work it out for your boat, we recommend two water tanks connected by a pipe with a shutoff valve. This recommendation is not only for safety in case one tank develops a leak, but also for convenience in case you must take on poor-quality water and wish to reserve one tank for drinking purposes. A water-purifying unit (Everpure Purifier) is now marketed which uses chlorine tablets.

Take along at least a few gallons of bottled water as a reserve supply. Bottle it in polyethylene bottles or jugs, or buy Poland Water.

Don't forget to carry a five-gallon can and a funnel reserved for filling water tanks only. You can't count on finding a dock and convenient water hose when taking on water in out-of-the-way places.

STOVES AND FUELS

TYPES OF STOVES AND FUELS

Your choice of a stove should depend on the type of boat you have, the climate you will be sailing in, and the fuel you wish to burn for reasons of safety and availability in your cruising ground. The size of your pocketbook should be but a minor factor. If you can afford a boat at all, you can afford the best stove for her type. The listing of stoves in this section does not pretend to be all-inclusive of every make of stove. It will give you a picture of the types in general use and some specific makes which we know are excellent.

In general, coal- and wood-burning stoves are the choice of those who sail in cold, offshore waters in stable craft which sail on their bottoms. Week-end cruisers, warm-water sailors, and owners of small craft who do most of their sailing between the Fourth of July and Labor Day favor the pressure stove burning alcohol, kerosene, or liquefied petroleum gas with a portable Sterno canned heat kit as an auxiliary or emergency cooking unit.

When it comes to rating stoves by the fuel they burn in order of safety, the fuels should be classified as (1) electricity; (2) coal, coke, or wood; (3) canned heat; (4) alcohol; (5) kerosene; (6) liquefied petroleum gas.

Electricity is as yet impractical for small-craft cooking. Alcohol takes fire more easily than kerosene, is cleaner, and can be extinguished with water. From the personal experience of numerous cruising skippers, a quarter of a gallon of alcohol per person per week is indicated as a minimum allowance of fuel for cooking and washing. For ordinary cruising we recommend a more generous allowance of half a gallon per person per week. Kerosene burns with a hotter flame than alcohol, has a lower fuel consumption rate, is cheaper, and in general has better distribution in both domestic and foreign ports, although some of the yellowish stuff sold as "coal oil" in country stores fouls up your burners in no time. Fire Protection Standards state that *gasoline stoves shall not be used on boats.*

Yachtsmen who sail coastal waters which are dotted with first-rate service ports where high-grade alcohol fuels can be purchased are apt to pay the price and use alcohol. Kerosene is often the choice of the more rugged breed of sailorman who sails (or plans all his life to sail) less frequented waters and likes to economize where he can. Experienced kerosene-users ask for "water-white kerosene," such as Mobil kerosene. Signaloil, used by railroads, is a kerosene which has been recommended to us.

COAL STOVES

Recommended makes of coal-, charcoal-, and wood-burning stoves include the cast-iron Shipmate (Richmond Ring Co., Souderton, Pa.), and a more expensive, insulated stove, known as the Constant Cooker (Rudman and Scofield, Inc., 275 Pearl Street, New York).

A coal stove means a warm, dry boat, an oven to cook in, and a kind of cozy companionship no other type of stove can give. It requires a smoke head on deck, is relatively heavy, and cannot be swung in gimbals. The only smoke head in our experience which will draw under even the most unfavorable conditions of down-draft from sails is the Concordia Head, Concordia Company, Inc., South Dartmouth, Mass. Use of charcoal briquettes for a quick fire and red-ash anthracite for lasting heat is a combination of fuels which makes a coal stove almost as handy as a liquid-fuel pressure stove. A grate suitable for pea coal is recommended. Users of the Constant Cooker tell us that it is so well insulated that the heat it gives out to the cabin can be controlled by opening or keeping closed the oven door.

KEROSENE STOVES

There are many good makes of kerosene stoves on the market today, but in our opinion Swedish Primus is the best. Of the many other satisfactory brands, we can also recommend a Shipmate kerosene pressure stove equipped with two Primus burners, which can be supplied in gimbals, and a one-burner Sea Swing, also Primus-equipped (see description under Jellied Fuel Stoves).

Perhaps more important than specific names of makes are a few general safety regulations in conformity with the National Fire Protection Association standards for both kerosene and alcohol stoves. For example, either pressure or gravity-fed burners are permissible, but bubble-feed, wick-type burners, or any system which might be affected by the motion of the vessel, should not be used. Pressure tanks may be installed integrally with stoves, provided they are protected from the heat of the burners; but gravity tanks should be well secured in an area remote from the stove, where they can be filled and vented outside the galley. All fuel tanks should be constructed of corrosion-resistant metal with welded or brazed joints and fittings, and the fuel lines should be continuous from tank to stove. Check any pressure stove you may select to be sure it has a catch pan at least ¾ inch deep that extends under all burners. Sterno is a safer priming fuel than alcohol.

ALCOHOL STOVES

For the past twenty-five years, an alcohol stove has been our choice, and we feel it has several advantages over kerosene. Alcohol is easier to light, it gives off less odor and a less intense heat, it evaporates when spilt, and an alcohol fire can be put out with water.

There are several well-known makes of two-burner alcohol

pressure stoves; these include the Perko (Perkins Marine Lamp and Hardware Corp., Brooklyn, N. Y.), Sea Cook (Willcox-Crittenden, Middletown, Conn.), Shipmate (Richmond Ring Co., Souderton, Pa.), Mariner (Homestrand, Inc., Larchmont, N. Y.). The Heritage Co., Huntington, L. I., N. Y., makes several deluxe alcohol stoves in various sizes. The Heritage stove has a flat, heavy aluminum top and an insulated oven large enough for roasting meats.

If you prefer a gravity-fuel alcohol stove, be sure to install a shut-off valve in the fuel line at the tank and also at the stove, according to the National Fire Protection Association.

FUEL-OIL STOVES

Regular Shipmate coal ranges with oven are available equipped with fuel-oil burners. These burners are equipped with a necessary blower which requires a reliable source of electricity. In a pinch, roarer-type Primus stoves can be coaxed into burning No. 2 fuel oil.

GAS STOVES

Gas stoves are less used on small craft than stoves burning other types of fuel. Safety requires that gas tanks be located on deck. Refilling gas containers is not as simple as purchasing supplies of other fuels from the village store. The installation of liquefied petroleum gas "systems" (i.e., gas cylinder and regulator assembly) is comparatively expensive, and any gas line leaks which develop are very dangerous, since the petroleum gases used are heavier than air.

We personally would not go to sea with any gas appliance —refrigerator, hot-water heater, cabin-space heater, or stove. Our opinion in this matter is confirmed by an enthusiastically written article in the March 1960 *Yachting* entitled "Now you're cooking with gas." This article summarizes the recommendations contained in "Fire Protection Standards for Motor Craft" issued by National Fire Protection Association, 60 Batterymarch Street, Boston, 10, Mass. The list of safety do's and don'ts, including a biweekly gas-system test, is enough to shy us away from the convenience of gas on a boat until a heating gas is made which is lighter than air. Gas is also dangerous because it is under pressure, and vaporizes immediately to create explosive conditions.

JELLIED-FUEL STOVE

Sterno (canned heat) is useful on board small craft as a priming fuel for kerosene pressure stoves and as an auxiliary or emergency source of heat. Sterno makes a two-flame galley stove, each flame equipped with a "heat intensifier," which is a great improvement over the familiar little folding can-holders.

The "Sea Swing" gimbal stove, which takes about one cubic foot of space, is a really practical addition to any galley. It is highly recommended, especially for offshore cooking. Be sure to buy the "heat intensifier" accessory to this unit. Specially designed utensils (aluminum) are sold to fit this unit by The Crow's-nest, 16 East 40th Street, New York 16, N. Y. It will accept many standard utensils, too.

HEATING STOVES

For cruisers in cool climates and areas where fog is prevalent, there is nothing more useful than to install two stoves in your cabin, a liquid-fuel stove for cooking, and a coal-, charcoal-, or wood-burning stove for cabin heating and for broiling, simmering, and toasting. The best of these for larger boats, in our opinion, is the Concordia Cabin Heater, Concordia Co., Inc., South Dartmouth, Mass. Seagoing soapstone fireplaces are also available.

STOVES AND FUELS

Even for small craft, miniature briquette and wood-burning cabin heaters such as Tiny Tot or Fatsco Pet are also very satisfactory. While their prime purpose is to give heat, they will keep a coffee-pot hot and will serve as a "one burner" cook stove when your regular stove goes back on you somewhere east of civilization. We use a Pet, which we understand was developed originally to heat milk wagons in Minnesota.

GASOLINE STOVES

Gasoline stoves (also gasoline lanterns and ice machines operated by flame) are positively banned for use on boats by the fire underwriters. If you insist on using them, your boat is probably not insurable against fire. In the case of gasoline stoves and lamps the principal reason for this prohibition is not the equipment, which is very well made and quite safe for camp or farm use. It is the nature of gasoline itself and its explosive heavier-than-air fumes which collect in bilges and boat compartments. As the *U.S. Coast Guard Motor Boat Regulations* puts it: "An atmospheric concentration (of gasoline) as low as $1\frac{1}{4}\%$ is practically odorless but is sufficient to create a mixture which may be exploded by a slight spark."

FIRE IN THE GALLEY

AVOIDING GALLEY FIRES

It is easier to avoid fire than to fight it. From our own experience and from off-the-record discussions with various people in the fire insurance and prevention business, these are the danger points in normal galley procedure:

1. Filling stove tank so full that there is no air space left in the tank. This may cause leakage when you pump up pressure.

2. Filling a tank located over or under the stove burners in the middle of preparing a meal, or priming a stove when the burners are hot. This is especially dangerous with gasoline pressure stoves.

3. Squirting too much liquid priming into the priming cup and then lighting up. When lighting a stove under way we prefer chunks of Sterno to liquid alcohol.

4. Failing to preheat alcohol burners long enough to cause full vaporization. Even though the burner may light, it may also still drip raw alcohol into the priming cup, causing an eventual dangerous flare-up.

5. Failing to check joints of fuel pipes from fuel tank to each burner.

6. Ignoring dirty burners until they choke and flood. Use of high-grade fuel is the best way to minimize cleaning of burners, but they should be easy to get at and should be cleaned regularly.

7. Allowing fat or grease to catch fire. No recipe in this book calls for deep-fat frying, but even an unwatched pan of bacon will catch fire if left alone long enough.

8. Use of galley pots as emergency receptacles to hold small quantities of gasoline. Believe it or not, at least two boats burned one year recently from pots set on the stove to boil which a post mortem revealed held gasoline instead of water.

Carelessly handled or overfilled ash boxes are apt to make trouble, especially if they are dumped overboard in a seaway. Transfer your ashes and live clinkers to a bucket before going on deck.

Gasoline should never be used as a priming fuel. Lighting a wood- or coal-burning stove with kerosene or gasoline is a famous cause of galley fire.

FIRE IN THE GALLEY

TYPES OF EXTINGUISHERS

Most galley fires involve inflammable liquids—greases, etc. —where a blanketing or smothering effect is essential to put them out. These are classified by the Underwriters Laboratories as Class B fires. It is stated that they may be put out with a foam extinguisher (such as Foamite) or a carbon dioxide extinguisher (such as Kidde) or a dry chemical (such as Ansul). They may also be extinguished by a vaporizing liquid extinguisher with a carbon tetrachloride base (such as Pyrene), but this type of extinguisher is no longer approved for boat use. These approved makes and many others are listed in "Fire Protection Equipment List" issued by Underwriters Laboratories, 161 Sixth Ave., New York, or see "Equipment Lists" of items approved under Maritime Inspection and Navigation Laws issued by the U. S. Coast Guard.

Standards for the number and type of fire extinguishers recommended on boats of various lengths are specified in Coast Guard regulations in accordance with the Federal Boating Act of 1958. The net of the matter is that within reach of the cook there should be either two hand-extinguishers of a type suitable for Class B fires (foam, carbon dioxide, or dry chemical), each with an Underwriters Laboratories inspection label reading "B-I," or one larger extinguisher of the same type, labeled "B-II." We use two Kidde (pistol-grip) carbon dioxide extinguishers. We have not had first-hand experience with dry chemical extinguishers or foam.

In the first edition of this book we wrote "We do not recommend any carbon tetrachloride extinguisher for cabin use, for the fumes may be as dangerous as the fire. If you have to use one of these extinguishers, send everyone else on deck and join them yourself as soon as possible." Current Federal regulations discontinue approval of these extinguishers for

28

boat use.

We should point out that our recommendations above for two "B-I" extinguishers for the cook's use may not satisfy Federal requirements for fire extinguishers on your boat. These regulations vary with boat length and are primarily set with regard to gasoline-engine fire hazards. No boat should be equipped, however, without at least one "B-I" extinguisher.

So much for the galley fire hazard. While most boat fires are caused by gasoline engines, nothing is more foolish than to install a stove of doubtful design or a second-hand miscellaneous assembly of different makes of stoves. For further information on this whole topic, consult the Yacht Safety Bureau, or the National Fire Protection Association.

BURNS

MILD BURNS

Dr. Sheldon, in *First Aid Afloat*, says: "Fortunately the usual burn is a mild affair which gets well without leaving a disfiguring scar, regardless of the type of treatment used. There may be pain but infection seldom takes place, and after the first hour or so, the pain is not severe. The usual treatment for this sort of thing is to apply a wet compress of soda in cold water (two tablespoons of soda bicarbonate or baking soda in a quart of water) or a compress of undiluted milk of magnesia. If pain is sufficient to warrant it, remember that aspirin or the like may bring greater relief than what you do to the burned area. A sleeping pill may help the victim through a rough night.

"Once your patient is comfortable, remove the soda compresses and lay onto the burned skin a thin sheet of gauze or some cloth like a clean handkerchief dipped in mineral oil or spread with white vaseline. A clean or boiled table knife makes a good spreader for this cloth. Over the vaseline gauze place dry gauze or cloth padding, and secure with an ordinary or ace bandage. The vaseline gauze layer next to the skin can remain in place for several days. Healing takes place beneath it, and when changed, it will not stick to the new skin.

"Though white vaseline is recommended for protecting wounds while healing, one can use 'burn ointments,' mineral oil or even olive or salad oil in place of vaseline."

COOKING GEAR
GENERAL ADVICE

However snug or spacious your galley may be, two enemies beset every cook who works afloat—rust and sudden motion.

Each piece of equipment on your boat lives in a constant atmosphere of salt damp. Everything susceptible rusts thoroughly and comparatively quickly, from tin cans forgotten in the back of a locker to the cast-iron skillet you scoured so clean last night. Aluminum oxide, one of the less digestible forms of rust, appears all too easily in aluminum ware.

Under way or tied up, everything on a small boat that is not nailed down is subject to an unexpected and violent tendency to leap into the air without warning.

So consider, before you buy any piece of galley equipment, whether it can live a useful life in a world of salt air and sudden bumps. Otherwise it will let you down when you need it most.

As essential cooking gear on small boats adds up to relatively few items, it pays to buy only first-grade hardware. Enamelware is the best buy for the money, but it rusts where it chips and is not as good a conductor of heat as uncoated metal. Iron, copper, and aluminum ware have their advantages in household cookery, but the best metal for most seagoing pots and pans is stainless steel. In the case of frying pans, stainless steel with a copper bottom is better than solid stainless steel. However, in our opinion, a heavy cast-iron skillet is worth all the trouble its rusting may make. A drop of olive oil or cooking oil or a small amount of bacon grease rubbed on after each use will keep your iron skillet rust-free. As any old-timer will tell you, iron ware should never be cleaned with soap—just hot water, paper towels, and elbow grease.

A Dutch oven (heavy metal pot with cover) can be one of the most useful all-purpose pots in the galley. The classic

Dutch oven is made of heavy cast iron which has the same seagoing disadvantages and requires the same care as the cast-iron skillet. However, for a minimum of scorching and burning, successful slow cooking over pressure burners, and retention of heat after cooking, the cast-iron Dutch oven is hard to equal. Enameled cast-iron frying pans and Dutch ovens are a good solution for seagoing cooks who value cast iron and wish to avoid the rust problem.

Some seagoing cooks claim wonders from box-type, top-of-the-stove ovens. Insulated stainless steel ovens are available from Rudman and Scofield, and Hill Marine Specialties, 7422 Belden Street, Philadelphia, makes a folding oven which is easy to stow. (However, for ready-mix and other simple baking, we find the Connolly oven entirely practical.)

CHECK LIST OF GALLEY EQUIPMENT

The following lists of cooking equipment (pots and pans and other galley equipment), divided into "essential" and "useful," are submitted as a basis for a galley where meals are usually cooked for not more than six persons. You doubtless will develop or have developed your own set of favorite utensils. If you know their characteristics or enjoy their special qualities, keep your old pots and pans as you keep your old friends. The equipment listed below may be obtained generally at hardware stores or by mail from Lewis & Conger, Sixth Avenue and 45th Street, New York, or other source as noted.

COOKING EQUIPMENT

ESSENTIAL	RECOMMENDED TYPE
Asbestos pads (for stove burners)	Metal or wire screen backed pads are preferable to plain ones. Metal Flame Tamer
Bottle opener	
Bread knife	Case (chrome, vanadium steel)

COOKING EQUIPMENT (*continued*)

ESSENTIAL	RECOMMENDED TYPE
Can openers (hand type), 3	Westco, rotary with wooden handle
	Beer can opener
	Anchor opener
Carving knife and fork	Case (chrome vanadium steel)
Cheesecloth	
Chopping board, wooden, about 8" x 12"	
Colander, 9" diameter at top	Carlton (stainless steel)
Corkscrew	Korkmaster (stainless steel)
Egg beater	Ekco Best beater, chrome, rotary.
Grater	
Ice pick	Single prong
Juice (orange, lemon, lime) extractor	Standard glass type
Knife sharpener	Steel or Carborundum stone
Measuring cup, 1-cup size	Pyrex
Measuring spoons, set of 4	
Mixing bowl, 9" diameter	Carlton (stainless steel)
Pancake turner	Carlton (stainless steel)
Salt and pepper shaker	
Spoons, cooking, 3	Carlton (stainless steel, solid and slotted) and wooden
Strainers (8" and 3" diameters)	
Vegetable knife	Case (chrome vanadium steel)

USEFUL BUT NOT ESSENTIAL	RECOMMENDED TYPE
Apple corer	
Can opener (wall type)	
Hot-can remover	Ordinary pliers
Ladle	Carlton (stainless steel)
Meat grinder	Stanete (aluminum)
Oven thermometer	

COOKING GEAR

COOKING EQUIPMENT (*continued*)

USEFUL BUT NOT ESSENTIAL	RECOMMENDED TYPE
Pan liners	Panette or Chef aluminum foil
Potato peeler	
Timer	Presto timer
Toastmaker	Toast-et
Wire salad basket	French spherical wire basket
Wooden bowl (about 10″ diameter at top)	

POTS AND PANS

ESSENTIAL	RECOMMENDED TYPE
Coffeepot	Nicro (stainless steel, vacuum type) or Carlton (stainless steel, drip type) or enamelware percolator type
Double boiler, 2-qt. insert	Carlton (stainless steel) straight-sided pots
Dutch oven	Griswold (cast iron); Revere (stainless steel, copper bottom); Le Creuset (porcelain solid iron ware), Bazaar Français, 666 Sixth Ave., New York City, N.Y.
Frying pan with cover (10″ diameter)	Griswold (cast iron); Revere (stainless steel, copper bottom)
Frying pan (8″ diameter)	Revere (stainless steel, copper bottom); Le Creuset
Kettle, 5-qt.	Large top opening, lip-spout type, "Farberware" (stainless steel), Macy's, New York; Le Creuset
Mixing bowl (fits kettle as a double boiler insert)	See mixing bowl in list above
Potato baker, 10″ diameter	Connolly oven
Pressure cooker, 4-qt.	Revere (stainless steel, copper bottom)

34

POTS AND PANS (*continued*)

ESSENTIAL	RECOMMENDED TYPE
Saucepan, 1-qt.	Revere (stainless steel, copper bottom); Carlton (stainless steel)

(For stoves with built-in ovens only)

Casserole baking dish	
Pan, roasting	Polar or Carlton (stainless steel)

USEFUL BUT NOT ESSENTIAL	RECOMMENDED TYPE
Cocktail shaker	
Pail, with bail handle, 12-qt. capacity	Polar (stainless steel)
Pans, baking	Connolly oven set of 3 round pans, or standard blocked tin pans
Pitcher, 2-qt.	Carlton (stainless steel)

OTHER GALLEY EQUIPMENT

ESSENTIAL	RECOMMENDED TYPE
Fire extinguishers, 2	See section on Fire in the Galley
Fuel	See section on Stoves and Fuels
Funnel (for liquid fuel stoves)	
Funnel (for filling water tanks)	
Matches	Diamond, water-resistant
Priming can (for kerosene pressure stoves)	Pump-type oil can, or Primus priming can
Stove	See section on Stoves and Fuels

USEFUL BUT NOT ESSENTIAL	
Asbestos gloves	
Canvas bag and mallet	
Ice tongs and ice carrier bag	
Icebox food containers	Flexible plastic bowls with covers; transparent plastic wrap; aluminum foil
Insulated bag	Fiberglas insulated bag or pail
Paper bags	Garbage bags

OTHER GALLEY EQUIPMENT (*continued*)

USEFUL BUT NOT ESSENTIAL	RECOMMENDED TYPE
Oven, box type, folding	Hill Marine Specialties (stainless steel)
Vacuum bottles	Stanley stainless steel (all metal)

CLEANUP GEAR
GENERAL ADVICE

The best way to keep a galley clean is never to allow it to get dirty.

"Clean up as you cook" is a primary rule. Wash your pots and pans, whenever possible, just after they have been used and before the remnants of cooked food freeze on hard. Hang a roll of paper towels in a handy place and use them freely. Spread newspapers over working space. Pick up and wipe up every morsel or drop that spills to the floor at once before it is tracked all over your boat.

Save yourself cleaning by serving directly from pots. One of the reasons that we like stainless steel pots is that nothing sticks to them—not even oatmeal or scrambled eggs. Panettes (aluminum-foil throw-away skillet liners) are a great luxury for jobs which leave a sticky residue in ordinary frying pans.

Everyone has his own washing-up system. A few principles are of general application. Scrape well. A Chore Boy or Chore Girl copper sponge, obtainable everywhere, is invaluable. Start with boiling water. Wash glasses and cutlery first. A Polar stainless steel bucket is useful to boil water and makes a good dishpan. If you use Vel, Dreft, Glim, or other detergent you can swish the plates clean in hot salt or fresh water by twisting the bucket back and forth slowly. Rinsing after using detergents is advisable but, from our experience, not essential.

Save strong kraft paper bags (or take along regular garbage bags) to line your garbage pail. As a matter of common sense and common courtesy, don't throw garbage overboard in any anchorage. If you are tied up, take it ashore, or else drop it under way in an open bay.

To clean the copper bottom of your Revere stainless steel frying pan use the heel of a lemon into which a generous dash of salt has been poured.

To keep the top of your cast-iron stove black and shiny, rub a rag over the moist side of a cake of brown laundry soap and scrub the stove top when it is cold. Wiping the top of your cast-iron stove, when hot, with wax paper will also keep it clean and shiny.

Don't use soap to clean your icebox. Use washing soda or Clorox.

INSECT CONTROL

Cleaning out insects from the galley is generally associated with tropical cruising. Three types of bug control are D.D.T., Chlordane, and Pyrethrum. The first two are poisonous to man. Pyrethrum is a safe remedy and will not injure man or pets. Although D.D.T. usually comes in a 5 per cent solution and Chlordane in a 2 per cent solution, frequent use in a confined galley work area could deposit a sufficient residue of the poison to be dangerous. We suggest that it is wise to play safe and use a spray based on Pyrethrum without added poison.

Bug powders such as sodium fluoride (poisonous) or Pyrethrum are apt to cake up in damp weather on small boats, in which case the bugs can crawl merrily over the stuff without injury. Phosphorus paste bug and rat poison works with increased effect in a moist atmosphere and is less messy than scattered powder if smeared on a piece of cardboard which is then rolled into a tube (paste inside) held together with string.

CLEANUP GEAR

CHECK LIST OF CLEANUP GEAR

The following check list of cleanup gear may prove useful in outfitting your boat.

USEFUL CLEANUP GEAR	RECOMMENDED TYPE
Washing soda, or Clorox	
Cleaning powder	Bon Ami, Bab-O, Ajax, etc.
Detergents	Vel, Dreft, etc. (powders); Glim (liquid); I. C. DeGreaser (a stronger liquid)
Dish mop	
Dishpan	Polar bucket (stainless steel) or enamel pan
Dish towels	
Drying rack	
Dustpan	
Floor mop	(Cut down the handle for convenience)
Insect spray (non-poisonous)	Pyrethrum type
Insect poison	Phosphorus type
Paper towels	
Soap	
Scouring aids	Chore Girl, Chore Boy, copper wool, Brillo pads, etc.
Scrubbing brush	
Spray gun	Spray pump attachment to fit a standard quart can
Whisk broom	

TABLE GEAR
GENERAL ADVICE

No two skippers agree as to the best small-boat tableware. Our preference happens to be for good-grade, normal-weight household china plates, generous-size china soup bowls, broad-bottomed china coffee mugs, and standard glassware. (William

H. Plummer, Ltd., 734 Fifth Avenue, New York, is the place to go if you want "yacht china" complete with crossed house and yacht club flags.)

Breakage is a relatively minor consideration for coastwise cruisers. On the other hand, deepwater voyages where replacement would be difficult or impossible call for unbreakable tableware throughout. Our preference is white enamelware, as it is easy to clean, holds heat fairly well, and is attractive to use. Some sailors, however, like to eat off tin pie plates. Many prefer paper plates for some or even all meals. Stainless steel plates, bowls, and cups can be purchased at campers' supply houses (such as Abercrombie & Fitch, Madison Avenue at 45th Street, New York) or at hardware stores which carry Carlton Ware products. Tupper (flexible plastic) cocktail shakers and bowls are inexpensive and useful if they appeal to you. Melmac (plastic) plates are heavier than most plastic ware and can be purchased from retail stores. American Cyanamid Company, Plastics Division, 34 Rockefeller Plaza, New York, will, on request, give you a list of manufacturers specializing in Melmac tableware. When it comes to cutlery we recommend stainless steel flatware, which is now available in full place settings and can be bought in complete sets for 4, 6, or 8 persons. The less expensive grades can be secured at such stores as Woolworth's or Kresge's. The better-finished and more expensive kinds are available at most house furnishing stores. The International Silver Company, Meriden, Conn., manufactures three fine grades which have general distribution.

Masslinn non-woven fabric napkins (Chicopee Sales Corporation, 47 Worth Street, New York) are much better than paper napkins and make useful disposable dishcloths. These can be bought in department stores and can be obtained by mail from S. S. Pierce Company, Boston, Mass.

There are a number of salt and pepper shakers on the market designed to prevent caking. We have tried them all,

39

including the reliable salt-mill type. These gadgets are fun to experiment with. However, a small beef-extract jar with its original cork, filled with regular or, when available, kosher salt, has served us for years.

STOWAGE

Before you load your boat up with food, give real thought to the places where you intend to stow different categories of canned food such as meat, milk, soup, fruit, fruit juices, etc. We mention this elementary rule of household organization because it is so often overlooked on small boats in the rush of sailing day. It is also well worth the trouble to tack a location list of ship's stores on the back of a locker door and a "remember-to-buy" pad alongside this list.

If you are undertaking an extended cruise or an ocean race, it is advisable to establish one emergency locker of canned goods such as a few cans of fruit juices, evaporated milk, bacon, chicken, potatoes, peas, corned beef hash, soup, and fruit. Also a can of cocoa, Baker's chocolate, a jar of instant coffee, a small folding Sterno stove and cans of canned heat, a box of Diamond water-repellent matches in a tin container, and a roll of toilet paper.

Stowage is a matter of common sense and experience. A few general observations from our experience follow.

DRY STAPLES

The best place for most dry staples which are not packed in cans is in a tin can with a friction top (tobacco-can type), such as can be purchased from local camping supply stores or from Abercrombie & Fitch, Madison Avenue and 45th Street, New York. Some dry staples such as cereals, rice, and flour will keep well enough in their non-metal packages for alongshore cruises if small-size packages are favored. Stow dry staples in well-ventilated shelves, cupboards, or lockers unless they are sealed in tins and may be treated like canned goods.

Some cruisers in stable boats rig a shelf of screw-top jars or chemists' square glass jars with deep stoppers for salt, flour, sugar, rice, and cereal. Square, unbreakable polyethylene containers are also useful for such storage. A condiment shelf made to fit cans of spices, herbs, etc., is something you will want if you really use this book. Be sure these shelves are deep enough to prevent their contents from jumping out in a seaway. Rice, peas, or beans in the bilges will clog a pump and can become a source of real danger on the day when "everything goes wrong at once."

CANNED GOODS

Canned goods may be stowed almost anywhere, provided they don't change the trim of your boat or the deviation of your compass.

Take our advice and either remove can labels before they go into the bilges, marking the content of each can in waterproof crayon, china marking pencil, or, for major cruises, varnish or dip them, labels and all, in Plasti-pak, type A, obtainable in gallon cans from Standard Varnish Works, 2589 Richmond Terrace, Staten Island, N.Y. We will long remember one ocean race when can labels clogged the bilge pump and the cook had to guess the contents of cans by shaking them, with some amazing and disappointing results.

The outside of cans may be covered with rust and the food within will still be perfectly good, if no air leak has developed. Cans may be bashed all out of shape without losing their airtight property. If a can bulges at the ends, however, the chances are its contents are spoiled.

As to leaving food in open cans, a release by the U.S. Department of Agriculture states:

It is just as safe to keep canned food in the can it comes in—if the can is cool and covered—as it is to empty the food into another container. Thousands of housewives are firm in the faith that canned goods ought to be emptied as soon as the can is opened, or at least before the remainder of the food goes into the refrigerator —one of the persistent food fallacies. . . . Whether in the original can or in another container, the principal precautions for keeping food are—Keep it cool and keep it covered.

PERISHABLES

Meat. Meat, including fowl, will keep longer if wiped with a clean wet cloth and rewrapped in fresh waxed paper or clear plastic wrap or aluminum foil before being placed in the galley icebox. Never stow meat wrapped in brown paper only. Frozen meat keeps slightly longer in an icebox than fresh meat, and makes your ice last longer. Sliced bacon in its original package will keep at least two weeks in a cool place such as the back of a shelf or locker near the planking below the water line. Bacon in a flitch (uncut) and uncooked smoked hams will keep almost indefinitely. Canned cooked ham and chicken (such as Hormel packs) will keep indefinitely in the can in a cool place.

The best guide to spoiled meat is your nose. If you have any doubts, don't eat it. Pork and veal spoil more quickly than other meats. Beef will turn a dark red color and become somewhat slimy as it "hangs" or ages in a non-frozen state. If this layer of meat is cut off revealing firm, pink meat underneath, the inside meat is still edible. In general, meat surrounded by fat lasts better than unprotected lean meat. For this reason lamb, mutton, and ribs of beef will outlast a steak or chopped meat.

Eggs. Really fresh eggs will keep five weeks in a cool place if they are turned over once a week. They will keep for months if dipped in hot lard and packed in table salt. Painting eggs with white vaseline is also an effective method of keeping them edible. General store eggs are seldom really fresh and cannot be counted on for more than one week unless kept in the icebox. Your icebox should have a shelf designed to fit a few standard egg boxes. Rotten eggs float in water, edible eggs sink. Probably no egg which you can bring yourself to eat will poison you. Open doubtful eggs in a cup rather than in the frying pan or mixing bowl to avoid spoiling a batch of opened good eggs with one bad one.

Butter, cheese. Butter, in quarter-pound wrapped bars, will keep two weeks in a cool place and longer if left floating in water. Margarine will outlast butter. For long cruises canned butter should be carried.

Wax-covered cheeses such as Edam, and foil-wrapped cheeses such as Gruyère will, until opened, keep for months in a ventilated dry locker. Processed cheeses in packages and jars are also good for months without refrigeration. Cuts of store cheese will keep well if wrapped in cloth moistened with vinegar. Another useful trick is to butter cut surfaces.

Bread. Unsliced bread will outlast sliced. Bread should be kept in a tin container or, if your boat is too small, in the grocer's brown-paper bag with the top twisted tight. Some people remove the wax paper, but we leave it on, since mildew spreads fast from one bad loaf. As bread may be several days old when you buy it, no two batches seem to act alike. Whole wheat may outlast white, and vice versa. Painting bread with vinegar is said to retard mildew. Our advice is to buy bread every three or four days. If this is impossible, use either canned bread or the sailor's best friend, pilot biscuit. Ordinary bread mold is unpalatable but not poisonous.

Packaged cake may be stowed in the same manner as bread and will last a month and more.

Milk. Fresh milk, like eggs and bread, will have varying degrees of "freshness" when you buy it. Milk should go in a rack (in the coldest part of the icebox) designed to hold the bottles or containers upright. Homogenized milk stays sweet longer than regular milk. A half teaspoon of salt added to a quart of milk will preserve its freshness several days. Milk is perfectly safe to use as long as your palate will accept it. Half a teaspoon of baking soda in a cup of slightly sour milk will make it a fresh-milk equivalent for cooking purposes.

Vegetables. Keep winter vegetables (potatoes, onions, carrots, etc.) in string shopping bags in a ventilated dark locker. Nylon string bags are now available. (If you don't find them, write to our favorite store, the Salamander Shop, Vinalhaven, Maine.) As onions will sprout readily in damp air, get them in relatively small quantities. Never bury fresh vegetables under a bunk or in the forepeak, especially potatoes. For short trips keep winter vegetables in the paper bags they come in and take the leftovers ashore with you. Other fresh vegetables last best in the icebox. Frozen vegetables, to taste fresh, should be eaten within twenty-four hours after they thaw out.

Fruits. Most fruits will keep better if wrapped in tissue paper to avoid bruising and the spreading of rot. On long trips where stowage space is at a premium a crate of oranges will keep two weeks on deck if covered from direct sunlight. Citrus fruits keep three weeks in a cool climate in string bags in a well-ventilated place below decks. Other fruit should go in the icebox, except bananas. Bananas ripen in the dark and spoil in the sunlight. In tropical waters, stow a bunch of green bananas (inspect for spiders first) in the forepeak or the engine room and they will ripen to perfection in about a week. As we learned in New Guinea during the war, dipping the bunch in salt water hastens the ripening process.

ICEBOX SUBSTITUTES

Enough ice for drinks may be stored in a large-mouth vacuum bucket, if your boat has no icebox. Frozen foods may be carried in insulated picnic bags (without adding ice) for at least two days in a cool climate. An exception to this generalization is frozen French-fried potatoes and other precooked frozen foods.

In cold waters, hang milk and other perishables overboard in a market bag. Set meat on deck at night. A porous water bag will keep drinking water cool in hot climates, and a small quantity of fruit juice of any kind, canned or fresh, makes even tepid drinking water surprisingly palatable.

LEFTOVERS

Flexible plastic boxes or bowls with covers are ideal for icebox leftovers. Never stow anything uncovered in the icebox. Whatever is stowed there should be placed to avoid shifting about when the boat lays over to the breeze or the sea kicks up. Don't overload your icebox with leftovers, for they steal your ice and, try as you will, they spill now and then with foul and even poisonous results.

In short, unless they are to be part of tomorrow's planned menu, the best place to stow most cooked leftovers is overboard.

FOOD PLANNING

GENERAL ADVICE

In general, plan your ship's stores by computing how many breakfasts, lunches, and dinners you will have on your trip. If you are methodical, you can plan menus for the entire trip, realizing that you will undoubtedly deviate from your plans even though you make them as a food-buying guide. This method is recommended for cruises up to two weeks and for at least the first two weeks of longer cruises in waters where supplies may be purchased easily. For cruises of more than two weeks you will probably want to buy as you go as regards staples, but stock up for the entire trip with a number of items which cannot be purchased everywhere.

When you cruise to ports where food is hard to buy, or if you are planning an ocean trip, we recommend that you do

STOWAGE

some careful menu planning and make up your supply list from this firm foundation of what you will need.

One of the greatest helps in food planning is to obtain a good catalog of food produce from a large distributing house. Without such a catalog to guide you in what is available, your food buying will fall into the same rut year after year.

SUGGESTED MENUS AND LIST OF SUPPLIES FOR A TWO WEEKS' COASTAL CRUISE

There follow menus for a two weeks' cruise (16 days, as three week ends are included) with a complete list of supplies for four people for the entire cruise and preparation time for each meal.

For shorter cruises, the list may be broken up into as many units as necessary.

FOOD PLANNING

MENUS FOR A TWO WEEKS' COASTAL CRUISE

SATURDAY

BREAKFAST
Minimum Time
30 Minutes
Fresh Fruit or Juice
Wheatena (No. 291)
Bacon (No. 95)
Fried Eggs (No. 277)
Toast & Jam
Coffee (No. 326)

LUNCH
Minimum Time
25 Minutes
Appleton Street Soup
(No. 1)
Rye Bread & Liverwurst
Sandwich (No. 238)
Milk
Apple & Cheese (No. 311)
Candy

DINNER
Minimum Time
1 Hour
Cocktails (Nos. 329–336)
Pan-broiled Hamburger
(No. 68)
Green Beans (No. 141)
Bread & Butter
Green Salad (No. 229)
Cheese & Crackers
Blancmange (No. 304)
& Raspberry Jam
Coffee

SUNDAY

BREAKFAST
Minimum Time
25 Minutes
Fresh Fruit or Juice
Shredded Wheat
Molasses & Milk
Bacon (No. 95)
Fried Eggs (No. 277)
Toast & Butter
Coffee

LUNCH
Minimum Time
20 Minutes
Pea Soup with Frank-
furters (No. 127)
Canned Chicken Sand-
wiches (No. 238)
Cream Cheese &
Gooseberry Preserves
Milk

DINNER
Minimum Time
1¼ Hours
Cocktails
Pan-broiled Steak (No. 53)
Baked Potatoes (No. 181)
with Butter
Waldorf Salad (No. 234)
Bread & Butter
Rum Boiled Custard
(No. 306) over Cake
Coffee

MONDAY

BREAKFAST
Minimum Time
30 Minutes
Apple Sauce
Shredded Wheat
Molasses & Milk
Ham Omelet (No. 262)
Toast & Butter
Marmalade
Coffee

LUNCH
Minimum Time
25 Minutes
Black Bean Soup
with Ham (No. 3)
Raw Sliced Carrots
Canned Beef Sandwiches
Canned Baked Apples
(cold)

DINNER
Minimum Time
1 Hour
Cocktails
Fried Chicken (No. 113)
Mashed Canned Sweet
Potatoes (No. 190)
Canned Beet Greens
(No. 208)
Bread & Butter
Sliced Pineapple
Coffee

47

TUESDAY

BREAKFAST	LUNCH	DINNER
Minimum Time	*Minimum Time*	*Minimum Time*
25 Minutes	*20 Minutes*	*30 Minutes*
Fresh Fruit or Juice	Hot Chocolate (No.328)	Cocktails
Cream of Wheat (No.288)	Lettuce with French	Norton & Jones Beef Stew
Milk & Sugar	Dressing (No.235) (½	(No. 118)
Boiled Eggs (No. 258)	head per person)	Sliced Tomatoes
with Butter	Spam Sandwiches	with French Dressing
Whole Wheat Toast		(No. 235)
Gooseberry Jam &		Bread & Butter
Butter		Apple Snow (No. 302)
Coffee		Coffee

WEDNESDAY

BREAKFAST	LUNCH	DINNER
Minimum Time	*Minimum Time*	*Minimum Time*
30 Minutes	*20 Minutes*	*1 Hour*
Canned Apricots	Cream of Mushroom	Cocktails
Corn-Meal Mush	Soup	Steak Pan-broiled in Salt
(No. 286)	Canned Hamburger	(No. 54)
Bacon (No. 95)	Sandwiches (cold)	Boiled Potatoes
Scrambled Eggs (No. 270)	Raw Cauliflower Dipped	with Butter (No. 179)
Toast	in Mayonnaise	Spinach (No. 196)
Butter & Jam	Apple & Cheese (No. 311)	Chocolate Blancmange
Coffee		(No. 304)
		Coffee

THURSDAY

BREAKFAST	LUNCH	DINNER
Minimum Time	*Minimum Time*	*Minimum Time*
25 Minutes	*25 Minutes*	*1¼ Hours*
Canned Prunes	Corned Beef & Chicken	Cocktails
Oatmeal (No. 289)	Succotash (No. 134)	Baked Potato Soup (No. 2)
Sugar & Milk	Bread & Butter	Vegetable Salad (No. 233)
Boiled Eggs (No.258)	Milk	Mushroom Omelet
with Butter	Apple & Cheese (No. 311)	(No. 261)
Toast & Butter		Bread & Butter
Marmalade		Peach Condé (No. 315)
Coffee		Coffee

FRIDAY

BREAKFAST
Minimum Time
20 Minutes
Fresh Fruit or Juice
Shredded Wheat
Boiled Eggs (No. 258)
  with Butter
Toast & Butter
  & Marmalade
Coffee

LUNCH
Minimum Time
25 Minutes
Scrambled Eggs with
  Kippered Herring
  (No. 271)
Bread & Butter & Cheese
Canned Apricots
Cocoa

DINNER
Minimum Time
45 Minutes
Cocktails
Baked Codfish (No. 24) or
  Fresh Flounder (No. 28)
Boiled Potatoes (No. 179)
Lima Beans (No. 144)
Lettuce & French Dressing
  (No. 235)
Butterscotch Pudding
Coffee

SATURDAY

BREAKFAST
Minimum Time
25 Minutes
Canned Prunes
Wheatena (No. 291)
  with Milk & Sugar
Bacon (No. 95)
Fried Eggs (No. 277)
Toast, Butter & Jam
Coffee

LUNCH
Minimum Time
30 Minutes
Black Bean Soup with
  Ham (No. 3)
Tomato, Onion, & Let-
  tuce Salad, Mayonnaise
Crackers & Cheese
Sliced Pineapple

DINNER
Minimum Time
1 Hour
Cocktails
Wiener Schnitzel (No. 89)
Mashed Potatoes (No. 188)
Sliced Tomatoes,
  French Dressing
  (No. 235)
Bread & Butter
Rum Boiled Custard (No.
  306) over Plain Cake
Coffee

SUNDAY

BREAKFAST
Minimum Time
45 Minutes
Fresh Fruit or Juice
Pancakes (No. 292)
  Butter & Syrup
Sausages (No. 102)
Coffee

LUNCH
Minimum Time
45 Minutes
New England Clam
  Chowder (canned)
Pilot Biscuit
Lobster Salad (No. 225)
Milk
Preserved Strawberries
Cookies

DINNER
Minimum Time
1 Hour
Cocktails
Tongue (canned) with
  Madeira Sauce (No. 247)
Cauliflower Butter Crumb
  (No. 160)
Lettuce & French Dressing
  (No. 235)
Fruit
Coffee

FOOD PLANNING

MONDAY

BREAKFAST	LUNCH	DINNER
Minimum Time	*Minimum Time*	*Minimum Time*
20 Minutes	*30 Minutes*	*1¼ Hours*
Fruit	French Toast (No. 314)	Cocktails
Corn Flakes, Milk & Sugar	Butter & Syrup	Pot Roast, Pressure-
Boiled Eggs (No. 258)	Milk	Cooked (No. 63)
with Butter	Tomato slices with	Boiled Potatoes (No.
Toast, Butter &	Mayonnaise	179), Onions (No. 173),
Marmalade	Crackers & Cheese	Carrots (No. 157)
Coffee		Bread & Butter
		Stewed Apricots
		Coffee

TUESDAY

BREAKFAST	LUNCH	DINNER
Minimum Time	*Minimum Time*	*Minimum Time*
30 Minutes	*30 Minutes*	*40 Minutes*
Canned Prunes	Cold Pot Roast	Cocktails
Shredded Wheat	Sandwiches	Lamb Chop, Pan-broiled
Molasses & Milk	Vegetable Salad (No. 233)	(No. 76)
Ham Omelet (No. 262)	Hot Chocolate (No. 328)	Eggplant Provençale
Toast, Butter &	Raw Apple	(No. 168)
Marmalade		Lettuce with French
Coffee		Dressing (No. 235)
		Crackers & Cheese
		Canned Fig Pudding
		Coffee

WEDNESDAY

BREAKFAST	LUNCH	DINNER
Minimum Time	*Minimum Time*	*Minimum Time*
30 Minutes	*25 Minutes*	*1 Hour*
Fresh Fruit	Chicken & Cream of	Cocktails
Corn-Meal Mush (No.	Corn Soup	Crab Flake Cakes (No. 44)
286) Milk & Sugar	Tongue Sandwiches	Boiled Potatoes (No. 179)
Bacon (No. 95)	Tomato & Lettuce	Creamed Spinach (No. 198)
Fried Eggs (No. 277)	Salad, Mayonnaise	Waldorf Salad (No. 234)
Toast, Butter &	Canned Black Cherries	Crackers & Cheese
Marmalade	Milk	Coffee
Coffee		

THURSDAY

BREAKFAST
Minimum Time
45 Minutes
Canned Apricots
Pancakes (No. 292)
  Butter & Syrup
Sausages (No. 102)
Coffee

LUNCH
Minimum Time
25 Minutes
Purée Mongole with
  Frankfurters
  (No. 127)
Lettuce & Tomato Salad
  with Mayonnaise
Crackers & Cheese
Fresh Fruit

DINNER
Minimum Time
1 Hour
Cocktails
Chicken Curry (No. 111)
Rice (No. 296)
Blancmange (No. 304)
  with Maple Syrup
Coffee

FRIDAY

BREAKFAST
Minimum Time
25 Minutes
Canned Prunes
Shredded Wheat, Milk
  & Sugar
Boiled Eggs (No. 258)
Toast, Butter &
  Marmalade
Coffee

LUNCH
Minimum Time
35 Minutes
Lobster Newburg (No. 49)
Toast
Lettuce & Tomato Salad
  (No. 230)
Crackers & Cheese
Beer

DINNER
Minimum Time
45 Minutes
Cocktails
Flounder Sautéed
  Meunière (No. 28)
Boiled Potatoes (No. 179)
Green Beans (No. 141)
Bread & Butter
Coffee

SATURDAY

BREAKFAST
Minimum Time
25 Minutes
Fresh Fruit or Juice
Shredded Wheat,
  Molasses & Milk
Bacon (No. 95)
Fried Eggs (No. 277)
Toast, Butter &
  Marmalade
Coffee

LUNCH
Minimum Time
30 Minutes
Hot Chocolate (No. 328)
Canned Hamburger
  Sandwiches
Mixed Green Salad
  (No. 229)

DINNER
Minimum Time
1¾ Hours
Cocktails
Green Turtle Soup
Chicken Cromwell
  (No. 116)
Wild Rice (No. 300)
Lima Beans (No. 144)
Bread & Butter
Blueberry Blancmange
  (No. 304)
Coffee

FOOD PLANNING

SUNDAY

BREAKFAST	LUNCH
Minimum Time	*Minimum Time*
30 Minutes	*45 Minutes*
Fresh Fruit or Juice	Appleton Street Soup (No. 1)
Corn Flakes	Chicken Salad (No. 228)
Sausage Omelet (No. 268)	Whole Wheat, Cream Cheese
Toast, Butter & Marmalade	& Olive Sandwiches
Coffee	Milk

SHOPPING LIST FOR 16-DAY CRUISE

Shopping list of supplies for foregoing menus for cruise of 16 days (2 weeks plus 1 week end). It is expected that perishables will be picked up from time to time at ports of call. Fresh meats are listed in order of appearance in menus.

MEATS, FRESH

Hamburger, 2 lb.
Beefsteak, 3 lb.
Chicken, fryers, 4 lb.
Beefsteak, 3 lb.
Cod or flounder, 3 lb.
Veal cutlets, 2 lb.

Pot roast, 4–5 lb.
Lamb chops, 2 lb.
Chicken, roasting, 4 lb.
Flounder (or other fish), 3 lb.
Chicken, broilers, 2½ pounds each, 2

STAPLES, PERISHABLE

Bacon, 6 lb.
Milk (Canned milk can be substituted), 31 qt.
Cream, ½ pt.
Butter (or margarine), 8 lb.
Eggs, 12 doz.
Cheese, 4 lb.
Cream cheese, 3 pkg.

Pilot biscuit, 1 box
Cakes, sponge, 2
Crackers, saltines, Hi Ho's, etc., 3 boxes
Bread or cracker crumbs, 1 box
Bread, 12 loaves
Cookies

VEGETABLES AND FRUITS, FRESH, FROZEN, OR CANNED

Potatoes, 18 lb.
String beans, 4 lb.; 4 pkg. or cans

Lettuce, 11 heads
Cauliflower, 2 heads

52

Celery, 5 bunches
Carrots, 4 bunches
Beet greens, fresh, 2 lb.; 1 can
Tomatoes, 36
Spinach, fresh, 6 lb.; 3 pkg. or
 cans
Mushrooms, 1 6-oz. can
Mixed vegetables, 2 cans
Lima beans, fresh, 3 lb.; 5 cans
 or pkg.
Eggplant, 1

Corn, 1 can
Sweet potatoes, 5 lb.; 2 cans
Turnips, 1
Onions, small white, 4 lb.
Lemons, 12
Apples, 24
Fresh fruits, oranges, grapefruit,
 berries, melons, peaches,
 pears, or plums, 50 individ-
 ual servings

SOUPS, CANNED

Asparagus, 2 cans
Black bean, 4 cans
Chicken, 4 cans
Clam chowder, New England,
 4 cans
Consommé, 6 cans

Corn, 1 can
Green turtle, 1 can
Mushroom, cream of, 2 cans
Split pea, 2 cans
Purée mongole, 2 cans
Tomato, 1 can

MEATS AND FISH, CANNED

Liverwurst, 1 can
Spam, 1 can
Deviled ham, 3 cans
Tongue, 2 cans
Frankfurters, 2 cans
Corned beef, 2 cans
Lobster, 2 cans

Chicken, boned, 3 cans
Kippered herring, 1 can
Hamburgers, 2 cans
Sausages, 3 cans
Crab meat, 2 cans
Canned roast beef, Swift's, 3
 cans

FRUITS AND DESSERTS, CANNED

Fruit juice, 16 cans
Prunes, 4 cans
Apple sauce, 2 cans
Baked apples, 1 can
Pineapple slices, 3 cans
Apricots, 4 cans
Strawberries, preserved, 1 can

Blueberries, 1 can
Black cherries, 1 can
Gooseberry preserves, 3 cans
Fig pudding, 1 can
Raspberry jam, 2 jars
Orange marmalade, 2 jars
Butterscotch pudding, 1 pkg.

FOOD PLANNING

CEREALS

Corn flakes, 2 medium boxes	Corn Meal, 1 lb.
Oatmeal, 1 box	Flour, 1 5-lb. bag
Wheatena, 1 box	Wild rice, 1 lb.
Cream of Wheat, 1 box	Pancake mix, 1 box
Shredded Wheat Biscuits, 4 boxes	Rice, Minute, 4 boxes; regular, 1 lb.

STAPLES, DRY

Sugar, white, 5 lb.	Vinegar
Sugar, brown, 1 lb. (optional)	Mayonnaise, 1 pt.
Coffee, 5 lb.	Olives, 2 bottles
Chocolate, sweet, 2 lb.	Raisins, 1 box
Cocoa, 1 box	Candy, hard, 3 lb.
Cornstarch, Duryea's, 1 box	Walnut meats, 1 can (optional)
Chutney, 1 jar	Whiskey (or other spirits), 5 bottles
Maple syrup, 1 pt.	
Molasses, 1 pt.	Vermouth, bitters, etc.
French dressing, 1 pt.	Beer
Olive (or other cooking oil)	

CONDIMENTS

Salt	Cinnamon (optional)
Pepper	Garlic salt (optional)
Cayenne (Red) Pepper	Coconut, dry, shredded (optional)
Paprika	
Nutmeg	Escoffier Sauce Robert (optional)
Mustard, dry	
Mustard, prepared	Red wine, 1 pt.
Curry powder	White wine, 1 pt.
Vanilla extract	Sherry, 1 bottle
Worcestershire sauce	Madeira, 1 bottle
Bouillon cubes	Rum, 1 pt.
Garlic, 1	Brandy, 1 pt.

FOOD FOR AN OCEAN RACE

Ocean racing may be divided into two general types, the long Pacific and transatlantic races and the shorter Bermuda,

Mackinac, and many other races for which small craft must be provisioned for three days up to a week, plus a reserve in case of trouble.

Food for races which may last two weeks or more should be as varied as for cruising. The best list we know is the one Paul Hammond worked out for *Landfall* in the 1931 transatlantic race. This food list is reprinted in Uffa Fox's *Sailing, Seamanship and Yacht Construction,* pages 37–39 (Charles Scribner's Sons, 1934). Worked out for a crew of twelve, this food list contained plenty of variety for the three weeks' race, with a generous reserve. *Landfall* carried a professional cook. The crew ate in two shifts. Meals were served for half an hour, fifteen minutes before and fifteen minutes after the change of watch, at 7:45 A.M., 12:45 P.M. and 6:45 P.M. (the Swedish system of watches was used). As life was fairly regularized, it was important to have a normal variety at mealtime.

For the shorter races, however, the emphasis should be on simple, easy-to-prepare food. Variety is not essential. Nourishing, hot food is required, but as it may have to be prepared by any member of the crew, a large assortment will prove confusing and a waste of valuable time and energy in digging it out.

Rod Stevens has evolved a basic short race provisioning list used with real success on board *Mustang* in a Bermuda Race. This list, with Rod Stevens' comments on it after the race, follows. Our own comment is that it lacks red meat, such as a few raw steaks and a home-cooked roast of beef.

OCEAN RACING FOOD LIST
(Bermuda Race, three weeks' food for seven persons.)

BREAKFASTS

Perishables	*Remarks after race*
½ crate of fresh oranges	A few too many
3 doz. fresh grapefruit	
12 doz. eggs	
12 loaves Arnold thin-sliced bread . . .	Thin-sliced O.K. Right amount
6 coffee cakes	

FOOD PLANNING

Perishables (Cont.)
Remarks after race (cont.)

42 qts. homogenized milk . . . . . . 36 qts. enough. Lasted 6 days

12 half-pts. cream . . . . 9 half-pts. enough. Lasted 8 days

3 lbs. fresh butter . . . . Sufficient for 1 week. Two more
lbs. would have been good

2 doz. bananas

Dry Staples

6 Corn flakes (medium size)

4 Krumbles (medium size)

4 Grape-Nut Flakes (medium size)

1 Quick Quaker Oats

1 Wheatena

8 jars Borden's Instant Coffee

6 lbs. sugar (in 2-lb. boxes) . . . . . 4 lbs. would have been enough

1 bottle maple syrup

1 box Bisquick

Canned Goods

2 doz. #2 cans sweetened orange and
grapefruit juice mixed . . . . . White Rose very good. Perhaps
½ doz. more

4 cans sausage

6 cans bacon (Hygrade)

12 cans canned butter . . . . Superior, packed for Charles &
Co. Very good

LUNCHES

Perishables

4 heads lettuce

1 doz. tomatoes . . . . 2 doz. would have been better

Dry Staples

4 jars mayonnaise

2 jars homogenized Peter Pan Peanut Butter

6 cheese spreads (3 Vera-Sharp, 3 cheese and bacon)

6 jars currant jelly (White Rose) . . . 2 or 3 more jars of jelly could
have been used

4 jars grape jelly (Welch's)

3 bottles catsup

Mustard

Canned Goods

6 large tongues (tins)

8 cans baked beans (Heinz)

16 cans Armour's corned beef hash . . . Take more. Also beef stew

Canned Goods	*Remarks after race (cont.)*
6 cans potatoes (Premier)	One can serves only 4 people
8 cans spaghetti and tomato sauce . . .	4 would be enough
6 jars chicken and noodles (Diplomat) . .	Take more. Good with boned chicken to help it; 2-to-1 ratio

SUPPERS

Perishables	
1 cooked ham	Very good. Will keep for 2 weeks
1 cooked turkey	Very good. Gravy excellent. Stuffing not eaten
21 Idaho potatoes	14 (for 2 meals) enough for hot weather
2 fresh cakes	Big cake lasted 9 days. Good

Dry Staples

Pepper
Salt
 4 small Ritz crackers
 1 box Uncle Ben's rice
 5 lbs. onions

2 cartons Hershey's almond bars, small . .	Too much

Canned Goods (Mostly #2 Cans)

12 cans Herbex soup	Needed only half as much
12 cans cream of mushroom soup	
12 cans cream of pea soup	
12 cans cream of tomato soup	
12 cans tomato juice	
4 cans sweet potatoes	Take more. Premier very good
12 cans peas	
8 cans green asparagus	Either get less or a better brand
8 cans string beans	Kane's green beans, French-sliced, very good
6 cans halved peaches	Take more fruit. Apricots, figs, prunes, peaches
6 cans cherries	
6 cans apple sauce (Premier)	
6 cans cranberry jelly (Ocean Spray)	
3 tins FFV cookies (colonial, orange, & lemon)	Scotch Shortbread very good
6 cases canned beer	Ale also would have been good

FOOD PLANNING

ROUGH-WEATHER MEALS

A Word on Seasickness

The rough-weather menus suggested below are designed for ease of preparation and to avoid seasickness. The only sure cure for seasickness is to go home and sit down under an apple tree. When you feel like eating an apple you are well. The medical profession describes seasickness as a form of nervous shock induced by motion which upsets your balance mechanism either via the inner ear or through your eyes, or both. This process takes a different length of time for different people and even for the same person under varying circumstances.

Dr. Sheldon, in *First Aid Afloat,* says: "Volumes have been written on this subject, and many drugs tried. Undoubtedly the newer, longer-acting, anti-motion drugs have markedly decreased seasickness aboard ships. Whether they are really helpful to any great degree aboard small boats in rough seas is still open to debate. Some think these no better than the older remedies which depend on belladonna and hyoscine. If you have no special favorite anti-motion pill, you might try Marezine, dose is a 50 mgm. pill taken (if possible) a half-hour before the motion begins and repeated as necessary four to six hours later."

We suggest the following advice for minimizing seasickness which may be of practical value to you and your crew. If you are one of the five out of a hundred who are chronically seasick, do not try to be a sea cook. Avoid alcoholic binges and big, heavy meals just before going to sea unless you are sure of your sea legs. Once on board, avoid eyestrain. For example, don't read fine print, and, if you use them, wear dark glasses. Try to keep warm and busy in the open air. Postpone engine-room and cabin jobs while the going is rough.

Hot food is preferable to cold. Avoid foods which are hard to digest, such as pork or baked beans. Keep "on the alkaline side." Favor creamed soups or black bean or pea soup over vegetable or oxtail or clam chowder with tomato (Manhattan). Baked potatoes, oatmeal, corn-meal mush, and dry cereals with milk and sugar have a way of staying with you. Liquids (including coffee, tea, beer, and highballs) taken on an empty stomach sometimes bring on seasickness. Sugar helps some people in difficult moments, especially in the form of hard candy, such as sourballs or Life Savers. A nip of iced brandy is another preventive often recommended, as is gin and bitters.

Don't worry about seasickness, don't talk about it, and don't be embarrassed when it hits you. Only the novice boasts of being a good sailor, since the man is not yet born who will not have a few bad days in an otherwise carefree seafaring career.

Rough-Weather Menus

Heavy-weather menus are designed to make cooking easy and to stand by you after you have eaten them. Rough-weather cooked foods are generally served in bowls and can be eaten with a spoon. Ability to boil water is all that should be required of the cook when the going is really bad. Always use large pots with as small a quantity of liquid in them as possible, and keep your rubber boots on as a safeguard against a scalded leg or foot.

A good way to heat canned food without having to watch it or even stay below in an airless galley is to boil the cans in four inches of water in a large pot well secured to the stove. Wedge the cans in the pot so they won't turn over. Prick the top of each can with an ice pick before heating. Never heat unopened cans directly on stove top or in an oven, as they will explode. Unopened cans will not explode in boiling water.

Remember that in heavy weather hot food, not variety, is the spice of life. While breakfast, lunch, and dinner have little

59

significance in rough weather, we have divided the menus into these conventional categories for convenience in listing.

Heavy-Weather Breakfasts

1. Canned fruit juice
   Soft- or hard-boiled eggs with butter and broken crackers
   Coffee, tea, or cocoa
2. A whole orange
   Oatmeal, Wheatena, or Cream of Wheat; sugar or honey; milk (add cut-up dates if you like them)
   Coffee, tea, or cocoa
3. Canned fruit juice
   Corn-meal mush (heat in can); syrup, sugar, or honey; milk
   Coffee, tea, or cocoa
4. Canned stewed prunes (heat in can)
   Shredded Wheat, molasses, and hot milk
   Coffee, tea, or cocoa

Heavy-Weather Lunches

1. One of the following canned soups (if condensed, made with milk): Pea, black bean, cream of celery, cream of chicken, cream of corn, cream of mushroom, or cream of potato, with broken crackers
   Sandwiches
   Canned fruit or dried figs
   Hard candy (sourballs)
2. Dry cereal with raisins added; sugar or honey; milk
   Peanut butter or cheese, and crackers
   Cocoa or chocolate
   Hard candy (Life Savers)
3. Cold meat sandwiches (raw chopped beef is easy to digest)
   Cheese and crackers

Milk, cocoa, or chocolate
4. Canned tomatoes (heat in can) with broken crackers
   Canned prunes (cold)
   Milk
   Chocolate or hard candy

Heavy-Weather Dinners
1. Minute rice (or canned potatoes) and chicken à la king
   (heat in can)
   Canned pears or dried figs
   Coffee, tea, cocoa, or milk
   Hard candy (sourballs)
2. Baked potato soup (see recipe No. 2)
   Whole orange or banana
   Coffee, tea, cocoa, or milk
3. Chicken and noodles fortified with canned chicken in ratio
   of 2 to 1 (heat in cans)
   Apple sauce (canned)
   Coffee, tea, cocoa, or milk
4. Corned beef hash and small canned potatoes in ratio 1 to
   1 (heat in cans, if too rough to use frying pan)
   Fresh fruit or canned apricots
   Coffee, tea, cocoa, or milk
5. Minute rice and chipped beef or tuna (heat in cans; add
   butter or cream sauce if you can)
   Fresh fruit or canned black cherries
   Coffee, tea, cocoa, or milk
6. Sherry flip (see recipe No. 348)
   Baked or boiled potato with plenty of butter
   Stewed prunes (canned)
7. Canned beef stew and canned potatoes in ratio 1 to 1 (heat
   in cans)
   Canned apple sauce or dried figs

Milk

8. Soft-boiled eggs and cut-up canned tongue and crackers (heat can in egg water)

    Canned fruit and figs or dates

    Cocoa or chocolate

9. Hard-boiled eggs cut up into canned black bean soup made with milk

    Canned brown bread (heat in can) and butter

    Cocoa or chocolate

    Hard candy (Life Savers)

10. Fried steak (see recipe No. 56) or hamburger sandwiches

    Canned prunes or dried figs

    Coffee, tea, or milk

CHECK LIST OF BASIC PROVISIONS

The following list of basic provisions has been generalized to a considerable degree, since a detailed enumeration is not really helpful as a check list. For a useful list and description of non-perishable staple foods consult the catalog of S. S. Pierce & Co., Boston, Mass.

BASIC PROVISIONS THAT CAN BE BOUGHT IN ADVANCE AND KEPT FROM WEEK TO WEEK

Baking powder
Beer and ale
Bread, canned
Butter, canned
Cereals, hot (oatmeal, Wheatena, Cream of Wheat, etc.)
Cheese, processed and in jars
Chocolate, cooking
Cocoa, chocolate syrup in cans or jars
Condiments and herbs (see list, p. 65)
Coffee, in cans
Coffee, instant

Cornmeal
Cornstarch
Desserts, packaged (Jello, My-T-Fine, Royal, etc.)
Fish and shellfish, canned (see list, p. 115)
Fish, smoked (kippers, codfish, etc.)
Flour
Fruits, canned (see list, p. 261)
Fruits, dried (apricots, dates, figs, prunes, etc.)
Galley supplies (see list, p. 32 and p. 38)
Gelatin
Hot-bread mixes, prepared (Bisquick, Flakorn, Duff's, etc.)
Jams, jellies, marmalade, honey
Juices, canned (see list, p. 261)
Liquor (whiskey—Scotch, rye, bourbon; gin, brandy, rum, vermouth)
Macaroni, spaghetti, noodles; also canned (see list, p. 163)
Meats, canned (see list, p. 162)
Milk, evaporated, powdered
Molasses
Nuts
Oil, olive and other cooking
Pancake mix
Pickles and olives
Pie-crust mix
Rice, Minute and/or regular
Salad dressings (French dressing, mayonnaise)
Shortenings (Crisco, lard, margarine)
Soft drinks (ginger ale, Coca Cola, soda, etc.)
Soups, canned (see list, p. 88)
Spreads (peanut butter, apple butter, etc.)
Sugar (granulated, brown, powdered)
Syrup (corn, maple)
Tea
Vegetables, canned (see list, p. 204)
Vinegar
Wines (white, red, sherry, Madeira)
Water, bottled or canned reserve

FOOD PLANNING

Biscuits and crackers (Triscuits, Pilot, Saltines, Graham, Ritz, etc.)

Bread (white, rye, raisin, wheat, etc.)

Bread, dry (melba toast, zwieback, Holland rusk, etc.)

Butter, fresh

Candies (chocolates, candy bars, hard candies, etc.)

Cereals, cold (corn flakes, Shredded Wheat, Pep, etc.)

Cheese (Edam, Roquefort, cream, etc.)

Coffee, regular

Crackers, sweet (gingersnaps, Fig Newtons, Sultanas, Hydrox, etc.)

Eggs

Fish, fresh (cod, halibut, shad, etc.)

Fruit, fresh (apples, berries, melons, oranges, lemons, grapefruit, peaches, pears, etc.)

Ice

Meats, fresh (beef, lamb, veal, chicken, etc.)

Meats, smoked (bacon, ham, tongue, ham butts, sausage, frankfurters, etc.)

Milk, fresh

Vegetables, fresh (potatoes, onions, carrots, peas, lettuce, tomatoes, etc.)

Water, for your tanks

Check List of Condiments, Basic Ingredients, Frills and Garnishes

The following list of condiments, basic ingredients, frills, and garnishes are the materials which you will need to use in cooking as you follow the recipes of this book.

If the list of condiments (seasoning and flavorings) seems long, remember that the quantities required are small and non-perishable.

Some of the items listed as basic ingredients (such as apples, eggs, or consommé) are themselves used as staple foods. In the basic-ingredient list they are considered in their capacities as flavoring, mixing, and binding elements. A small supply of those basic ingredients listed as "essential" should, whenever possible, be kept on hand for cooking purposes. This simply means, for example, that you should not drink up all your consommé as soup, since you will undoubtedly want plenty of it for sauce as well.

The frills and garnishes listed below are optional. To some a Martini is a failure without its olive. To others garnishes are strictly nuisances to be left ashore. We remember that on one ocean race the most popular single food item on board was an enormous can of sweet midget gherkin pickles. Unfortunately it lasted only two days.

CHECK LIST OF CONDIMENTS

Essential to Complete Recipes in This Book

Angostura Bitters	Paprika
Bay leaves	Pepper, black
Catsup	Peppercorns
Cayenne (red) pepper	Rum
Curry	Salt
Garlic	Sherry and/or Madeira
Marjoram	Vanilla extract
Mustard	Worcestershire sauce
Nutmeg	

Useful, but less often called for

Basil	Dill
Brandy	Escoffier Sauce Robert
Bouillon cubes	Garlic salt
Capers	Ginger, crystallized or pre-
Chili sauce	served
Chives	Horseradish
Chutney	Mint, dried
Cinnamon	Parmesan cheese
Cloves	Parsley, fresh or dried
Coconut, dry, shredded	Rosemary
Cordials—Kirschwasser,	Sage
Curaçao	Sour cream

Useful, but less often called for (continued)

Soy bean sauce

Summer savory

Tarragon

Thyme

Tomato paste

White wine

CHECK LIST OF BASIC INGREDIENTS

Essential to Complete Recipes in This Book

Bacon

Baking powder

Bread or cracker crumbs

Butter

Carrots

Cheese

Chicken soup (clear)

Consommé

Corn meal

Eggs

Flour

Lemons, fresh

Margarine

Milk, fresh and evaporated

Mushrooms, canned

Oil, olive and/or other cooking oil

Onions, small white, not canned

Sugar, granulated, brown, and powdered

Tomato soup

Vinegar

Useful, but less often called for

Apples

Anchovy, fillets or paste

Celery

Chocolate, unsweetened

Cider

Cornstarch

Corn flakes

Corn syrup

Cream cheese

Deviled ham

French dressing, prepared

Gelatin

Ginger ale

Green peppers

Hollandaise sauce, canned

Holland rusk

Honey

Jams and jellies

Limes, fresh

Maple syrup

Mayonnaise

Molasses

Oranges, fresh

Pimientos, canned

Raisins

Salt pork

Sugar, powdered

Zwieback

Almonds
Candied fruit and fruit peel
Cherries, candied and maraschino
Citron
Gherkin pickles
Lemon peel, candied
Mixed fruits, candied

Olives
Onions, baby or pearl pickled
Orange peel, candied
Pickles
Pineapple, candied
Radishes
Walnut meats

HINTS AND SHORT CUTS

To core apples:

If you have no other corer, the small end of a funnel will serve.

To peel peaches:

Drop peaches for a moment in boiling water. Remove and cool. Skins will slip off easily.

To sort peas:

When peas have been shelled, put in cold water and discard those that float, as they are no longer good.

To peel onions without tears:

Hold a crust of bread in your mouth, or peel them under cold water.

To peel onions quickly:

Cover with boiling water. Let stand for 5 minutes. Cut off bud and root ends and skins will slip off.

To get rid of onion smell:

Wash hands in soap and water immediately, or scrub them with salt and wash them, or rub hands with a slice of lemon.

To extract juice from onions:

Cut onion in two and rub and twist cut part of halves against a grater. Or cut a slice off the root end and scrape the center of the larger piece with the edge of a tablespoon.

To dice, chop, or mince onions:

Cut the root end off and cut the surface into squares of the

size needed. Then slice onion across cuts and the right size
pieces will fall from the edge of the knife.

To peel tomatoes quickly:

Drop tomato into boiling water for 3 minutes, take out, and
skin will slip off easily. Or hold tomato on the end of a fork
close to burner flame, turning slowly until skin wrinkles
and splits. Cool, and skin will peel off easily.

To peel beets:

Do not peel until after beets are cooked, as they will bleed
and lose their flavor. When they are cooked, the skins, root,
and stump of tops will slip off in your fingers.

To cook potatoes quickly:

Cut into quarters or smaller before boiling for mashed
potatoes and boiled potatoes (except for boiled new potatoes,
which should be boiled whole).

To prepare potatoes ahead of time:

Potatoes may be peeled for several meals ahead if kept
covered with cold water. Water should be changed if they
are in it for more than two days.

To have better carrots:

Do not peel or scrape carrots before cooking, as the real
good of them lies under the very thin outer skins. Boil carrots whole, then rinse in cold water for a minute; skins will
slip off easily. Carrots can then be cut up, warmed with a
little butter, and served.

To freshen lettuce and other greens:

When wilted, all greens can be refreshed by rinsing in cold
water for a few minutes and then wrapping in a damp cloth
and placing in the icebox for as long as possible.

To obtain a small quantity of lemon juice:

Don't cut the lemon. Puncture it with an ice pick, squeeze
out what juice you want, and wrap the lemon in waxed
paper.

To cut parsley and other fresh herbs:

Use scissors. It is easier and quicker, and does not lose the fine essence as chopping in a bowl does.

To dress up fruits:

Add a couple of tablespoons of cordial or liqueur to cut-up fresh or canned fruit. Kirsch is our favorite, with Grand Marnier second.

To keep eggs:

Keep in icebox if possible. Never wash, as it removes protective coating.

To determine bad eggs:

If you are in any doubt about your eggs, put them in cold water just before you use them. Those that float to the surface are not fit to eat. Those that rise just below the surface are all right but not the best. Those that sink are fresh.

To slice hard-boiled eggs:

Draw the edge of a sharp knife across the surface. Do not press down hard.

To break eggs neatly:

Crack egg on the *inside* of the bowl. Otherwise the white runs down the outside and is messy.

To separate eggs:

Dent the shell by tapping gently, and open with the ends of your thumbs. Holding one half in each hand, empty the half that is all white. Then transfer the yolk to the empty shell, letting the white slip out between. You may have to repeat several times to get out all the white.

To measure eggs:

Where recipe calls for part of an egg, beat egg and then measure.

To keep bowls from slipping:

When you are beating something in a bowl, place bowl on a folded damp cloth, such as a dish towel.

To clean egg beater:

After beating eggs, wash beater immediately in *cold* water;

after cream, mashed potatoes, or mixtures with flour in them, use warm water. Try to keep cogs of beater out of water. If cogs need lubrication, use olive oil, cooking oil, or glycerine. Machine oil will flavor food.

To mix flour for thickening:

If flour is to be mixed with cold water or milk for thickening gravies, put flour and liquid in a jar with screw top and shake well. If flour is to be mixed with butter, do it with your fingers. Form a ball which can be dropped in the sauce or stew, where it will dissolve slowly and blend with the liquid to be thickened.

To keep flour, coffee, and tea:

All must be kept in tightly covered containers. At sea 1 quart of good flour, if left open, can absorb 1½ cups of water, making it difficult to use any recipe without adjustment. Coffee and tea lose their flavor quickly when uncovered. Keeping coffee in the icebox helps to keep it fresh, if you can find room for it.

To keep herbs and spices:

Keep in tightly closed glass jars with screw tops, as sea air quickly robs them of strength and flavor.

To prepare butter for sandwiches:

Let stand at galley temperature and then work it around in the bowl with a wooden spoon until it is creamy. It will spread more evenly and with much less waste.

To measure butter and other fats:

Pack firmly into the measuring spoon and scrape out with a knife. When cup is used for measure, pack so firmly into it that it retains the shape of the cup when it is turned out. When parts of a cup are called for, fill cup partially with water and add fat. For instance, where ½ cup of butter is called for, fill half the cup with water and then add butter until water comes up to the one-cup mark.

To melt chocolate:

First butter or grease the pot in which chocolate is to be melted; then melt over boiling water.

To freshen bread or rolls:

Let cold water run over them for a moment; put into a paper bag and put in a moderate oven (350°) for a few minutes. A few rolls at a time can be treated this way in a Connolly oven.

To whip cream:

Cream will whip more surely if the bowl and beater are first chilled.

To whip evaporated milk:

Put can of evaporated milk in boiling water for about ten minutes. Then chill in the icebox for at least half an hour. Pour into chilled bowl and beat fast. If plenty of sugar and a little vanilla are used, it is hard to distinguish from fresh whipped cream.

To keep cheese fresh:

Lightly butter the cut side and wrap in waxed paper, or wrap in a cloth wrung out with vinegar. Keep in icebox when possible. Keep in a cool place if icebox is too crowded. Soft cheeses such as Camembert or processed Gruyère should, of course, be kept in their regular wrappings.

To keep bread, cake, or cookies:

Keep in a tin bread box, with tight cover, which should be scalded and sunned at least once a week to prevent mold.

To keep chopping board clean:

The board on which you cut up fish, meat, and vegetables should always be washed with soap and water, rinsed well, rubbed with a freshly cut lemon, dried, and sunned for a few minutes if possible.

To season new cast-iron frying pans and Dutch ovens.

Scrub with hot water and soap. Rinse and dry. Place over flame or in oven, with about 4 tablespoons of grease in each utensil. Let heat for 15 minutes, twisting so that hot fat reaches all inside surfaces. Pour off fat and rub out utensil with newspaper or paper towels. It is much better to wipe out frying pans and Dutch ovens than to wash them, as it prevents rust on the inside of the pans, where it can do harm. However, it is sometimes necessary to scrub them out. In that case, wipe them over with a little grease as soon as they are dry. While on board, they should never be left ungreased.

To clean copper utensils:

Rub with the cut end of a lemon dipped generously in salt; or you can use one of the commercial polishes. Lemon and salt will clean, not polish.

To prevent enamelware from chipping:

Heat *slowly,* or the quick change of heat may crack the enamel and lay the surface beneath open to rust.

To stop fat fires:

Throw generous handfuls of salt on the flame. *Never* put water on flaming fat as it will spread the flame.

To prevent food on stove from smoking:

When food has boiled over on the stove, or in the oven, throw salt on it at once, and it will not smoke.

To clean a burned pot:

A badly burned pot can be cleaned by boiling vinegar in it. Vinegar will also remove the odor of fish from a pot.

To clean wooden spoons:

Wooden spoons are desirable, as they don't scratch the bottom of pots or bowls and the handles remain cool even when left in the cooking pot. However, they do absorb grease. To remove it, wet the spoon with ammonia and scrub with soap and hot water. Rinse carefully with hot water and dry.

To substitute for a cocktail shaker:

A mason jar with rubber and top will serve.

To remove pin feathers:

A small pair of tweezers will be a great help in removing the pin feathers of a not-too-well-plucked fowl. Lacking them, the edge of a knife blade held against the ball of the thumb will do the job.

To keep glasses from cracking:

When pouring hot liquids into glasses, hot whiskey, for instance, put a spoon in the glass before you begin to pour, and the glass won't crack.

To keep food hot:

If one dish must be finished before the others, to keep the stove top clear, place the pot with the cooked food on top of one of the pots in which food is still cooking—on the double-boiler principle. Sometimes it will be necessary to have several pots, one on top of the other. We call this "pagoda cooking."

To open boiled cans:

If heated cans have not been punctured before being placed in boiling water, place a dishcloth over the hot can and pierce can through the cloth with an icepick. Then cut top about three-quarters around with a rotary hand can opener (Westco is good), bend opened can top up, and pour out hot contents, using can opener as a handle.

To keep liquids from boiling over:

Butter edge of pan to the depth of an inch from the top. To keep spaghetti and rice from boiling over add 2 tablespoons of butter or margarine to the boiling water.

To repair small icebox leaks temporarily:

Should you have a small leak in your icebox, it can be repaired temporarily by a thick coating of melted paraffin.

To remove hot-dish marks from varnished or polished wood:

Immerse thick cloth in boiling water. Wring out; place, bunched-up on the marred surface; let it rest a minute. Remove; rub place with a dry cloth. Repeat until marks disappear. Wax and polish wood (no need to revarnish).

To be sure of proper flavor:

Underseason and taste. You can always add more. In fact, you must taste all the time when you cook, even at the expense of your own appetite.

Part Two

TWO-BURNER RECIPES

TABLE OF COOKING TIMES
Under 15 Minutes

COOKING TIMES

Under 15 Minutes

|---|---|---|---|---|
VEGETABLES (*continued*)				
Beet Greens	Pressure-cooked			150
Beet Greens		Canned		208
Brussels Sprouts	Pressure-cooked		Preparation Time 15 Min. (Optional)	152
Brussels Sprouts, Creamed		Canned		209
Cabbage, Boiled			Preparation Time 30 Min. (Optional)	154
Cabbage	Pressure-cooked		Preparation Time 30 Min. (Optional)	155
Carrots	Pressure-cooked			158
Cauliflower	Pressure-cooked		Preparation Time 30 Min.	161
Corn on the Cob				162
Corn on the Cob	Pressure-cooked			163
Cucumbers, Boiled				164
Eggplant	Pressure-cooked			166
Greens	Pressure-cooked			170
Onions, Creamed		Canned		215
Onions, Glazed		Canned		216
Peas, Green	Pressure-cooked		Preparation Time 30 Min. (Optional)	177
Potatoes, Creamed		Canned		218
Potatoes, Mashed	Pressure-cooked		Preparation Time 30 Min.	189
Spinach	Pressure-cooked			197
Spinach, Creamed		Canned		223
Squash, Summer	Pressure-cooked			200
Sweet Potatoes	Pressure-cooked			191
Tomatoes	Pressure-cooked			203
SALADS				
French Dressing				235
Green Salad				229
Vegetable Salad			Preparation Time 1 Hour (Optional)	233
Wintertime Salad				226
SAUCES				
Brown Roux				240
Brown Sauce				242
Cream (White) Sauce				241
Egg Sauce				244

Under 15 Minutes

Recipe
Number

SAUCES (*continued*)

	Recipe Number
Horseradish Sauce	246
Mornay Sauce	248
Mustard Sauce	249
Newburg Sauce	251
Olive Sauce	252
Onion Sauce	253
Poulette Sauce	255
Velouté Sauce	257
White Roux	239

EGGS

Eggs, Boiled	258
Eggs, Boiled, Cinderella	259
Eggs, en Cocotte	275
Eggs, Fried	277
Eggs, Marlou	259A
Eggs, Poached	276
Eggs, Scrambled	270
Eggs, Scrambled, with Cheese	272
Eggs, Scrambled, with Kippers	271
Eggs, Scrambled, with Tomato Paste	273

BREADS, CEREALS, PANCAKES, SPAGHETTI, AND RICE DISHES

Oatmeal	Pressure-cooked	289
Ralston	Pressure-cooked	290
Rhode Island Johnny Cake		293

DESSERTS

Apple Snow	302
Bar-le-Duc	310
Cheese and Apple	311

15 to 30 Minutes

SOUPS

Appleton Street Soup	1
Black Bean Soup, Improved	3

FISH

Boiled Fish, All Sorts	16
Clams, Steamed	39
Codfish, Boiled	21
Codfish (Dried) Down East	32

79

15 to 30 Minutes

		Recipe Number
FISH (*continued*)		
Codfish (Fresh), Pan-fried		23
Codfish, Poached		22
Clams Southside		33
Flounder, Baked		29
Flounder, Sauté Meunière		28
Haddock Hash		31
Kippered Herring (or other Seafood) Cutlets	Canned	47
Lobster, Boiled		30
Lobster (or other Seafood) Kedgeree	Canned	48
Lobster Newburg	Canned	49
Mussels Bonne Femme		35
Oyster Pie		41
Pan-fried Fish, All Sorts		19
Poached Fish, Most Sorts		17
Scallops Sautéed Meunière		37
Scallop Stew		38
Shrimps, Curried	Canned	52
Steamed Fish, All Sorts		18

MEATS

		Recipe Number
Beef, Dried	Canned	126
Beef Stew	Canned	117
Beef with Gravy	Canned	119
Chicken à la King	Canned	122
Chicken, Boned	Canned	120
Chicken Fricassee	Canned	123
Chicken, Whole	Canned	121
Corned Beef—Plain	Canned	124
Corned Beef Hash	Canned	125
Frankfurters	Canned	127
Ham, Deviled	Canned	129
Hamburgers	Canned	128
Hamburgers, Pan-broiled		68
Lamb Chops, Pan-broiled		76
Lamb Stew	Canned	130
Roast Beef Hash	Canned	131
Sausage, Fried		102
Steak, Pan-broiled		53
Steak, Pan-broiled in Salt		54

15 to 30 Minutes

			Recipe Number
MEATS *(continued)*			
Tongue	Canned		133
Veal Scallopini			88
Wiener Schnitzel			89
VEGETABLES			
Artichoke Hearts Newburg	Canned		205
Asparagus			139
Beets	Pressure-cooked		147
Brussels Sprouts, Boiled		Preparation Time 15 Min. (Optional)	151
Cabbage and Apples	Canned		210
Carrots Burgundy	Canned		211
Carrots Burgundy	Pressure-cooked		159
Carrots, Glazed	Canned		212
Cauliflower, Boiled		Preparation Time 30 Min.	160
Corn-Meal Mush, Fried	Canned		213
Eggplant, Boiled			165
Greens			169
Mushrooms, Creamed			172
Mushrooms in Cream Sauce	Canned		214
Mushrooms Fried in Butter			171
Onions	Pressure-cooked		174
Peas, Green, Country Style	Canned		217
Potatoes	Pressure-cooked		180
Potatoes, Boiled			179
Potato Cakes			195
Potatoes, Creamed	Pressure-cooked	Preparation Time 25 Min.	185
Potatoes, Fried		Preparation Time 35 Min.	186
Potatoes, Fried	Canned		219
Potatoes, Hashed Brown			187
Potatoes, Hashed Brown	Canned		220
Potatoes, Mashed			188
Potatoes, Salt Glazed			182
Spinach, Boiled			196
Spinach, Creamed			198
Squash, Fried			201
Summer Squash, Boiled			199
Sweet Potatoes, Candied	Canned		222
Sweet Potatoes, Fried	Canned		221

COOKING TIMES

<u>15 to 30 Minutes</u>

		Recipe Number
VEGETABLES (*continued*)		
Sweet Potatoes,		
Mashed	Pressure-cooked	192
Tomatoes, Fried		204
Tomatoes, Scalloped	**Canned**	224
Tomatoes, Stewed		202

SALADS

Deviled Eggs	237
Fruit Salad	232
Mayonnaise Dressing	236
River Salad	227
Tomato Salad	230
Waldorf Salad	234

SAUCES

Curry Sauce	243
Madeira Sauce	247
Mushroom Sauce	250
Parsley Sauce	254
Tomato Sauce	256

EGGS

Cheese Omelet	263
Crab Omelet	264
Eggs, Scrambled, with Creamed Onions	274
Ham Omelet	262
Jelly Omelet	265
Mushroom Omelet	261
Plain Omelet	260

BREADS, CEREALS, PANCAKES, SPAGHETTI, AND RICE DISHES

Corn-Meal Mush	Pressure-cooked	287
Cream of Wheat	Pressure-cooked	288
Pancakes		292
Rice, White or Wild	Pressure-cooked	301
Wheatena	Pressure-cooked	291

DESSERTS

Apples Normandy	303
Crepes	312
French Toast	314
Rum Omelet	323

TABLE OF COOKING TIMES

15 to 30 Minutes

COOKING TIMES

30 to 45 Minutes

TABLE OF COOKING TIMES
45 Minutes to 1 Hour

Recipe
Number

SOUPS

Baked Potato Soup		2
Fish Chowder		10A
New England Clam Chowder		9

MEATS

Beef Stew	Pressure-cooked	67
Chicken Curry		111
Chicken Fricassee	Pressure-cooked	107
Chicken, Fried		113
Chicken, Roast	Pressure-cooked	115
Chicken, Smothered		112
Chicken Stew	Pressure-cooked	110
Lamb, Roast, 3 lb.	Pressure-cooked	81
Pork, Roast Loin of	Pressure-cooked	94
Steak, Pan Fried, French Style		57
Steak, Sour Cream	Pressure-cooked	59
Veal Chops		87
Veal, Roast	Pressure-cooked	84
Veal Steak		82

VEGETABLES

Beans, Lima	144
Carrots Burgundy	159
Eggplant, Fried	167
Eggplant Provençale	168
Onions, Creamed	175
Peas, Green, Country Style	178
Potatoes, Baked	181

BREADS, CEREALS, PANCAKES, SPAGHETTI, AND RICE DISHES

Rice, Chinese	297
Rice, Fried	298
Rice, Wild, Boiled	300

DESSERTS

Blueberry Pie	322
Hetty's Betty	321
Vanilla Blancmange	304

85

COOKING TIMES

1 Hour to 2 Hours

			Recipe Number
Soups			
Court Bouillon			20
Fish Chowder			9A
Mary's Lobster Stew			8
Fish			
Galley Shore Dinner			36
Shrimps, Boiled			40
Meats			
Beef, Roast		Preparation Time 40 Min.	60
Beef, Roast	Pressure-cooked		61
Chicken, Braised			103
Chicken Cacciatore			104
Chicken Cromwell			116
Chicken Fricassee			106
Chicken Stew, Cream			109
Corned Beef and Cabbage	Pressure-cooked		73
Ham Butt	Pressure-cooked	Preparation Time 3 Hours	101
Lamb, Roast, over 3 lb.	Pressure-cooked		81
Lamb Stew			77
New England Boiled Dinner	Pressure-cooked		65
Pork Chops, Braised			91
Pot Roast	Pressure-cooked		63
Tongue, Boiled Smoked Beef	Pressure-cooked	Preparation Time 12 Hours	75
Veal, Roast			83
Veal Stew			85
Vegetables			
Beets, Boiled			146
Salads			
Potato Salad			231

Breads, Cereals, Pancakes, Spaghetti, and Rice Dishes

	Recipe Number
Corn Bread, Steamed	278
Corn-meal Mush	286
Rice, Wild, Alice	299

1 Hour to 2 Hours

Recipe
Number

DESSERTS

Apple Pie	319
Bavarian Cream	307
Charles Gregory's Poor Man's Apple Pie	320
Coffee Crème	309
Condés	315
Marion's Dessert	308
Norwegian Prune Pudding	316
Pot de Crème Chocolat	317

Over 2 Hours

MEATS

Beef Stew		66
Chicken Pot Pie		108
Chicken, Roast		114
Corned Beef and Cabbage	Preparation Time 2 Hours	72
Ham, Boiled or Baked		96
Ham Butts	Preparation Time 6 Hours	100
Lamb, Braised Roast		79
Lamb, Roast Leg		80
New England Boiled Dinner		64
Pork, Roast Loin		93
Pot Roast		62
Tongue, Boiled Smoked Beef	Preparation Time 12 Hours	74

DESSERTS

Blueberry Flummery	305

SOUPS

Time and time again your cold, tired, hungry crew will crave something hot and quick—and soup is it! From the lordly green turtle and sophisticated Vichyssoise to the humble bean, nearly every kind of soup may be had in cans in numerous brands, most of them with considerable merit. Canned soups are everything that soup should be aboard a small boat: easy to prepare . . . nourishing . . . satisfying. For instance, a cup of black bean soup which can be prepared in ten minutes has almost as many calories as a good-sized chunk of steak.

Our experience with dehydrated soups is limited. They are made by reputable manufacturers and enjoy wide sales, which should prove their merit. We have tried a number of kinds and have never quite warmed up to them. They never seem to have quite the body and richness we have come to expect from canned soups. Yet we recognize their merit. They are easy to store, are light in weight, and their labels stay intact. They are quick to prepare and have simple-to-follow directions on each package. You probably ought to try them. Don't take our word for it. Find out for yourself.

Canned soups fall into two categories—condensed, to which milk or water should be added, and ready to serve. Listed below are the canned soups, most of which are readily available anywhere.

Asparagus	Bean, Lima	Beef Bouillon
Asparagus, Creamed	Bean with Bacon	Beef Consommé,
Bean	Bean with Ham	Jellied
Bean, Black	Beef	Celery

Celery, Creamed	Corn, Creamed	Pepper Pot
Chicken	Fish Chowder	Purée Mongole
Chicken Broth	Gumbo Creole	Quahaug Chowder
Chicken Consommé,	Julienne	Scotch Broth
Jellied	Minestrone	Shrimp, Creamed
Chicken, Country Style	Mulligatawny	Soup Stock
Chicken, Creamed	Mushroom	Soups for Babies
Chicken Gumbo	Mushroom, Creamed	Spinach, Creamed
Chicken Noodle	Mutton Broth	Tomato
Clam Broth	Noodle	Tomato, Bretonne Bean
Clam Chowder,	Okra	Tomato, Creamed
New England Style	Onion	Tomato Okra
Clam Chowder,	Onion, Creamed	Turtle, Green
New York Style	Onion, French Style	Turtle, Mock
Clam Consommé	Ox Tail	Vegetable
Consommé	Oyster	Vegetable Beef
Consommé, Madrilene	Oyster, Creamed	Vegetable, Vegetarian
Consommé, Printanier	Pea	Vermicelli
Corn Chowder	Pea, Creamed	Vichyssoise

Justly favorite combinations of canned soups are:—

Green Pea and Tomato
Chicken and Cream of Mushroom
Chicken Broth and Mushroom Broth
Consommé and Asparagus
Cream of Onion and Asparagus
Chicken Gumbo and Vegetable
Green Turtle and Green Pea
Ox Tail and Split Pea with Mustard
Chicken and Cream of Corn

To these marriages you will add, of course, the combinations which particularly please you, or you can experiment with endless variations. Further variety is also available in the use of such flavorings and seasonings as you may have on board. Curry powder, for instance, mustard, Worcestershire, Angostura bitters (particularly in cream soups), sherry, Madeira, or brandy. If your taste runs toward fancier cooking, try onion juice, grated orange or lemon peel, bay leaves, cloves, and such dried herbs as marjoram, dill, summer savory, chives, and tarragon. As a wholesome change, use the vitamin-loaded water in which your vegetables have been cooked to dilute condensed soup.

Garnishes are worth while if you are in the mood. Croutons made of small cubes of stale bread fried in a couple of tablespoons of butter; leftover rice or spaghetti; tiny hamburgers (seasoned with salt, pepper, a pinch of dill, or chopped parsley, if you have them, boiled ten minutes in the soup itself or in well-salted water); slices of hard-boiled eggs, lemon, lime, or oranges.

Consommé is useful in so many ways that it should be stocked in really large quantities. Not only can it be used in the combinations mentioned in this book, but is good alone. Put on the ice for six or seven hours, it jellies and is refreshing on a hot night. Further, it can be used for making sauces, to step up the flavor of pallid stews, and for braising meats or vegetables. Next most useful are chicken soup, split pea, black bean, and mushroom. Following are a few suggestions for dressing up canned soups.

(Each recipe serves 4.)

1 Appleton Street Soup

Cooking time 30 minutes

Combine in the top of a double boiler **1 can Condensed Asparagus Soup** with **1 can Consommé, 2½ cups Fresh or Diluted Evaporated Milk, 1 teaspoon Curry Powder,** and **a few grains Cayenne (Red) Pepper.** Keep over boiling water at least 20 minutes, and just before serving add ½ **cup Cream or an additional** ½ **cup Undiluted Evaporated Milk.** This is enough for four. For six, add an extra can each of **Consommé** and **Milk** and ½ **teaspoon Curry.**

2 Baked Potato Soup

Cooking time 1 hour

Bake until the skin is crisp and the potato mealy, 4 **Medium-sized Potatoes** (see No. 181). Into the top of a double boiler pour **4 cans Chicken Soup.** We prefer College Inn Clear Chicken Broth for this. Season with **a few grains Cayenne (Red) Pepper** and ½ **teaspoon Nutmeg** (optional). Work the newly baked potatoes through a coarse strainer or colander with the back of a spoon into the soup. Stir well and bring to a boil. Beat up the **Yolks of 2 Eggs** in ½ **cup Cream or Undiluted Evaporated Milk.** Pour slowly into the soup, stirring well. Keep hot over boiling water in double boiler. (Do not let this soup come to a boil again or it will curdle.) Add ½ **teaspoon Salt.** Serve with **a dash of Paprika** on top (optional).

3 Improved Black Bean Soup

Cooking time 30 minutes

Into the top of a double boiler pour **4 cups Black Bean Soup.** (Dilute as directed on can, if soup is in concentrated form.) If you have any **scraps of Cooked Ham,** cut them up fine and add **8 Tablespoons,** or add **a small can of Underwoods,** or other **Deviled Ham** stirred well into the soup and simmered for 5 minutes. Then add the **Juice of** ½ **Lemon.** Stir well. Put over boiling water for at least 20 minutes. Just before serving, add **4 Tablespoons Sherry** (optional). If possible, have the bowls hot, and in each put a **thin slice of Lemon** and a **slice of Hardboiled Egg** (optional). The egg can be cooked in the bottom of the double boiler while the soup is cooking in the top.

4 Corn Chowder

Cooking time 40 minutes

Cut into very small pieces ½ **pound Bacon** (easy if you use scissors) and fry in the bottom of a large pot or bucket. Remove bacon as soon as slightly brown and save to be used later. In the remaining **Bacon Grease**, fry **4 Medium-sized Sliced Onions** until soft (8 minutes). Add **4 Medium-sized Potatoes,** peeled and cut into small pieces. Cover onions and potatoes with water and boil until potatoes are soft (15 minutes). Add **1 can Corn, 1 can Tomatoes** and **1 pint Fresh or Diluted Evaporated Milk.** Add cooked bacon (previously set aside). Thicken by mixing **2 Tablespoons Flour** with a little of the cold milk. Pour slowly into chowder. Stir well and bring to a boil. This is a full meal for four or a soup course for six. When doubled or tripled, an excellent meal for a large party. Serve with **Crackers** broken into bowls.

5 Cream of Onion Soup

Cooking time 35 minutes

In the top of a double boiler over the flame, boil until soft (20 minutes) **20 Very Small or 12 Medium-sized Peeled Onions** (or use a #2 can **Boiled Onions**) in **1 can Consommé** and ¾ cup **Fresh or Diluted Evaporated Milk** and 1½ cups **Water.** Add a few grains **Cayenne (Red) Pepper,** 1 teaspoon **Curry Powder,** a pinch of **Marjoram** (optional), ½ cup **Cream or Undiluted Evaporated Milk.** Cook together 15 minutes and serve with **a dash of Paprika** on top.

6 Onion Soup

Cooking time under 10 minutes

There are so many makes of good canned onion soup that a complete recipe is not included here. However, canned onion soup can be very much improved if a couple of **Large Onions** (Spanish onions are best) sliced thin are fried in **Butter** until almost black and canned soup added and brought to a boil. Put 1 teaspoon of **Whiskey** in each cup, pour in soup and sprinkle with **Grated Parmesan Cheese.**

7 Cream of Tomato Soup Wupperman
Cooking time under 10 minutes

Make cream of tomato soup as directed on the can. Add, 10 minutes before serving, for each four portions, **1 teaspoon Angostura Bitters,** and ½ teaspoon **Dried Marjoram.**

8 Mary's Lobster Stew
Cooking time 1 hour 20 minutes (plus 6 to 12 hours, optional)

Into a pot which can be tightly sealed (or a pressure cooker if you have one large enough) put **1 cup Boiling Water** (sea water is better if you are offshore in clean water), **1 Tablespoon Salt, 4 Small Live Lobsters** (about 1 to 1½ pounds each). (Any pot which has a lid can be tightly sealed by inserting a round piece of wrapping paper or a brown paper bag, well oiled with any cooking oil or bacon grease, between pot and lid and putting a weight on the lid.) Cook until done, about 10 minutes in pressure cooker, 20 minutes in sealed pot. Save water. As soon as lobsters are cool enough to handle, remove all meat from shell, saving the juices and keeping the green tomalley. (This is the liver and is particularly delicious.) Remove meat, lay lobster on its back and cut through shell with sharp knife, or use scissors or can opener. Cut from head to tail. Open lobster, pull tail meat out, and remove intestine (the black vein which is just under the shell along the back). All the rest of the meat is good. Crack claws to get out claw meat. Remove meat over a plate to save juice. Fry the **Tomalley and Red Roe,** if there is any, in **6 Tablespoons Butter** or **Margarine** for 7 minutes. Add **Lobster Meat** broken into small pieces, and water in which lobsters were steamed and all the juices and scraps. Leave pot on brisk fire for 10 minutes more. Let pot cool slightly and add **3 cups Warm Milk** and **1 cup Cream or Undiluted Evaporated Milk,** stirring constantly. When stock is a rich salmon color, it is done (about 12 minutes). Season with **Salt** and **Pepper** if desired, cool, and let stock "age" for at least six hours. Overnight is better, as the flavor improves with age. Heat and serve. *This is the best lobster stew we have ever known.* It is well worth the trouble.

9 New England Clam Chowder

Cooking time 1 hour

You can buy very good canned New England Clam Chowder, but it will not equal this if you want to go to the trouble. Wash **3 dozen Quahaugs (Hard-shell Clams)** in several waters, scrubbing with a brush to remove all sand and grit. Place clams in a pot, which can be tightly sealed, and add ⅔ **cup Water.** Cover pot and place over flame and let clams steam until they open (about 10 minutes). Remove clams from shells, saving the liquid in which they were cooked. Separate the soft and hard parts of the clams and chop hard parts into small pieces (or they can be put through a meat grinder, if you have one). Cut a **2-inch Cube of Salt Pork** into ½-inch cubes and place in pot in which chowder is to be made. Cook slowly, and when the cubes are brown, remove and save for later use. Into the pork fat put the cut-up hard parts of the clams and a **Large Onion** minced fine.

Cook slowly until onion is soft (about 6 minutes). Then stir into this mixture **3 Tablespoons Flour** (or 6 of roux—see No. 239). When this is well blended, add **3 Large Potatoes,** peeled, and cut into ½-inch dice (about 2 cups). Add liquid in which clams were steamed plus enough water to cover. Simmer until the potatoes are soft (about 10 minutes), then add the soft parts of the clams and browned pork pieces. Add **4 cups**

Heated Milk and 4 Tablespoons Butter or Margarine. Season with ⅛ teaspoon Pepper, and Salt if necessary.

This chowder should be served with pilot biscuits. Sometimes several biscuits are crumbled fine and cooked in the chowder for the last 10 minutes before serving. This should make about two quarts or enough to serve four people as a main course, or eight people as a soup course. As with most chowders, it keeps well and is even better when warmed up a second time.

9A Fish Chowder

Cooking time 1 hour 30 minutes or 1 hour

Cover skin, bones, and head from 2½ pounds Cod, Haddock, a combination of both, or other White-fleshed Fish, with 5 cups Cold Water to which 1 teaspoon Salt has been added. Bring to a boil and simmer for 20 minutes. Strain. Cut 2 cups Potatoes into small dice and boil until soft, about 10 minutes, saving liquid. This stock-making step may be eliminated and the potatoes cooked in 4 cups boiling water. Meanwhile, cut a 1½-inch cube of Salt Pork into small dice, and fry in a heavy pot (a Dutch oven is swell) until lightly brown. Add ¾ cup Finely Chopped Onions and cook until onions are soft, about 5 minutes. Sprinkle onions with 2 Tablespoons Flour, stir in well and cook for 5 minutes. Add potatoes and liquid in which they have been cooking, stirring well for 3 minutes. Then add the 2½ pounds fish cut into 2-inch pieces. Simmer until fish is cooked, about 25 minutes. Add ¼ teaspoon Pepper, ½ teaspoon Nutmeg, if you have it, 2 cups Hot Fresh or Diluted Evaporated Milk, and 2 Tablespoons Butter or Margarine. Add 4 Hard Crackers, Boston Common, Pilot Biscuit, or Saltines. Cook 10 minutes more. Taste, add more salt if necessary, and serve very hot with hard crackers on the side. This chow-

95

der will be much improved if it "rests" for a couple of hours and is reheated before serving.

10 Oyster Stew

Cooking time 10 minutes

Simmer **1 quart Opened Oysters** in their liquor until the edges of the oysters curl (about 4 minutes). Add **1 quart Warm Fresh Milk** or **1 pint Milk and 1 pint Cream** together with **2 Tablespoons Butter**. Bring this to a boil. Add **⅛ teaspoon Pepper, 1 Tablespoon Worcestershire Sauce, ¼ teaspoon Salt**. Serve in bowls with **a dash of Paprika** and a small lump of butter on top.

For recipes **10A Fish Chowder, 10B Persian Soup, 10C Greek Lemon Soup, 10D French Peasant Soup** see pp. 288–289.

FISH

Fish, whether fresh, salted, or smoked, is inexpensive, quick, and easy to prepare. Allow at least one-half pound of cleaned fish per person when planning. However, if more is cooked than can be eaten at one meal, it can be made into many appetizing leftover dishes. (See Nos. 31, 48.)

Fresh fish is good when it is stiff and the flesh firm. When poked with the finger, it should show no dent. The eyes should be bright, and the gills pink. Fresh fish sinks when put into water. Keep fish well wrapped when on the ice, preferably in waxed paper or parchment, both because its smell is transferable to other things, and because it loses its own flavor in direct contact with ice. Never leave fresh fish soaking in water, as it will become flabby and tasteless.

FISH COOKING TABLE

FISH	BOIL 6 to 10 min. per pound (# 16)	STEAM 12 to 15 min. per pound (# 18)	POACH 15 min. per pound (# 17)	PAN-FRY 15 min. (# 19)	BAKE 10 min. per pound
Bass (sea)	x	x	x	x	x
Bass (striped)		x	x	x	x
Bluefish		x	x	x	x
Codfish	x	x	x	x	x
Eel				x	
Finnan haddie		x	x	x	
Flounder	x		x	x	x
Grunt	x				x
Haddock	x				x
Hake	x	x	x	x	x
Halibut	x		x	x	x
Herring	x				
Kingfish	x			x	x
Mackerel	x				x
Marlin	x	x		x	x
Mullet	x			x	x
Perch	x			x	x
Pompano	x		x		x
Porgies	x		x	x	x
Salmon	x	x	x	x	x
Sardines				x	x
Scrod	x		x	x	x
Shad	x	x	x	x	x
Sheepshead	x			x	x
Smelts				x	x
Snappers	x				x
Sturgeon	x	x			
Swordfish	x		x	x	x
Trout (sea)	x		x	x	x
Tuna	x	x	x		x
Turbot	x			x	x
Weakfish	x		x	x	x
Whitefish	x		x		x
Whiting	x		x	x	x

11 To Clean a Fish

Place the fish on a newspaper-covered board. Pin the tail of the fish to the board with the point of an ice pick. If you keep your hands covered with salt, the fish will not be so slippery or so difficult to handle. With a fish scraper, a saw-edged knife, or a knife not too sharp held at a slant, scrape from tail to head until each side is free of scales. Make a large enough slit in the belly from the gills toward the tail to remove entrails. (To clean mackerel, cut down the middle of the back.) Wrap up and dispose of waste in the newspaper. Wash fish carefully in cold water and dry carefully. If fish is to be cooked whole, leave on head and tail. If it is to be served in fillets, steaks, or chunks, cut off head and tail. They may be saved to make stock or court bouillon in which fish can be poached. Don't cut off fins at the top and bottom of a fish that is to be cooked whole. When the fish is cooked, pull them, and the fin and the small bones attached to them will come out easily.

12 To Skin a Fish

When fish has been cleaned as above (it is not necessary to scale a fish to be skinned), run the tip of a sharp knife down either side of the entire length of the backbone. Cut the skin across the body at the tail. With tip of knife and fingers, loosen skin and gently pull from tail to head. Reverse fish and skin the other side. If fish is large and skin does not come off easily, cut into fillets, steaks, or chunks with the skin on and drop pieces to be skinned into boiling water for a minute or so. Skin will come off easily.

13 To Bone a Fish

After skinning, slit fish along belly through flesh to spine and lay flat on a newspaper-covered board. Scrape meat from

97

bones and backbone with the back of a knife. Remove long backbone with ribs attached. Go over fish carefully and remove all small bones with a pair of tweezers or a short-bladed knife. Save all bones for stock or court bouillon.

14   To Fillet

Fillets are usually the meat cut lengthwise from one side of a fish and free of skin and bones. Used whole in small fish, such as flounder, fillets are cut into convenient pieces when the fish is larger. Divide fish—cleaned, skinned, and boned, as described above—into two pieces along the back with a sharp knife. Each piece can be divided into smaller convenient-sized pieces, if desired.

15   Steaks and Chunks

Steaks are usually slices ½ to 1 inch thick of a fish from which the entrails have been cleaned, cut across the fish at right angles to the backbone. The skin is usually removed. For boiling, slices of large fish are cut as for steaks but much thicker, usually from four to five inches through. In this book these will be referred to as chunks.

WAYS TO COOK FISH

Fish should never be dull. It can be fried, poached (gently boiled), steamed, broiled, or baked. Because many small-boat galleys are not equipped with ovens or grills where fish can be baked or broiled, this book does not put much emphasis on these two methods of cooking. It concerns itself rather with the proved easy ways of cooking on the top of the stove.

In whatever way you may cook a fish, do it gently, slowly, with no extremes of heat.

16 To Boil a Fish

Fish with dry flesh such as cod, haddock, hake, halibut, salmon, tuna, and whiting, are good boiled. The pieces to be boiled should be washed, dried, and placed on a saucer or inverted pot cover which will fit, with room to spare, into the pot in which the fish is to be cooked. A piece of cheesecloth should then be wrapped around saucer (or pot cover) and fish, and the whole lowered into the boiling water. While the fish can be poached or boiled in gently simmering water flavored with ½ teaspoon Salt and 1 Tablespoon Lemon Juice or Vinegar per cup, it will have a much finer flavor if it is cooked in court bouillon (described in No. 20). It should be cooked at a temperature just below a boil. Where the stove cannot be turned down to allow simmering, use an asbestos pad between pot and flame and quench the boil by adding to the liquid in the pot a small amount of cold water or cold court bouillon each time pot comes to a rolling boil. Most fish will be cooked in about 6 to 10 minutes to the pound. Don't overcook so that fish flakes apart. It is done when the meat separates easily from the bones. Drain and serve on a hot platter or plates with a suitable sauce. Mustard, curry, horse-radish, creamed egg, Hollandaise, anchovy, or butter sauce is recommended with hot boiled fish. A cupful or so of the liquid in which the fish has been cooked makes, when strained, a wonderful base for any of these sauces.

17 To Poach a Fish

To poach a fish use less liquid than for simmering. Baste often. Frequently a bed of chopped onion or carrots or parsley is made in the pan in which the fish is to be cooked. The fish is laid on this and a small amount of **White Wine, Court Bouil-**

lon, or Water, with 1 Tablespoon Lemon Juice or Vinegar is poured over the fish. A cupful would be enough for a 2-pound fish. This is continuously spooned over the fish to keep it moist. Cook until done, when bones and flesh separate, usually about 15 minutes to the pound.

18 To Steam a Fish

Any fish that can be boiled can be steamed with less attention from the cook. Place fish, previously sprinkled with **Salt and Pepper** (and other seasoning, such as herbs, as desired) and wrapped in cheesecloth, in a colander over rapidly boiling water in which vegetables or other food may be cooking. Fit cover tightly over colander and let steam. The cooking time should be slightly longer than for boiled fish, about 12 to 15 minutes to the pound. Serve in the same manner as boiled fish.

19 To Pan Fry a Fish

This is an excellent way to cook small fish or fillets of larger fish. Dip for a moment or two into **Milk** which has been well salted (**1 Tablespoon Salt per pint of Milk**). Drain and then roll in **Flour or Corn Meal** (less digestible) which has been seasoned with **Pepper** and **Salt**. (To **1 cup Flour or Corn Meal** add 1 teaspoon Salt and ½ teaspoon Pepper.) An easy way to coat fish with flour is to put seasoned flour or meal in a paper bag and shake the fish in the bag. Fish can be cooked in frying pan in which **3 Tablespoons Butter, Margarine, or Bacon Grease** is at the bubbling stage.

An alternate method is to dip the fish in a mixture of **1 Egg** beaten with **1 Tablespoon Cold Water,** then roll in **Dried**

Bread Crumbs or Crushed Corn Flakes. The fish should then be put into a hot frying pan in **2 Tablespoons Butter, Margarine,** or **Bacon Grease** which has been brought to a bubbling stage.

Cook slowly (use asbestos pad if pan gets too hot) until one side is brown (about 4 minutes) and then turn and brown other side. Do not overcook. Do not let fat burn. When fish is done (rarely more than 6 minutes on each side, except in the case of fine-textured, moist fish such as sandfish), place on a hot platter or plates. *Do not use butter in which fish has been fried as a sauce,* but melt fresh butter seasoned with a little **Lemon Juice, Paprika,** and **Parsley** (if available).

20 Court Bouillon
Cooking time 1 hour 30 minutes

Lots of people ashore as well as at sea just won't take the trouble to make court bouillon. However, we are including it because we do make it when we want fish to be particularly delicious.

Court bouillon is a highly seasoned broth which imparts additional flavor to the fish simmered or poached in it. Instead of using boiling water, as indicated below, most French cooks always make fish stock by boiling head, bones, skin, and scraps of fish which has been cleaned, boned, and filleted, in 2 quarts (8 cups) of water for 30 minutes to get a stock with a strong fish flavor. The fish remains are strained out and the stock is used to make a stronger court bouillon as indicated below.

Into a pot put **2 quarts (8 cups) Boiling Water or Fish Stock** (see above), ½ cup **Scraped and Sliced Carrots,** ¼ cup **Finely Sliced Onions,** ¼ cup **Cut-up Celery,** if you have it, **10 Peppercorns, 3 Whole Cloves, 1 Bay Leaf, 1 cup White Wine** or ½ cup Vinegar. Bring to a boil and let simmer for 40 minutes. Strain, pour into pot in which fish is to be simmered or poached. This can be strained after use and used again and again. Keep in a well-capped jug or bowl in the icebox. This court bouillon can also be used for making the sauces to be served with the fish.

21 Boiled Codfish

Cooking time 25 minutes

If small, a cleaned fish can be cooked whole in a baking pan. The fish should be cooked barely covered with court bouillon, at the simmering point, or covered with water seasoned with ½ teaspoon Salt and 1 Tablespoon Lemon Juice or Vinegar per quart. The liquid should be allowed to simmer gently until the fish is tender (when bones separate easily), about 12 minutes to the pound. If fish is large, it should be cut into convenient-sized chunks, placed on a saucer. Both fish and saucer should be wrapped in cheesecloth and lowered into a pot with enough court bouillon or water to cover. Liquid should be kept simmering until fish is tender.

22 Poached Codfish

Cooking time 30 minutes

Chop fine 4 Large Onions and 3 Carrots. Add a pinch of Dry Marjoram if you have it, and place in frying pan with 1 Tablespoon Butter or Margarine and ½ cup Strong Court Bouillon, White Wine or Fish Stock (water in which bones, head, and skin of fish have boiled for 40 minutes), or Water seasoned with ½ teaspoon Salt and 1 Tablespoon Vinegar per quart. Place 2 pounds Cleaned Cod Fillets on this bed. Cover pan. If pan does not have a lid, cover with oiled paper, being careful that edges of paper do not extend far enough beyond pot sides to catch fire. Cooking must be very gentle. Do not let liquid boil. Baste fish with liquid frequently until done, about 20 minutes. Remove fish, keep warm, and cook down liquid to be used as a base for the sauce or as the sauce itself.

23   Codfish (Fresh) Pan-fried

Cooking time 16 minutes

Have 2 pounds Fresh Cod cut into convenient-sized pieces— either fillets or steaks. Dip into **Seasoned Fresh or Diluted Evaporated Milk,** seasoned with **2 teaspoons Salt per cup;** drain, and roll in **Flour or Fine Corn Meal** until completely covered. Flour should be allowed to set for a few minutes; then fish should be put into frying pan in which **2 Tablespoons Butter, Margarine, or Bacon Grease** has been brought to the bubbling stage. Cook slowly until one side is brown (about 4 minutes) and with pancake turner turn carefully and brown other side. Remove fish from pan and pour off grease in which it was cooked. Melt **1 Tablespoon Fresh Butter** in pan. Squeeze about 1 Tablespoon Lemon Juice into butter and pour over fish. Good with **Chopped Parsley,** if you have it, and slice of **Lemon.**

24   Baked Codfish

Cooking time 40 minutes

(For galleys with an oven.) Fillet a good-sized codfish—3 or 4 pounds. (See No. 14) Make a bed in the bottom of a baking pan of ½ cup **Chopped Onions** and ½ cup **Chopped Carrots.** Place one of the fillets of codfish on the onions and carrots. Add ⅛ teaspoon **Pepper** and ½ teaspoon **Salt.** Sprinkle with 3 **Tablespoons Bread or Cracker Crumbs** and dot with ½ **Tablespoon Butter or Margarine.** Cover with another fillet, add ⅛ teaspoon **Pepper** and ½ teaspoon **Salt.** Lightly sprinkle with **3 Tablespoons Bread or Cracker Crumbs**, dot with ½ **Tablespoon Butter**. Pour into pan ¾ **cup Fresh or Diluted Evaporated Milk** or ¾ **cup White Wine, or Water** to which **1 teaspoon Vinegar** has been added, or ¾ **cup Court Bouillon**, if available. Bake 30 minutes in 350° oven.

DRIED FISH

There are many kinds of canned and dried fish ready to serve. If fresh fish is not available these can give variety to the diet. Dried fish, either salted or smoked, in cans or in bulk, may usually be purchased anywhere. Some fish, such as cod and haddock, are salted, and others, such as salmon and herring, are smoked. Salted fish should be soaked in fresh water for several hours, changing the water several times. Where time makes this soaking impractical, put fish in frying pan, cover with fresh water, and bring to a boil. Pour off water, add fresh water, and bring to a boil. Repeat this 4 times, and fish will no longer be too salty to use. Always soak salted fish flesh side down so that the salt will go to the bottom of the pan.

(Each recipe serves 4.)

25   Codfish Balls

Preparation time 6 hours
Cooking time 40 minutes

There are many excellent brands of canned codfish balls. If available, these products can be easily prepared by following directions on can. Often the addition of a slightly beaten egg is an improvement. Form balls and cook as below. If you wish to make codfish balls from dried codfish, prepare as follows.

Let **2 cups Shredded Dried Codfish** stand for 6 hours in fresh water, changing water once or twice. Drain and carefully pick out pieces of bone. Peel and cut into small pieces **4 Large**

Potatoes, enough to make 4 cups. Put fish and potatoes into pot. Cover with water and boil until potatoes are soft (about 10 minutes). Drain off all water. Shake pot over fire until fish and potatoes are quite dry. Mash until potatoes are soft and fluffy. Add **2 Well-beaten Eggs, 2 Tablespoons Butter or Margarine, ⅛ teaspoon Pepper.** Beat well. If you have an egg beater on board, beat it with that until mixture is soft and fluffy. Ordinarily, this mixture would be made into balls 2½ inches through and fried in deep fat. Because of the fire hazard of deep-fat cooking in a small galley, we recommend pan-frying in **3 Tablespoons Butter, Margarine, or Bacon Grease.** For this, flatten balls on two sides. Keep soft. Do not squeeze into hard ball. Dip flattened sides into **Flour** and put into frying pan when fat is bubbling. Fry until one side is brown—usually about 6 minutes. Turn and brown the other side.

26   Brandade of Codfish (Salt or Fresh)
Preparation time 24 hours or 1 hour
Cooking time 40 minutes

Soak **1 pound Shredded Salt Codfish** in fresh water for 24 hours, changing water several times. If it is not practical to soak the fish as long as this, put fish into fresh water, bring to a boil, pour off the water, add fresh water, and bring to a boil. Do this 4 times. In the top of a double boiler placed directly over flame, cover fish with water and bring to a boil and simmer for 15 minutes. Pour off all water. Shake pot with fish in it over fire until fish is quite dry. Still in top of double boiler, pound fish hard with a heavy spoon, a wooden one if you have it, until fish is in shreds, soft and pliant. Add ½ **Tablespoon Lemon Juice,** stirring well into fish. Add very slowly, a few drops at a time, **3 Tablespoons Olive or Other Cooking Oil** per pound, stirring constantly. This will stiffen the mixture. Add slowly **3 Tablespoons Warm Cream or Undiluted Evap-**

orated **Milk.** Season with **a few grains of Cayenne (Red) Pepper** and ¼ teaspoon **Nutmeg.** Heat again in a double boiler, and serve (optional) decorated with sliced sweet gherkins.

When fresh codfish is used for this recipe, the fish should be poached in court bouillon or white wine until done—about 20 minutes. (See No. 17). It should be salted slightly and pounded as with cooked salted codfish. If you wish this to be a one-pot meal, boil potatoes in the bottom of the double boiler. This is a famous French dish.

27 Poached Flounder (Filet de Sole)
Cooking time 40 minutes

In a heavy frying pan in **4 Tablespoons Butter or Margarine,** cook **3 Tablespoons Finely Chopped or Grated Onions** until soft and brown (about 8 minutes). Add **½ cup Fish Stock or Strong Court Bouillon** to which has been added **2 Tablespoons Lemon Juice** and **½ cup Madeira or Sherry.** (If none of the above are available, use **1 cup Water** with **1 teaspoon Vinegar.**) In this liquid place **2 pounds Flounder Fillets.** Simmer covered until fish is cooked—about 15 or 20 minutes. In a saucepan put **1 Slightly Beaten Egg.** Add **1 cup Sour Cream (Sweet Cream or Undiluted Evaporated Milk** can be used). Season with **Salt** and **Pepper** and **Paprika.** Bring this to the boiling point, stirring gently all the while. Pour this over the fish. Bring up to the boiling point, stirring constantly. Do not boil.

28 Flounder (Filet de Sole) Sautéed Meunière
Cooking time 18 minutes

Dip into seasoned **Fresh or Diluted Evaporated Milk (1 teaspoon Salt to a cup) 2 pounds Flounder Fillets.** Roll in **Flour** and pan-fry gently in **3 Tablespoons Butter or Margarine** until golden brown on both sides (about 6 minutes on each side). Place fillets on hot plate or platter. Pour used butter out of frying pan. Add **2 Tablespoons Fresh Butter** with **1 Table-spoon Cut-up Parsley**, if you have it, and **1 teaspoon Lemon Juice**. Heat to the sizzling point and pour over the fish. Serve with a quartered **Lemon**.

29 Flounder (Filet de Sole) Baked

Cooking time 30 minutes

(For galleys with ovens.) After seasoning **2 pounds Flounder Fillets** with **1 teaspoon Salt**, ⅛ **teaspoon Pepper**, and ⅛ **teaspoon Nutmeg**, place in well-oiled baking dish. Sprinkle with **3 Tablespoons Finely Chopped Onions**. Over fish pour **1 cup Dry White Wine** mixed with **2 Tablespoons Lemon Juice**. If wine is not available, substitute water. Wine and lemon juice should just cover fish. Bring to a boil very slowly on the top of the stove, covered. If pan has no cover, cover fish with oiled brown paper (a torn paper bag does nicely), being careful that paper does not extend far enough beyond pan to catch fire. As liquid comes to a boil, remove cover and put pan in moderate oven (350°). Cook until fish is done, about 20 minutes, basting with liquid in pan and occasionally with **Melted Butter or Margarine**. Fish should be nicely glazed and sauce reduced to a tablespoon or so. This should be poured over the fish, which should be served with a **Quartered Lemon**.

30 Boiled Live Lobster

Following are three ways of boiling a lobster—all good.

Cooking time 15 minutes

1. Into **3 quarts Boiling Water** seasoned with **3 Tablespoons Salt** (or you can use sea water if you are offshore in clean water), drop **Lobster** head first, holding it by the back. Simmer lobster 5 minutes for the first pound and 3 minutes for each additional pound—time to begin when water comes to a boil after lobster has been immersed. Lobster should be bright red when done. Do not overcook, as meat becomes tough and stringy.

Cooking time 15 minutes

2. Cook as above in court bouillon. (Court bouillon can be strengthened for the next use by boiling in it the lobster shells after lobster meat has been removed. Simmer shells in court bouillon about 20 minutes; then strain.)

Cooking time 25 minutes

3. Into a pot which can be tightly covered, put **1 cup Boiling Court Bouillon,** or **Boiling Water** with **1 Tablespoon Salt** in it. Drop in **Lobster,** head first. Insert a round of wrapping paper or brown paper bag which has been oiled, large enough to fit, between lid and top of pot. Put weight on lid and steam over a hot fire for 20 minutes.

Whichever way it is cooked, split lobster down under side, crack claws, and serve with **Melted Butter.** Butter can be kept hot if a lump of it is floated on boiling water in a small bowl or cup and the lobster dipped in it.

At Maine clambakes, where a large number of lobsters are opened and eaten with the fingers, the following method is used: Break off the lobster tail at right angles to the body. Break off the tail fins at right angles to the tail. Push the hot tail meat forward and out of the tail shell with a spoon handle. Peel the top strip off the curled piece of tail meat, revealing the black cord. Clean out this cord, dip the tail in butter, and eat.

Lobster claws can be opened neatly as follows: Remove plug. Remove claw finger by bending it back at right angles to the claw. Separate claw from its two "arm joints." Lay the claw on its side and place a heavy knife at right angles to it at the place where the finger comes out. Tap the knife sharply, but not too heavily, with a hammer, mallet, rolling pin, or the bottom of a bottle. When you get the knack, the claw will crack right around at right angles to its length. The claw can be pulled apart in two sections, revealing the meat in perfect shape. This method avoids the bashing and splashing process by which lobster claws are usually opened.

31 Haddock Hash
Cooking time 15 minutes

Can be made with fresh hake, halibut, sandfish, or any dry-fleshed fish that has been previously cooked.

In a bowl mix **3 cups Cooked Haddock** broken into flakes (this may be a leftover from the day before) with **3 cups Diced Boiled Potatoes** (if canned boiled potatoes are used, cut into ½-inch dice). Season with ½ teaspoon Salt, ¼ teaspoon Pepper, ¼ **teaspoon Nutmeg.** Mix well. Place in frying pan in which **4 Tablespoons Butter, Margarine, or Bacon Grease** have been heated to bubbling point. Let hash brown on bottom; then stir well, mixing browned crust well into hash. Add **2 Tablespoons Fat** and let brown on the bottom again, about 6 minutes. Holding pan by handle in left hand, tip it toward you and with pancake turner fold one half of the hash over the other half as with an omelet. Slide or turn out of pan on hot platter with brown part on top. Or serve directly from pan. If mixture gets too dry in cooking, additional butter or bacon grease can be added.

32 Down East Dried Codfish
Preparation time 6 hours or 1 hour
Cooking time 20 minutes

Soak **1 pound Salt Codfish** for 6 hours in several changes of fresh water. Or, if there is insufficient time to do this, cover with fresh water and bring water to a boil. Pour off water, add fresh water, and bring to a boil. Repeat this 4 times. Dry fish carefully, either by pouring off water and tossing in pot over fire, or with towel. Break fish into small pieces and fry in **3 Tablespoons Butter or Margarine** in a heavy frying pan until nicely browned (about 15 minutes). Season with ⅛ **teaspoon Pepper** and ½ **teaspoon Nutmeg.** Barely cover with **about 2 cups ½ Cream and ½ Milk or Slightly Diluted Evaporated Milk.** Bring to a boil and serve.

33 Clams Southside (*Courtesy Stuart Crocker*)
Cooking time 15 minutes

Remove the hard parts from **1 quart Hard-shell Clams** (quahaugs) and chop the clams very fine. In **3 Tablespoons Butter** fry **1 Small Onion** chopped fine and **2 Tablespoons Parsley** chopped fine. When onion pieces are golden brown (about 4 minutes), add chopped clams and **a dash of Cayenne (Red) Pepper.** Cook for 3 or 4 minutes. Add **1 pint Heavy Cream** and simmer until cream is reduced by about half (6 minutes).

34 Steamed Mussels
Cooking time 15 minutes

Wash **2 quarts Mussels** carefully, scrubbing to get all of the sand and mud out of them. Carefully remove their beards, the seaweed-like stuff attached to them. Place them in a large pot and add **1 cup Boiling Water.** Place over flame, put cover on tightly and steam until mussels are opened—about 6 minutes. Remove from pot, strain the broth through two thicknesses of cheesecloth, and serve with the mussels. A little butter floated on very hot water should accompany them.

35 Mussels Bonne Femme
Cooking time 25 minutes

Remove the beards (the seaweed-like growth on the outside of the shells) from **2 quarts Mussels**. Scrub the mussels carefully in several changes of water until the shells are clean and free of sand. Put mussels in a pot, add **2 cups Dry White Wine, Court Bouillon,** or **Water** to which **2 teaspoons Vinegar** has been added. Add a **Good-sized Onion** in which a **Couple of Cloves** have been stuck, **1 clove of Garlic, 1 Bay Leaf,** ½ **cup Cut-up Celery,** and a **few sprigs of Parsley,** or as many of these as are available. Cover pot tightly and bring liquid to a boil. Cook until mussels are opened—about 10 minutes. Remove mussels from shells and keep hot. Remove garlic and bay leaf. Beat **2 Egg Yolks.** Add to eggs ½ cup **Warm Cream, Milk,** or **Undiluted Evaporated Milk,** and **2 Tablespoons Melted Butter.** Add this mixture slowly to liquid in which mussels were cooked, stirring constantly. Cook until just below boiling point. Add ¼ **teaspoon Pepper,** and **Salt** if necessary. Return mussels to pot and serve in pot. You can dip up sauce on shells and save washing spoons. Messy but delicious.

36 Galley Shore Dinner
Cooking time 1 hour 15 minutes

Boil **8 Good-sized Onions** for 25 minutes. Put in the bottom of a large pot or bucket **4 dozen Carefully Scrubbed, Cleaned Soft-shell Clams.** On top of the clams put **4 fillets of Fresh Codfish,** about ¼ pound each, wrapped in a piece of cheesecloth. On top of fish place **8 Sausages.** These, too, should be wrapped in a small piece of cheesecloth. Next add **8 Small Ears of Corn** with silk removed but the inner husks left on. Add onions wrapped in a small piece of cheesecloth. On top of these, put

4 Small Potatoes (White or Sweet). If you expect to feed very hungry people, 4 Small Live Lobsters can be added next. Pour 2 cups Boiling Water into pot. Put a round of oiled brown paper between top of pot and lid. Put weight on top of lid. Cook until potatoes are soft—about 40 minutes. Lift out the foods in their cheesecloth bags and keep hot. Serve broth first, then clams with melted butter, then fish, sausages, onions, potatoes and lobster. *Keep everything hot until served.* To do this, remove everything from the pot, pour broth into container or cups, and serve alone. Rinse sand out of bottom of pot. Put in 1½ cups Boiling Water with rest of food. Put lobster first, and so forth in the order in which they will be eaten. Serve with Butter Melted on boiling water in cup or bowl.

37 Scallops Sautéed Meunière

Cooking time 20 minutes

Heat 1 quart Cleaned Scallops. (Only central muscle is edible. Soft parts are thrown away.) Boil in their own liquor plus enough Water to cover, until they are soft and plump, about 6 minutes after they come to a boil. Drain off liquid. Put 1 Tablespoon Butter or Margarine into the pot with the scallops and shake over the fire until scallops are well covered with butter. Put ½ cup Flour and 1 teaspoon Salt in a bowl and roll buttered scallops in it, or put seasoned flour in a paper bag and shake scallops in it. Pan-fry the scallops in 2 Tablespoons Butter, Margarine, or Bacon Grease brought to the bubbling stage in a heavy frying pan. Scallops are done when lightly browned all over (about 10 minutes).

38 Scallop Stew

Cooking time 30 minutes

Put into a small bag of cheesecloth 2 Medium-sized Onions chopped fine, 1 Bay Leaf, 4 Tablespoons Chopped Parsley, if you have it, 4 Tablespoons Butter or Margarine. Simmer bag with these ingredients in it for 10 minutes in 4 cups Fresh Cream or 4 cups Fresh or Undiluted Evaporated Milk. Remove bag and add to liquid 4 dozen Clean Scallops and their liquor. (If deep-sea scallops are used, they should be quartered.) Let simmer for 20 minutes or until scallops are plump and tender. Season with ½ teaspoon Salt and a few grains of Cayenne (Red) Pepper. Serve hot in bowls with small lump of Butter floating on each and a few dashes of Paprika.

39 Steamed Clams

Preparation time 15 minutes
Cooking time 20 minutes

Thoroughly scrub 5 dozen Soft-shell Clams (steamers) with a brush to remove all sand or mud. Place in a large pot which can be tightly closed, together with 1½ cups Boiling Water. Cover and steam over low heat for 20 minutes or until clams are opened. Remove clams and strain broth carefully through two thicknesses of cheesecloth. Serve with cups of the hot broth, on which a lump of butter has been melted.

40 Boiled Shrimps

Cooking time 1 hour 35 minutes

In 2 quarts Water (8 cups) boil for 15 minutes 1 Small Sliced Onion, 1 clove of Garlic, 1 Small Lemon, sliced, 1 Bay Leaf, 10 Peppercorns, 2 stalks of Celery, 3 teaspoons Salt, or as many of these items as are available. After liquid has boiled 15 minutes, add 2 pounds Carefully Scrubbed Shrimp. Let shrimp simmer for 18 minutes and turn off fire so that shrimp can cool in the liquid. When cool, remove shrimp, dry, and then carefully remove shells. Be sure after removing shells to remove black vein (intestines) just under skin along back of each

113

shrimp. Shrimp can be eaten as soon as cool with a spicy sauce (either prepared cocktail sauce or a barbecue sauce), in salad, or can be reheated to be creamed (No. 241), curried (No. 243), or served in Newburg sauce (No. 251).

41   Oyster Pie

Cooking time 25 minutes

Into a large pot put 5 **Tablespoons Flour** and 5 **Tablespoons Butter**, ½ teaspoon **Salt**, and a few grains **Cayenne (Red) Pepper**, a large pinch of **Marjoram**, and a pinch of **Summer Savory**. Cook these together as for cream sauce (No. 241) about 4 minutes; then slowly add the liquor from 4 dozen **Oysters** and enough **Heated Fresh Milk** (about 1 cup) to make a thick white sauce. Add oysters to sauce. Meantime, boil 1 pound **Peeled Mushrooms** in a small quantity of **Water** (about ½ cup) until tender (about 10 minutes), (or use 2 6-oz. cans of mushrooms with liquid instead). Season mushrooms with ½ teaspoon **Salt**. Add mushrooms and liquid to the oyster mixture. Add 4 **Hard-boiled Eggs** sliced thin. Now add 1 cup **Fresh Cream**, 5 **Tablespoons Madeira or Sherry**. The dish should be kept warm until time to serve. 2 cups **Bread Crumbs** fried in 3 **Tablespoons Butter** until browned are sprinkled on the top. This oyster pie should be served from the dish in which it is cooked. It is a dish for special occasions only, but one well worth the trouble.

42   Fried Smelts (Sautéed Meunière)

Preparation time 25 minutes
Cooking time 12 minutes

Smelts are usually eaten whole, uncleaned. They can be cleaned, however, by opening the outer gill and with fingers or tweezers gently removing the inner gill. All inedible parts come away with the inner gill. Smelts should then be washed thoroughly and dried. While they are usually cooked and served with the heads and tails on, these can be cut off if desired.

Let **2 pounds Smelts** stand in the juice of **2 Lemons** for 20 minutes, turning over frequently so that all are exposed to the lemon juice. Roll smelts in seasoned **Flour (½ cup Flour** to 1 teaspoon **Salt** and ½ teaspoon **Pepper)**, or flour mixture can be put in paper bag and fish shaken up in it. Put smelts in a frying pan in which **2 Tablespoons Butter or Margarine** has been heated to the sizzling stage. Pan-fry until light brown, then turn and brown on the other side—about 3 minutes to each side. Place fish on a hot platter or on plates on which they are to be served. Empty used butter out of the frying pan. Melt **1 Tablespoon Fresh Butter** in the frying pan in which fish have been cooked. Add **1 teaspoon Lemon Juice** and pour over fish to be served.

WAYS OF USING AND IMPROVING CANNED SEAFOODS

Following is a list of the great variety of shellfish and seafoods which are available in cans. Most of them can be used directly from the can without preparation other than following the directions on the can. We have a friend whose idea of a really sumptuous meal is to open a can of tuna fish and eat it right out of the can, oil and all. However, not too many palates can adjust themselves to so rigorous a diet, so we are suggesting some of the things that can be done with offerings of the sea in cans. No doubt your own ingenuity will suggest many variations and additions.

Just see what a variety of canned seafood is available almost anywhere:

Alewives
Anchovies, whole
Anchovy paste

Caviar
Clam broth
Clam cakes

Clam juice
Clam nectar
Clams
Clams, minced
Codfish balls
Codfish cakes
Codfish flakes
Crabmeat
Crayfish
Eels
Eels, pickled
Eels, smoked
Finnan haddie
Fish flakes
Fish roe
Frogs' legs
Herrings
Herrings in tomato sauce
Herrings, kippered
Lobster
Lobster paste
Mackerel
Mackerel, tuna style
Mackerel fillets
Menhaden
Mullet

Mussels
Mussels, jellied
Oysters
Oysters, smoked
Pilchards
Salmon
Salmon, smoked
Sardine fillets
Sardine paste
Sardines in mustard sauce
Sardines in oil
Sardines in tomato sauce
Sardines, kippered
Shad
Shad, kippered
Shad roe
Shrimp, dry pack
Shrimp, wet pack
Squid
Sturgeon
Sturgeon in tomato sauce
Tonno
Trout, steelhead
Tuna
Tuna, creamed
Turtle

In many of the following recipes other canned seafood can be substituted for the one listed. For instance, while Lobster Newburg is the recipe listed, the same sauce is equally good for crab flakes, mussels, oysters, or shrimp.

43 Minced Clams in Cream Cheese Sauce
Cooking time 5 minutes

Melt **1 package (3 ounces) Cream Cheese** in a saucepan. Pour into it slowly the liquid from **1½ cups Canned Minced Clams.**

Add ½ teaspoon Garlic Salt, if you have it. If not, substitute ½ teaspoon Salt. Add ¼ teaspoon Mustard, 1 Tablespoon Worcestershire Sauce. Add the minced clams and bring to a boil. If sauce seems too thick add a little **Fresh or Diluted Evaporated Milk** to give the right consistency. Serve on toast or crisp crackers. This is a good canapé with drinks. It is also a good luncheon dish.

Crabmeat, fish roe, oysters, salmon, shrimp, or tuna fish can all be cooked and served in this manner. The difference in can sizes will make it necessary for you to make adjustments in the sauce.

44   Crab Flake Cakes

Preparation time 45 minutes
Cooking time 15 minutes

Crumble 4 slices Bread from which the crusts have been removed into a saucepan in which there is ½ cup Olive Oil or other Cooking Oil. Let crumbs soak in oil for ½ hour. Slightly beat 2 Egg Yolks, season with ⅛ teaspoon Mustard, ⅛ teaspoon Paprika, ⅛ teaspoon Nutmeg, ½ teaspoon Salt, and 4 teaspoons Worcestershire Sauce. Mix this thoroughly with the crumbled bread. Into this combination mix thoroughly 2 6½-oz. cans Crabmeat. Add the stiffly beaten Whites 2 Eggs, and fold crab mixture into them. Cut vertically down with a spoon, draw spoon across bottom of bowl, and bring it vertically up. Repeat about 15 times. Form into 1½-inch balls. Flatten slightly at the top and bottom and roll in Flour. Fry the cakes slowly in 2 Tablespoons Butter in a heavy frying pan. If the flame cannot be adjusted, use an asbestos pad between flame and pan. Cakes should be nicely browned—about 6 minutes on each side.

Minced clams, fish roe which has first been boiled for 10 minutes in enough salted water to cover, kippered herring, sardine fillets, or shad roe (this must also be boiled in enough water to cover), all make excellent cakes to be prepared in this way.

45 Clam Pancakes

Cooking time 15 minutes

Beat 1 Egg well and add to it, stirring in well, **1 cup Cream or Undiluted Evaporated Milk.** To this add ¾ cup Minced **Clams.** Sift together 1½ cups Flour with ½ teaspoon Salt and ½ teaspoon **Baking Powder.** Combine all ingredients. If cakes are too thick when cooked, add a little **Fresh or Diluted Evaporated Milk.** If they are too thin, add a little **Flour.** Heat a heavy frying pan and grease it with a piece of bacon on a fork or with a rag dipped in bacon grease. When pan sizzles if a few drops of water are sprinkled on it, it is time to pour in a little of the batter. When bubbles begin to break on the surface, lift edges of cake to see if it is browning. If satisfactory in color, turn and cook the other side. Grease the pan before each batch of cakes. If flame under pan cannot be controlled, use one or more asbestos pads until you arrive at the correct heat.

Pancakes can also be made with crab flakes, cut-up lobster, or shrimp.

46 Crabmeat à la King

Cooking time 15 minutes

Boil ¼ cup Chopped Green Peppers in a little salted water until soft or use ¼ cup Canned Green Peppers or Pimientos. Mix together 1 cup Crabmeat (1 6-ounce can) with 3 Hard-boiled Eggs chopped fine, 1 3- or 4-ounce can Mushrooms, and the cooked **Green Pepper.** Into a saucepan put 3 Table-spoons Butter or Margarine, 3 Tablespoons Flour, ½ teaspoon Salt, ½ teaspoon **Paprika.** Blend well together and add

2 cups Fresh or Diluted Evaporated Milk, stirring in slowly.
Let sauce come to a boil, stirring all the while. When it is at a
boil add the crabmeat mixture and let simmer for a few minutes. Add 2 Tablespoons Sherry and serve on toast or crackers.
This is particularly good on zwieback or Holland rusk.

Canned clams, lobster, frogs' legs, mussels, oysters, salmon,
and tuna are all good cooked this way.

47   Kippered Herring Cutlets

Cooking time 15 minutes

Remove the skin and bones from 1 can Kippered Herring.
Mix with 2 cups Cold or Hot Mashed Potatoes. Season with
½ teaspoon Salt and ¼ teaspoon Pepper. Form into 2-inch
balls, flatten, roll in Flour, dip in 1 Egg well beaten with
1 Tablespoon Water, roll in Bread Crumbs and fry slowly in
4 Tablespoons Butter, Margarine or Bacon Grease. If flame
cannot be controlled, use an asbestos pad between pan and
flame.

These cutlets can also be made with minced clams, codfish
flakes, crabmeat, lobster, salmon, shad, sturgeon, or tuna.

48   Lobster Kedgeree

Cooking time 30 minutes

In the top of a double boiler mix together 2 cups Cooked
Rice (No. 296), 2 6-ounce cans Lobster or 2 cups fresh Lobster Meat, 4 Hard-boiled Eggs chopped fine, 4 Tablespoons
Butter, ¾ cup Cream or Undiluted Evaporated Milk, 1 teaspoon Salt, ½ teaspoon Paprika. Heat thoroughly over boiling water.

This dish is good also with leftover or any of the following
canned fish: minced clams, crabmeat, finnan haddie, herring,
mackerel, mussels, oysters, salmon, sardine fillets, shad, shrimp,
sturgeon, or tuna.

49 Lobster Newburg
Cooking time 25 minutes

Melt **3 Tablespoons Butter** in a small frying pan or saucepan over a low flame or with an asbestos pad between flame and pan. In the butter fry **2 6-ounce cans Lobster** or **2 Cups fresh Lobster Meat.** Do not brown; keep turning. When lobster is nicely warmed through, add **1 cup Heavy Cream or Undiluted Evaporated Milk.** Cook slowly until the cream has been reduced to ½ its original quantity. (You can note how far up it comes on the pan when it first starts to cook.) Beat **2 Egg Yolks** and mix them with ¼ **cup Fresh Cream.** Take pan with the lobster in it off the fire and add the egg mixture, stirring all the while; then add 4 **Tablespoons Good Sherry,** ½ teaspoon Salt, **a few grains of Cayenne (Red) Pepper** and ¼ teaspoon Paprika. Heat pan but *do not bring to a boil,* or sauce will separate. Serve on toast or heated crackers.

Nearly every other kind of shellfish can be served with satisfaction in this sauce.

50 Creamed Lobster
Cooking time 8 minutes

Make **1 cup Medium Cream Sauce** (No. 241). Add **2 6-ounce cans Lobster** to it and add **a few grains Cayenne (Red) Pepper, 1 Tablespoon Lemon Juice,** or the same amount of **Sherry,** and simmer for a few minutes. Serve on toast or on crackers.

Clams, crabmeat, fish flakes, frogs' legs, herring, mussels, oysters, salmon, shad, shad roe, shrimp, or tuna can be served in this way.

Further variation is available to you by using any of the following listed under "Sauces": velouté sauce, curry sauce, egg sauce, mornay sauce, parsley sauce, poulette sauce, mushroom sauce, or Madeira sauce.

51   Oysters and Mushrooms on Toast
Cooking time 15 minutes

Empty the juice from 1 6- or 8-ounce can **Mushrooms** into a
small saucepan. Add to this **1 cup Fresh or Diluted Evaporated
Milk, 1 Small Onion** sliced thin, **1 clove of Garlic,** and **1 Bay
Leaf,** if you have one. Let this simmer together a few minutes.
Meanwhile, in larger saucepan melt **4 Tablespoons Butter or
Margarine** with **4 Tablespoons Flour,** ½ teaspoon **Salt,** ¼
teaspoon **Pepper.** Let this cook together for 2 minutes, stirring all the while, and then strain and add the milk and mushroom juice to it. Let this combination simmer for 5 minutes
and then add the mushrooms and **3 cups Canned Oysters** with
their juice. Bring to a boil. Take off the fire and stir in **2 Egg
Yolks** mixed with a little **Cold Fresh or Diluted Evaporated
Milk.** Put back on the fire, stirring all the while, until it begins
to thicken, about 4 minutes. Do not let boil again or the
sauce will separate. Serve on toast or crackers. Zwieback or
Holland rusk are good substitutes for toast. **3 Tablespoons
Sherry or Madeira** added at the last moment is considered
very good.

This same dish can be made with clams, crabmeat, lobster,
mussels, salmon, or tuna.

52   Curried Shrimp
Cooking time 30 minutes

An easy way to have this dish is to make curry sauce (No. 243)
and add **1 Tablespoon** more of **Curry Powder.**

A more authentic curry can be made as follows: Peel, core,
and slice thin **1 Tart Apple.** Peel and cut into small pieces
3 Small Onions. Cut **2 stalks of Celery** into small pieces. In a
heavy frying pan heat **4 Tablespoons Butter or Margarine.**
When this has reached the frothing stage add apple, celery, and

onion. Cook until all are soft, about 8 minutes. Then sprinkle on **2 Tablespoons Flour** and **2 Tablespoons Curry Powder.** Blend well together. Add **1½ cups Hot Consommé** (water can be substituted), stirring well until sauce has simmered 6 minutes. If it is too thick, add more consommé. If it is too thin, add more flour. The consistency should be a little thicker than heavy cream. Add **2 Tablespoons Seeded Raisins** and, if you have it, **3 Tablespoons Shredded Coconut.** Drain **2 6½-ounce cans of Shrimp** and take shrimp from cans. Be sure black vein along back (intestines) is removed.

Put shrimp into curry, let simmer a few minutes and serve, preferably with rice. Most of the other canned seafoods can be served in this way.

GOOD COMBINATIONS

You must not overlook the good dishes that are easily available by the marriage of canned seafoods and condensed soups. For instance, a can of tuna and a can of undiluted mushroom soup mixed with leftover rice or spaghetti or potato chips is a dish that is filling and tastes good. Put it in an oven dish, sprinkle with cheese, and brown in oven, if your galley carries one. Other fish can be substituted and other condensed soups —salmon and tomato, for instance. Try out your own combinations. It is hard to go very far wrong.

MEATS

Meats fall roughly into three classifications: fresh, smoked, and canned. There are advantages and disadvantages in each. Fresh meats require refrigeration. Smoked meats usually have to be soaked some hours before cooking. Canned meats are easiest to prepare and easiest to store, but because they must be packed to suit the average taste and pocketbook they do not always satisfy the better-educated and more fastidious palates. Realizing that fresh meat will be carried when possible, and smoked meats when there is time and space for soaking, we are devoting a separate section to suggestions for making canned meat more interesting and, where the variety on board is limited, less monotonous.

All fresh meat is better when taken off the ice one-half hour before cooking. Frozen meat, economical because it comes boned, is excellent when it can be used a few hours after it has been brought on board. Without low-temperature refrigeration, however, it deteriorates rapidly.

(Each recipe serves 4.)

BEEF

53 Pan-broiled Steak
Cooking time 12 to 30 minutes

There is probably no food closer to the heart of most men than a nice thick steak broiled over hickory coals. This is the traditional steak. Unfortunately most small boats offer only a two-burner alcohol or kerosene stove top. However, with a little ingenuity and care a passable substitute for the hickory-broiled wonder can be achieved.

Prepare a 2½- or 3-pound **Steak** by brushing with **Olive or other Cooking Oil** and sprinkling generously with salt. (It is better if this is done an hour or so before the steak is to be cooked.) Keep steak at galley temperature after it has been prepared. Heat a heavy frying pan until it is quite hot and then rub it with a piece of **Suet or a small piece of Fat** off the steak. The pan should be so hot that the fat sizzles. Then put the steak in the pan. Cook over a brisk fire. Sear it first on one side and then on the other, allowing about a minute for each side. Then keep turning steak every minute or so until done. This depends somewhat on the thickness of the steak and how well done you like it. Allow 8 to 15 minutes for a steak ¾ to 1½ inches in thickness; 18 to 25 minutes for a steak 1½ to 3 inches thick. If any fat collects, pour it off, as the point is to broil rather than fry the steak. Be careful not to pierce middle of steak in turning. Put fork in fat at the edge. When done to your taste, put steak on a hot platter, dot with **Butter,** sprinkle with a little **Pepper,** and serve.

54   Steak Pan-broiled in Salt
Cooking time 15 to 30 minutes

Put about ½ inch of **Salt** in a heavy frying pan and put over the flame. When salt becomes very hot, it begins to "boil" or seethe in the pan. Wipe a **3-pound Steak** with a damp, not wet, cloth and put into the pan. Sear first one side and then the other. Broil, turning about every 2 minutes. When steak has cooked the same length of time as you would customarily broil a steak of that thickness—8 to 15 minutes for a steak ¾ to 1½ inches; 18 to 25 minutes for a steak 1½ to 3 inches— hold it over the pan with a fork and with the back of a knife or some other handy tool knock off any salt that may be crusted on the steak. Put steak on a hot platter, dot with **Butter,** sprinkle with a little **Pepper,** and serve. This makes a very good steak, as the hot salt sears it and seals in the juices.

55   Potted Steak
Cooking time 45 minutes

Any kind of steak can be cooked in this way. It is a better way to cook round steak or any of the less tender cuts. Wipe a **2-pound Steak** with a damp cloth and rub **Pepper** and **Salt** well into it. Put **3 Tablespoons Flour** in a paper bag and shake the steak in it until it is well covered with flour. Peel and cut into thin slices **4 Medium-sized Onions.** In a heavy frying pan heat **4 Tablespoons Bacon Grease**. Fry onions in this until they are a light golden color (about 8 minutes). Then put in the steak and brown on each side, about 3 minutes to a side. When well browned add **1 can Consommé** and bring to a boil. Cover and simmer at low heat until meat is tender, about 15 minutes. Remove steak and thicken sauce with **2 Tablespoons Flour** mixed with **2 Tablespoons Butter**. Add **1 6-ounce can Mushrooms** (optional) and let sauce simmer for 5 minutes. Return steak to the pan, heat together for 2 minutes, and serve.

56   Fried Steak
Cooking time 18 to 40 minutes

Wipe a **3-pound Steak** with a moist cloth. Put **3 Tablespoons Flour** and **1 teaspoon Salt** in a paper bag. Shake up steak in this or rub flour well into steak with the fingers. Put **3 Tablespoons Butter, Margarine, or Bacon Grease** into a heavy frying pan. When the fat is sizzling, put in the steak. Fry first on one side for a minute, then turn and fry on the other side. Turn down flame or put an asbestos pad between flame and pan and put cover on pan. Turn steak about every 2 minutes until done, about 8 to 10 minutes for a steak ½ to ¾ of an inch thick, 15 to 30 minutes for a steak that is 1½ to 2½ inches thick, depending upon how rare you like your steak. Dot steak with **Butter or Margarine** and serve on a hot platter, or make gravy and season it with a little Worcestershire or other meat sauce.

57   Pan-fried Steak, French Style
Cooking time 50 minutes

Have **4 Individual Steaks** of ½ pound or more each. In a heavy pot or Dutch oven bring **4 Tablespoons Butter or Margarine**

to the sizzling stage. Sear steaks on each side and lightly brown
(1½ minutes on each side). Put on steaks 4 **Small Potatoes** cut
in ½-inch dice. Add 4 **strips Bacon, 2 cups Small Onions,**
peeled, 1 small (6-ounce) can **Mushrooms,** drained. Add 1
Small Bay Leaf and 4 sprigs **Parsley** if you have it, 1 **teaspoon Salt,** ½ teaspoon **Pepper,** ½ can **Consommé,** and ½
cup **White Wine** if you have it; if you do not, use a full cup
of consommé. Simmer over the flame for about half an hour
or until the steaks are very tender. Stir occasionally to get
vegetables well mixed. Serve on a deep platter or on individual
plates. For a heavy-weather dish, use canned potatoes and
canned onions instead of raw.

58 Mandarin Steak

Cooking time 35 minutes

In a covered saucepan simmer for 5 minutes 1 **can Cabbage**
(or 1 **Small Cabbage,** shredded), ½ cup **Chicken Broth** or
Canned Chicken Soup, 4 **Tablespoons Olive or other Cooking
Oil.** In a large saucepan simmer together for 5 minutes **3
Tablespoons Olive Oil,** 1 clove of **Garlic,** crushed, ¼ cup
Chicken Broth, ⅓ teaspoon **Salt.** Thicken with 2 teaspoons
Flour mixed with an equal amount of **Butter.** Add 4 **Tablespoons Soybean Sauce.** Let simmer gently. Cut a 2-pound **Sirloin or Round Steak** into strips ¾ of an inch thick and 2½
inches long. Salt lightly on each side. Heat a heavy frying pan
until a drop of water sizzles on it, rub it with a little fat from
the steak, and quickly brown strips of meat in it. Cook on both
sides about 1 minute each. Put steak strips into sauce and let
simmer for 5 minutes. Drain the cabbage and arrange it on a
small platter. Arrange strips of meat on the cabbage and pour
remaining sauce over.

59 Sour Cream Steak, Pressure-cooked
Cooking time 1 hour

Mix together 2 Tablespoons Flour, 1 teaspoon Salt, ¼ tea-spoon Pepper, and put them in a paper bag. Wipe with a damp cloth **2 pounds Chuck or Round Steak** and cut into 3-inch pieces. Shake steak up in paper bag until it is well covered with the flour mixture. With a rolling pin, heavy spoon, or the bottom of a heavy bottle, pound the steak thoroughly, pound-ing flour mixture well in and flattening steak pieces slightly. Melt **2 Tablespoons Butter, Margarine, or Bacon Grease** in a heavy frying pan and in it fry until soft but not brown **2 cups Peeled Onions** chopped fine (about 10 minutes). Brown steak pieces on both sides in this pan. Place steak in pressure cooker with **1 cup Water.** Cover cooker, and when steam comes out of the vent put indicator in place. Cook for 15 minutes after in-dicator reaches fifteen pounds pressure or the "cook" position. Cool cooker in cold water for a minute, open, and add cooked onions. Add remains of flour mixture in which steak was shaken, mixed with **1 cup Sour Cream.** Close cooker and bring up to fifteen pounds pressure or "cook" position on indicator. Cook for 2 minutes longer. Cool cooker and open. If sauce seems too thin, add a little **Flour** mixed with an equal amount of **Butter or Margarine.** Simmer a few minutes and serve.

60 Roast Beef
Preparation time 40 minutes
Cooking time 1 hour 40 minutes to 3 hours

This is possible only if your galley has an oven. Take a 5-pound **Rolled Rib Roast** off the ice and keep at galley tem-perature at least ½ hour before cooking. Wipe roast with a damp cloth and rub **Salt, Pepper,** and **Flour** well into the meat. (If roast is very lean, skewer or pin with a sail needle a little fat, salt pork, or bacon to the top of it.) Heat oven to 500°. Put roast in a pan with no water in it, fat side up. Cook for 20 minutes at 500°, then reduce temperature to 300° and continue until roast is done to your taste, about 16 minutes to the pound if you like it rare, 22 minutes to the pound if you like it medium, and 30 minutes to the pound if you like it cooked through. If your galley oven does not have a thermometer, heat oven over full flame for 10 minutes and then put roast in. At the end of 20 minutes reduce flame, or if your stove has a fixed flame put two asbestos pads under the oven.

61 Roast Beef, Pressure-cooked
Cooking time 1 hour to 1 hour 15 minutes

Wipe a 4-pound Rolled Roast of Beef, either Sirloin or Rib, with a damp cloth. Rub into it 1 teaspoon Salt and ¼ teaspoon Pepper. In cooker melt 2 Tablespoons Bacon Grease or Other Fat. Brown the roast in it, turning to get it browned evenly on all sides. Lift out roast and put rack in the cooker. Add ½ cup Hot Water, return roast to pot, cover cooker, and put over the flame. When steam comes out of the vent put indicator in place. Cooking time should be estimated from the time indicator reaches fifteen pounds or the "cook" position. For a rare roast cook 36 minutes, for a medium roast cook 40 minutes, and for a well-done roast cook 48 minutes. Cool cooker in cold water for a minute, then remove cover and serve roast.

If you want sauce, pour liquid in which roast was cooked into a cup or small pan. Cool in cold water so that the fat will come to the top. Skim off fat, thicken the sauce with 1 Tablespoon Flour mixed smooth with a little cold water, simmer a minute, and serve with meat.

62 Pot Roast

Cooking time 3½ hours

Nearly any cut of beef can be pot roasted. A rib roast should be ordered from the butcher rolled. A sirloin roast makes a very fine pot roast. However, the round, rump, cross-arm, clod, chuck, and blade bone all make good pot roasts if they are boneless. In fact, the tougher cuts of meat usually have the best flavor. Tie a **4-pound Roast,** if the butcher has not tied it, in a good shape with light twine. Rub it well with **Salt, Pepper,** and **Flour.** In a heavy pot (a Dutch oven is ideal) bring **3 Tablespoons Bacon Grease or Other Fat** to a sizzling heat. Put in the roast and brown it on all sides about 5 minutes. Pour over it **1 can Consommé** mixed with ½ can **Water.** Into this, slice **2 Onions, 1 Carrot,** and, if you have celery aboard, **2 or 3 Celery Tops.** This mixture should be boiling. There should be about ½ inch of liquid in the bottom of the pot. Cover pot tightly. Meat should simmer over low heat for 2½ hours, or until tender. Use asbestos pads under pot if flame cannot be turned down. Add a little water as necessary. Turn meat 3 or 4 times during cooking to cook all sides. When meat is done remove from pot and thicken juices with **1 Tablespoon or so of Flour** mixed with an equal amount of **Butter or Margarine.** Simmer in sauce for 5 minutes. Serve meat on a platter surrounded with boiled vegetables, onions, carrots, potatoes, and anything else you might like. You can cook **diced Potatoes, Carrots, Onions, Turnips, and Beets** with ¾ cup **Water** in pressure cooker together for 8 minutes. If beets are cooked, wrap them in a bit of aluminum foil with the ends tied up, as they will bleed and color other vegetables. Pour gravy over vegetables or serve on the side.

63 Pot Roast, Pressure-cooked

Cooking time 1 hour 15 minutes

Remove excess fat from a 4-pound **Pot Roast,** either sirloin, round, chuck, or brisket, and tie it into shape with white twine or string. Put **2 Tablespoons Fat** into cooker and in it brown ½ **cup Onions** chopped fine (about 5 minutes). Brown roast in fat, remove, and put rack in cooker. Place roast on rack and add **1 cup Consommé or Water** in which vegetables have been cooked. Sprinkle roast with **1 teaspoon Salt,** add **4 Small Carrots** washed and cut up fine, ½ **cup Celery** cut into small pieces, and **4 Tablespoons of Chopped Parsley,** if you have it. Cover cooker and place over flame. When steam comes out of the vent put indicator in place. Cook for 45 minutes after indicator reaches fifteen pounds or "cook" position. Cool a minute in cold water and take off cover. Remove roast from cooker. Lift out vegetables with a spoon with holes in it. If you want sauce, thicken liquid with **2 Tablespoons Flour** mixed smooth with a little cold water. Simmer for 5 minutes. Roast can be returned to cooker to keep it hot while sauce is simmering.

64 New England Boiled Dinner

Cooking time 4 hours

Rub a 3-pound piece of **Round or Chuck of Beef** with **Pepper, Salt,** and **Flour.** Brown it on all sides in **2 Tablespoons Bacon Grease or Other Fat** in a frying pan. Then place meat in the pot in which it is to be boiled (a Dutch oven is excellent). Cover with cold water and bring to a boil slowly. Skim off any scum that rises to the top. Add **6 Peppercorns** and a **Small Bay Leaf,** if you have one. Simmer covered for 2½ hours. Put in the pot **3 Small Parsnips, 2 Yellow Turnips** peeled and cut into 1-inch chunks, and **6 Carrots** cut into ¾-inch pieces. Simmer ½ hour more and then add **10 Small Onions,** peeled, and 6 **Medium-sized Potatoes** cut into quarters. Cook about 25 minutes more, until potatoes are tender, and then add 1 **small head of Cabbage** cut into eighths. Cook until stem of cabbage can be easily pierced, about 10 minutes more. Serve all together on a platter or directly from the pot, cutting meat into convenient portions. Horseradish sauce (No. 246) is very good with boiled beef.

65   New England Boiled Dinner, Pressure-cooked
Cooking time 1 hour 15 minutes

Remove the excess fat from a **4-pound piece of Brisket, Chuck, or Rump of Beef.** Tie the meat in shape with white twine or string. Place the meat on rack in the cooker with ½ **cup Peeled Sliced Onions,** ½ **Bay Leaf.** Sprinkle meat with **1 tea-spoon Salt** and pour in **2 cups Water.** Close cooker, and when steam comes out of the vent put indicator in place. Cook for 45 minutes after indicator shows fifteen pounds or reaches "cook" position. Cool cooker in cold water and remove cover. Add to meat in cooker **6 Medium-sized Potatoes,** peeled and cut into quarters, **3 Small Parsnips,** and **2 Yellow Turnips** cut into 1-inch chunks, if you have them, **6 Carrots** cut into ¾-inch pieces, and **1 small head of Cabbage** cut into eighths. Close cooker, and when steam comes out of the vent put indicator in place. Cook 8 minutes after indicator shows fifteen pounds or reaches "cook" position. Cool cooker a minute in cold water and remove cover. Remove meat, sprinkle vegetables with **1 teaspoon Salt** and ¼ **teaspoon Pepper.** Stir in **1 Tablespoon Butter or Margarine.** Cut meat into serving pieces and serve with vegetables.

66 Beef Stew

Cooking time 2½ hours

Heat **3 Tablespoons Bacon Grease** in a heavy pot (a Dutch oven is fine) until it is almost smoking hot. In this quickly brown, stirring and turning frequently, **2 pounds Beef Chuck, Rump, Neck, or Round** cut into 1-inch cubes which have been rolled in pepper, salt, and flour—or better, put **3 Tablespoons Flour, 2 teaspoons Salt** and **1 teaspoon Pepper** in a paper bag and shake meat in it. When meat is well browned add enough boiling water to cover meat (about 6 cups), add **1 Bay Leaf** and a few sprigs of **Parsley** or **Celery Tops** all tied together so they can be removed when stew is cooked. Bring to a boil and simmer over low heat for 1½ hours. Now add **6 Medium-sized Potatoes** cut into quarters, **1 cup Canned Tomatoes, 24 Small Peeled Onions, 6 Carrots** cut into ¾-inch pieces, and **1 cup String Beans,** if you have them handy. Cook until all the vegetables are tender (about 25 minutes). Season with 1½ teaspoons Salt, ¼ teaspoon Pepper and ½ teaspoon **Paprika.** Add **1 Tablespoon Flour** mixed with **1 Tablespoon Butter or Margarine** and simmer for 5 minutes more. If served in a bowl or platter, add **1 cup Canned Green Peas** on top. If served in individual portions, put **1 Tablespoon Peas** on top of each serving. This last is optional, of course, but it does make a stew attractive to the eye as well as to the taste and smell.

67 Beef Stew, Pressure-cooked

Cooking time 1 hour

Cut **2 pounds of Beef Chuck, Neck, Round, or Rump** into 1-inch cubes. Put **2 Tablespoons Flour, ⅛ teaspoon Pepper** and **1 teaspoon Salt** into a paper bag. Shake meat cubes in it until they are well covered with flour. In a heavy frying pan melt **2 Tablespoons Bacon Grease or Other Fat.** Brown the meat cubes in it. Put rack in cooker and put meat on it. Any bones there may have been in the meat should be tied in a piece of cheesecloth and added. Add **1 can Consommé** and **1 cup Water** or water in which vegetables have been cooked. Cover cooker and place over flame. When steam comes out of the vent put indicator in place. When indicator reaches fifteen pounds or "cook" position, cook 25 minutes. Cool cooker in cold water a minute and remove cover. Put into cooker **6 Medium-sized Potatoes** cut into small cubes, **12 Small Onions,** peeled, **6 Small Carrots** cut into ¾-inch pieces, **1 Tablespoon Parsley,** cut up fine, **1 teaspoon Prepared Mustard,** ½ **Tablespoon Worcestershire Sauce.** Cover and when steam comes out of the vent put indicator in place. Cook 5 minutes after indicator reaches fifteen pounds or "cook" position. Cool cooker in cold water for a minute and remove cover. If stew needs it, thicken with **1 Tablespoon or so of Flour** mixed with an equal amount of **Butter or Margarine.** Serve stew with cubes of bread, with zwieback, or with Holland rusk.

68 Pan-broiled Hamburger

Cooking time 30 minutes

In **3 Tablespoons Butter or Margarine** fry **3 Tablespoons Finely Chopped Onions, 1 Tablespoon Parsley** cut fine, and ½ **cup Bread Crumbs,** for about 8 minutes. Then add this mixture to **1½ pounds Lean Hamburger,** mixing well in. Add **1 teaspoon Salt** and ⅛ **teaspoon Pepper.** Beat **2 Eggs** and combine with this mixture. Press well together to make a cake about 1½ inches thick. In a heavy frying pan melt **2 Tablespoons Bacon Grease or Other Cooking Fat.** Place meat in pan and let brown on one side, shaking pan frequently to prevent the meat from sticking. Meat should be browned in about 6 minutes. Put 1 **Tablespoon more of Bacon Grease** in the pan and turn meat carefully. Brown other side and serve.

69 Hamburger Balls
Cooking time 35 to 40 minutes

Prepare hamburger as for pan-broiled hamburger (No. 68) and roll into 4 even-sized balls. Flatten bottoms and tops of balls in a dish in which there is a little flour. Melt **3 Tablespoons Bacon Grease** in a heavy frying pan. Put in hamburger balls and cook over a slow fire. If you cannot control flame, put asbestos pads between flame and pan. The hamburger balls should cook about 8 minutes on each side—less if you like them rare, more if you prefer them well done.

70 Crusty Hamburgers
Cooking time 35 minutes

This is an interesting variation from the usual hamburger and worth trying. Prepare hamburgers in balls as in hamburger balls (No. 69). Then dip in **1 Well-beaten Egg** and roll in **3 Tablespoons Flour** seasoned with **1 teaspoon Salt** and **½ teaspoon Pepper**. Then dip meat into beaten egg again and roll in **Bread Crumbs**. Fry in a heavy frying pan in **4 Tablespoons Bacon Grease or Other Cooking Fat**. Fry until hamburgers are golden brown, about 4 minutes on each side.

71 Swedish Meat Balls
Cooking time 45 minutes

In **2 Tablespoons Butter** fry **3 Tablespoons Chopped Onions**. When soft (about 6 minutes) add **1 Tablespoon Chopped Parsley**, if you have it. Mix this with **1 pound Hamburger** that has been put through the meat grinder 3 times. This is important. Your butcher will be glad to put the meat through the grinder a couple of times extra if you ask him. When onions, parsley, and meat are well mixed, add 1 **Slightly Beaten Egg** and ½ teaspoon **Dill**, if you have it. Form the meat lightly into balls about 1½ inches in diameter and flatten slightly. Have simmering in a small pot 2 **cans Condensed Consommé** mixed with 1 **can Water.** Put 6 or 7 meat balls into pot, enough to cover bottom. They will sink to the bottom. When they rise to the top, after about 3 minutes, they are done and should be scooped out and set aside in a warm place. Repeat until all meat balls are cooked. Heat in a small saucepan 3 **Tablespoons Butter or Margarine** and cook with it 3 **Tablespoons Flour** seasoned with ½ teaspoon **Salt** and a **few grains Cayenne (Red) Pepper.** When this has cooked 3 minutes, add, stirring all the while, half of the consommé in which the meat balls were cooked. To this add ½ jar (½ cup) **Heavy Sour Cream.** Mix well. Put the meat balls back in this sauce and heat together for 5 minutes. Do not let the sauce come to a hard boil.

72   Corned Beef and Cabbage
Preparation time 2 hours
Cooking time 4¾ hours

All corned beef is good, but the fancy brisket is enough better to warrant paying a slightly higher price. Wipe a 4-pound piece of **Corned Beef** with a damp cloth and tie into shape, if this has not been done by the butcher. Cover with cold water and soak 2 hours. Put into a heavy cooking pot (a Dutch oven is fine) and cover with fresh **Cold Water.** Bring very slowly to the simmering point. Take off all the scum that rises as the water heats. If you want a really well-cooked corned beef, never let the water come to a rolling boil but keep the pot simmering gently. This is of course difficult with a stove that has a fixed flame. However, by using asbestos pads and adding a little cold water from time to time if the water seems to be reaching a rolling boil, you can manage. When the meat has simmered for 4 hours and feels tender to a fork, add **6 Medium-sized Potatoes** cut into quarters, **6 Carrots** cut into ¾-inch pieces and **16 Small Peeled Onions.** Just before potatoes begin to be done (about 30 minutes) add **1 head of Cabbage** cut into 4 wedge-shaped quarters. Let cook 10 minutes more, drain, and serve meat surrounded with vegetables on a platter.

73 Corned Beef and Cabbage, Pressure-cooked
Cooking time 1 hour 30 minutes

Wipe a **4-pound piece of Corned Beef** (the fancy brisket is best) with a damp cloth. Put in the cooker and cover with cold water. With the cover off, bring to a boil and simmer for 5 minutes. Pour off the water. Put rack in the cooker. If corned beef has not been tied in shape, tie it with white twine or string. Add **3 cups Water** and **1 Bay Leaf.** Cover cooker. When steam comes out of the vent put indicator in place. Cook 60 minutes after indicator reaches fifteen pounds or "cook" position. Cool cooker in cold water for a minute and remove cover. If beef is not tender, replace cover and cook until it is. When tender, add **1 Medium-sized Cabbage** cut into eighths. Close cooker and cook for 3 minutes after indicator reaches fifteen pounds or "cook" position. Cool cooker for a minute in cold water, remove cover, and serve. Horseradish sauce (No. 246) is traditional with corned beef.

74 Boiled Smoked Beef Tongue
Preparation time 12 hours
Cooking time 3 to 4 hours

Soak a **3-pound Smoked Beef Tongue** in cold water for 12 hours. Put it in a large pot and cover it with fresh water. Add

1 **Large Onion,** sliced thin, 2 **Bay Leaves,** 12 **Peppercorns,** 1 **cup Chopped Celery and Leaves,** and 1 **Carrot,** sliced. Let simmer until tongue is tender—that is, tender enough to drop off a fork (3 to 4 hours). Let it cool in the water in which it was cooked. When cool enough to handle, skin tongue carefully and remove the small bones and the hard parts. The tongue can be served hot by heating again in the stock in which it was cooked or in the top of a double boiler. It can be served with Madeira sauce (No. 247) or horseradish sauce (No. 246).

75 Boiled Smoked Beef Tongue, Pressure-cooked
Preparation time 12 hours
Cooking time 1 hour 20 minutes

Soak a **3-pound Smoked Beef Tongue** covered with cold water for 12 hours. Put in the cooker with a **Bay Leaf** and **3 cups Water.** Cover cooker, and when steam comes out of the vent put indicator in place. When it shows fifteen pounds or "cook" position, cook for 1 hour and 15 minutes. Cool cooker in cold water for a minute and remove cover. Tongue should be tender when tested with a fork. If it is not, put back and cook for 20 minutes more.

LAMB
76 Lamb Chops, Pan-broiled
Cooking time 20 to 30 minutes

Wipe 4 or 8 **Rib or Loin Lamb Chops** with a damp cloth. Wipe with a little **Olive or Other Cooking Oil.** Sprinkle generously on both sides with **Salt.** Have frying pan so hot a drop of water sizzles. Smear it with a piece of fat off one of the chops. Put chops in frying pan. Sear quickly on one side and then sear other side. Turn down flame or put asbestos pad between flame and frying pan. If any fat collects in frying pan, pour it off, as you do not want chops cooked this way to fry. For chops ¾ inch thick cook 10 to 12 minutes. For double lamb chops allow from 15 to 20 minutes. Dot with **Butter or Margarine,** sprinkle a little **Pepper** on top and serve.

77 Lamb Stew

Cooking time 1 hour 30 minutes

Have 1½ **pounds Lean Lamb** cut into 1½-inch cubes. Any cut of the lamb will do, but the most economical are lean breast, neck, or shoulder. Heat **1 can Vegetable Soup** in a heavy pot and add meat and enough water to cover the meat. Simmer until the meat is tender, skimming off any scum that may come to the top, about 50 minutes. Then add **3 Medium-sized Potatoes** cut into quarters (or **1 can Boiled Potato Balls**), **1 cup Very Small Peeled Onions** (or **Canned Onions**), **1 cup Carrots** (or **Canned Carrots**), cut into ¾-inch pieces. Simmer gently until vegetables are tender, about 30 minutes if raw vegetables are used. Then thicken stew with **2 Tablespoons Flour** mixed with **2 Tablespoons Butter or Margarine.** Simmer for 5 minutes. Season with **Salt** if necessary and add about ⅛ teaspoon **Pepper.**

78 Lamb Stew, Pressure-cooked

Cooking time 40 minutes

Cut into 1-inch cubes **2 pounds Lamb** (shoulder or breast, if not too fat, is fine and less expensive). Put meat on rack in cooker and add **3 cups Water.** Sprinkle meat with **1 Teaspoon Salt** and ¼ teaspoon **Pepper.** Cover cooker, and when steam comes out of the vent put indicator in place. Cook for 15 minutes after indicator reaches fifteen pounds or "cook" position. Cool cooker in cold water a minute, open and add **4 Medium-sized Potatoes,** quartered, **12 Small Peeled Onions,** and **1** bunch **Small Carrots,** washed and cut into ¾-inch pieces. Cover cooker, and when pressure reaches fifteen pounds or indicator shows "cook," cook for 5 minutes longer. Cool cooker in cold water a minute, then take off cover. Thicken liquid in which meat and vegetables have been cooked with **2 Tablespoons Flour** mixed smooth with a little cold water. Simmer for **3** minutes more uncovered, stirring all the while. Check seasoning and add more salt if necessary.

79   Braised Roast of Lamb

Cooking time 2½ hours

Have a 4- or 5-pound **Shoulder of Lamb** boned and rolled by the butcher. In a heavy pot (a Dutch oven is fine) heat **4 Tablespoons Butter, Margarine, or Bacon Grease.** Rub shoulder of lamb with **3 Tablespoons Flour** mixed with **1 teaspoon Salt** and ½ **teaspoon Pepper.** Sear meat on all sides until light brown. Remove meat and in the same kettle fry ½ **cup Chopped Onions,** ¼ **cup Carrots** chopped fine, ½ **cup Celery with Leaves.** When the vegetables are soft, about 12 minutes, return the meat and add **6 Peppercorns,** ½ **teaspoon Salt, 1 Small Bay Leaf, 1** sprig **Parsley,** if you have it, and **2 cups Vegetable Soup (Canned)** plus **2 cans Boiling Water.** Put lid on tightly and simmer for about 2 hours or until meat is very tender. When meat is done pour off stock in which it has been cooked and thicken with **2 Tablespoons Flour** mixed with an equal amount of **Butter or Margarine.** Add **1 cup Hot Green Peas,** fresh or canned, if you have them. It adds much to the appearance. Serve meat surrounded with vegetables and gravy **in a separate bowl.**

80   Roast Leg of Lamb

Cooking time 2 hours 20 minutes to 3 hours

(For galleys with an oven.) Wipe a **4- or 5-pound Leg of Lamb** with a damp cloth. Rub with **Flour, Salt,** and **Pepper.** Heat oven to 500°. Put lamb in a pan with cut side of leg down. At the end of 20 minutes turn oven down to 300° and roast lamb without basting from 30 to 35 minutes to the pound. Serve lamb with the cut side of the leg down for easier carving. If you like your lamb pink, cook only 15 to 20 minutes to the pound.

81   Roast Lamb, Pressure-cooked

Cooking time 40 to 50 minutes or 1 hour to 1 hour and 15 minutes

Either a rolled shoulder or a leg of lamb can be roasted in the pressure cooker. The method and the timing are the same. Wipe with a damp cloth a **3- to 4-pound Leg of Lamb** from which the end bone has been cut so that it will fit in the cooker. Rub it well with **Salt and Pepper.** Put **1 Tablespoon Butter, Margarine,** or **Bacon Grease** in the cooker, and when it is very hot brown the leg of lamb in it, turning carefully to get it good and brown on all sides. Add ¼ cup **Water.** Close the cooker and put on the flame. When steam comes out of the vent put indicator in place. If you like your lamb pink, cook for 30 minutes for a 3-pound roast and 40 minutes for a 4-pound roast after the indicator reaches fifteen pounds or the "cook" position. If you like your lamb well done throughout, cook for 50 minutes for a 3-pound roast and 65 minutes for a 4-pound roast. When lamb has cooked the correct length of time, cool cooker in cold water for a minute and remove cover.

This is best served with a mint sauce. An easy-to-make method follows: Heat almost to boiling ½ **cup White Wine**

Vinegar. Take off flame and stir in **1 teaspoon Powdered Sugar.** Stir until well mixed and sauce is beginning to cool, then add ¼ **cup Chopped Fresh Mint Leaves,** or **3 Tablespoons Dried Mint Leaves.** Heat, but do not boil, and serve with the lamb.

VEAL

Veal is a tender but unusually fibrous meat. To be really good it should be pounded hard on each side with a rolling pin or the back of a heavy knife. You must remember too that veal has not a great deal of flavor, so it must be cooked with spices or vegetables that will supplement its flavor but not take it over entirely. Veal cutlets, which are slices of lean veal, can be cooked in a variety of ways. Most ways call for quick browning in a frying pan and then slow cooking, covered, with fried onions, tomatoes or sour cream, and various kinds of stock. European cookbooks are filled with numerous variations of this method, many bearing the hallmark of famous chefs. Make up some combinations of your own.

82 Veal Steak

Cooking time 1 hour

This is usually a cut across the round or top of the leg about 1 inch thick. Rub **Salt** and **Pepper** into **2 pounds Veal Steak** and then pound it well with the back of a heavy knife or rolling pin or bottom of a heavy bottle to about ¾ inch in thickness. Shake it up in a paper bag with **3 Tablespoons Flour.** In a heavy frying pan, melt **4 Tablespoons Butter, Margarine, or Bacon Grease** to which **1 Tablespoon Paprika** has been added. Fry ¾ **cup Thinly Sliced Onions** until they are soft but not browned, about 10 minutes. Then add the slice of veal and fry about 10 minutes until it is well browned on each side. Pour in ½ **cup Cream or Undiluted Evaporated Milk.** Add **1 Table-**

spoon **Lemon Juice.** Cover pan closely and cook over a low flame (use an asbestos pad between flame and pan if flame cannot be controlled) until steak is tender, about 35 minutes. Remove steak and thin material in which it has been cooked with **a little Hot Consommé or Water.** Serve over steak.

83 Roast Veal

Cooking time 1¾ hours to 2¼ hours

(For galleys with ovens.) The best cuts for roasting are the leg, loin, and rump. Have the butcher take out the bones and roll and tie up a 4- or 5-pound **Roast**—unless you want to stuff it, in which case you roll the meat around the stuffing and tie it into shape with white twine. Wipe the meat with a damp cloth. Rub a little **Pepper** and **Salt** into it and shake it up in a paper bag with **3 Tablespoons Flour** until it is well coated. Place strips of **Salt Pork or Bacon** over meat. Place in baking pan and sear for 15 minutes in an oven at 450° temperature. Reduce temperature to 300° and cook until tender, about 30 minutes to the pound. The roast should be basted every 20 minutes. If there is not enough liquid to baste, add **Hot Consommé or Water.** Gravy can be made with materials in pan.

84 Roast Veal, Pressure-cooked

Cooking time 50 minutes

Any of these cuts make good veal roasts: boned leg, rolled shoulder, blade, or rump. Wipe a 3-pound **Veal Roast** with a damp cloth and tie in shape with twine. Mix **2 Tablespoons Flour** with 1½ teaspoon **Salt** and ¼ teaspoon **Pepper.** Rub the roast well with this mixture. In the bottom of the cooker heat **2 Tablespoons Butter, Margarine, or Bacon Grease** until it is very hot; then brown the roast in it, turning all sides to get evenly brown all over. Put into cooker **2 Bay Leaves, 4 Tablespoons Chopped Parsley,** if you have it, and ¼ **cup Liquid** from Vegetables or Water. Put top on cooker. When steam comes out of the vent, put indicator in place. Cook for 45 minutes after indicator shows fifteen pounds or reaches "cook" position. Cool cooker in cold water for a minute and remove cover. Serve with mashed turnips or mashed sweet potatoes.

85 Veal Stew

Cooking time 2 hours

Cut into 1-inch cubes 1½ **pounds Veal**. Brown it in **2 Tablespoons Butter or Margarine** in a heavy frying pan. When brown, sprinkle it with **2 Tablespoons Flour** and brown again. Add **2 cups Consommé, Water in which vegetables have been cooked, or Plain Boiling Water**. Add **1 teaspoon Salt** and ½ **teaspoon Pepper**. Add ½ **cup Carrots** washed and cut in ¾-inch pieces, ½ **cup Potatoes** cut into 1-inch cubes, **1 Bay Leaf**, **1 6-oz. can Mushrooms**, juice and all. Cook slowly for 1½ hours. If necessary, thicken stew with **1 Tablespoon or more of Flour** mixed with an equal amount of **Butter or Margarine**. Let simmer a few minutes more. Sprinkle with **Paprika** and serve.

86 Veal Stew, Pressure-cooked

Cooking time 40 minutes

Cut 1½ **pounds Lean Veal** into 1-inch cubes. In cooker, melt **2 Tablespoons Butter, Margarine, or Bacon Grease**; brown veal cubes in it. Sprinkle browned meat with **2 Tablespoons Flour** and brown again. Sprinkle meat with **1 teaspoon Salt** and ⅛ **teaspoon Pepper**. Put into cooker **4 Carrots** cut into small pieces, **4 Small Potatoes** cut in dice, **1 6-oz. can Mushrooms**, juice and all, and **1 Bay Leaf**. Pour in **2 cups Water or Water in which vegetables have been cooked**. Cover cooker and place over flame. When steam comes out of the vent, put indicator in place. Cook for 18 minutes after indicator shows fifteen pounds or reaches "cook" position. Cool cooker in cold water for a minute and remove cover. Thicken stew with **2 Tablespoons Flour** mixed with an equal amount of **Butter or Margarine**. Sprinkle with **Paprika** and serve.

87 Veal Chops
Cooking time 1 hour

Brown in a heavy pot (a Dutch oven is fine) **4 Veal Chops** ¾ inch thick in **2 Tablespoons Butter**. Add **6 Slices Bacon** cut into small pieces (easy with scissors), **1 cup Small Peeled Onions,** and **1 cup Potatoes** cut into ¾-inch cubes. Fry for about 15 minutes, then cover and cook very slowly, about 35 minutes. If stove has no flame control, put an asbestos pad between flame and pot.

88 Veal Scallopini
Cooking time 30 minutes

Have 1½ **pounds of Veal Cutlet** (top of the round is best) cut into ½-inch thick cutlets. Then have butcher pound them well. Dip these cutlets in **Melted Butter** and roll them in **Finely Grated Cheese**. Parmesan is traditional, but for our taste it is too strong. Any cheese will do. In a heavy frying pan put what is left of the **Melted Butter** and enough more to make **4 Tablespoons** and fry until cutlets are light brown (about 8 minutes). In a separate pan gently fry **1 small can Mushrooms** in **1 Tablespoon Butter or Margarine**. Add to this **1 Bouillon Cube** melted in **3 Tablespoons Hot Water, 1 Tablespoon Butter or Margarine,** and **4 Tablespoons Good Sherry**. Season cutlets with **Salt** and **Pepper,** arrange on dish on which they are to be served, and pour the mushroom combination over it. Sprinkle with a little **Paprika** and serve at once.

89 Wiener Schnitzel
Cooking time 30 minutes

Certainly the best known of veal cutlet dishes all over the world, Wiener Schnitzel is probably made in as many ways as there are schools of chefs. The method that follows is a very good one, the best that we know and not too complicated.

Have **4 Veal Cutlets**, about **2 pounds**, cut from the round about ¾ inch thick. Mix **2 teaspoons Dry Mustard, 2 teaspoons Salt, 1 teaspoon Garlic Salt** if you have it, and **1 teaspoon Pepper** with enough **Worcestershire Sauce** to make a thick paste. Rub one side of a cutlet with some of this mixture, and then with a rolling pin, the back edge of a knife, or the bottom of a heavy bottle pound the cutlet until it is about ⅛ inch thinner. Turn cutlet over, rub with the seasoning mixture, and pound as you did the first side. Do this to all cutlets. It does not take long, about a minute or so each. Put **4 Tablespoons Flour** in a paper bag and shake cutlets up in it until they are well covered with flour. Next dip into **2 Well-beaten Eggs** mixed with **2 Tablespoons Water** and then roll in **Fine Bread or Cracker Crumbs**. Put into heavy frying pan **4 Tablespoons Butter, Margarine, Bacon Grease, or Olive Oil**, and when it is sizzling hot put in the cutlets, as many at a time as the pan will hold. When the cutlets are browned, about 6 minutes on each side, they are done. They are usually served with tomato sauce (No. 256).

PORK

Fresh pork is not a very satisfactory meat for use on a boat. It is a rather indigestible meat, and one which does not keep well unless carefully refrigerated. It must be cooked for a long time before it is tender, and it must be cooked thoroughly to eliminate all danger of trichinosis. Never eat pork that is pink. Do not cook thick cuts of pork less than 35 minutes to the pound. Always cook pork slowly.

90 Fried Pork Chops
Cooking time 45 minutes

Shake chops, which should be at least ¾ inch thick, in a paper bag with 3 Tablespoons Flour, 1 teaspoon Salt, and ½ teaspoon Pepper, until chops are well covered. Heat a heavy frying pan. Rub it with a little fat off one of the chops and put chops in pan. Brown chops on each side and then reduce heat either by turning down flame or placing an asbestos pad between flame and pan. Pour off fat as it accumulates. Cook until tender, about 25 minutes. Remove chops and fry Apple Rings (slices of 2 apples from which the cores have been removed) until brown on each side. Sprinkle with Nutmeg, Cinnamon, or a little Sugar and serve with the chops. Or for a change, try Sliced Pineapple.

91 Braised Pork Chops
Cooking time 1 hour 10 minutes

Sprinkle 4 Thick Pork Chops with Salt and Pepper. In a heavy pot (a Dutch oven is fine) melt 1 Tablespoon Bacon Grease. Sear chops until brown on each side. Add 1 cup Finely Chopped Onions, 2 cups Canned Tomatoes, and enough Water, if necessary, to cover, and simmer covered for 1 hour. If you have such herbs aboard, a pinch of oregano or marjoram adds a lot.

92 Pork Chops, Pressure-cooked
Cooking time 40 minutes

Cut most of the fat from 4 Pork Chops from ½ to ¾ inch thick. Melt the fat taken off in the pressure cooker. Mix 1 Tablespoon Flour, ½ teaspoon Salt, ¼ teaspoon Pepper in a paper bag. Shake the chops in it until they are all well covered with the flour. Brown the chops in the fat melted in the cooker. Remove chops and put the rack in the cooker. Return chops to rack. Peel 4 **Large Sweet or 4 Medium-sized White Potatoes** and 8 **Onions** and put them around chops. Add ½ **cup Water or Water in which vegetables have been cooked,** close cooker, and put on the flame. When steam comes out of the vent put indicator in place. Cook for 15 minutes after indicator reaches fifteen pounds or "cook" position. Cool cooker in cold water for a minute and remove cover. Remove chops and vegetables. Gravy can be made from liquid in the cooker by adding 2 **Tablespoons Flour** mixed smooth with cold water.

93 Roast Loin of Pork
Cooking time 3 to 4 hours

(For galleys with ovens.) Rub 3 teaspoons **Salt** well into a 3- or 4-pound **Loin of Pork.** Place in pan fat side up and sear in a hot oven (500°) for 20 minutes. Reduce oven to 350° and cook without basting until the pork is tender, about 50 minutes to the pound.

94 Roast Loin of Pork, Pressure-cooked
Cooking time 40 to 55 minutes

Wipe with a damp cloth a **3- to 4-pound Loin of Pork.** Mix 2 **Tablespoons Flour,** 1 teaspoon **Salt,** ⅛ teaspoon **Pepper,** and 1 teaspoon **Sage.** Rub this mixture well into the pork. Meanwhile heat ½ **Tablespoon Bacon Grease** in the cooker. Brown the roast well in it, being careful to brown on all sides. Add ¼ **cup Water or Liquid in which vegetables have been cooked.** Put top on the cooker. When steam comes out of the vent put the indicator in place. Cook for 36 minutes for a 3-pound roast and 48 minutes for a 4-pound roast after the indicator

147

reaches fifteen pounds or "cook" position. Cool cooker in cold water for a minute and remove cover. Take out roast. Add **2 Tablespoons Flour** mixed with a little cold water to the mixture in the cooker. Stir well and bring to a boil. Simmer 2 minutes. Check for flavoring and serve. Roast pork is at its best when served with plenty of apple sauce, either cold or hot.

95 Bacon

Cooking time about 7 minutes

To fry, place **8 strips of Bacon** in a cold, heavy frying pan and cook slowly over low heat, turning frequently until bacon begins to turn golden brown. Then lay bacon strips on paper towels or newspaper to drain. Serve while good and hot. If stove has no low-heat adjustment, use asbestos pad between flame and frying pan. If large quantities of bacon are being cooked at the same time, keep pouring off the fat so that bacon will be crisp.

96 Ham, Boiled and Baked

Most butchers now have ham in three degrees of preparation: cooked whole ham, tenderized ham, and smoked ham. The cooked ham, while convenient to use, is in our judgment rather tasteless. Its convenience, however, is a great advantage, as it can be eaten as is, fried, baked, or treated as any other ham.

The tenderized hams can be baked at once without soaking or boiling first to make them palatable. To our taste, the old-fashioned sugar-cured smoked ham has the best flavor. However, it should be soaked for a few hours before it is boiled. Hams for boiling should be well scrubbed and then put into a pot with cold water. As water heats, remove any scum that comes to the top. The ham should be boiled until tender, about 25 minutes to the pound. It can be served this way or can be baked.

To bake, take skin off ham, stick top with **Cloves** if you have them, and cover top of ham with **Brown Sugar.** Put into a 425° oven for 20 minutes or until nicely browned. While its flavor is really superior, it is doubtful whether on a boat it is worth the extra time and effort involved.

97 Ham Steak, Pan-fried
Cooking time 10 to 15 minutes

Grease a heavy frying pan with a little of the ham fat. Place **Ham Steak** about ¾ inch thick in frying pan over flame. Brown on one side, turn, and brown other side. Cook about 7 minutes to a side. If eggs are to be fried, pour off most of the fat and fry slowly, turning down flame or using an asbestos pad between flame and pan, after removing ham—preferably to a hot platter.

98 Ham Steak Cooked in Fruit Juice
Cooking time 45 minutes

Rub a ¾-inch **Slice of Ham** with **1 teaspoon Prepared Mustard** and stick in a few **Cloves** if you have them. Sear ham on both sides in a hot frying pan. Cover with **Orange Juice, Grapefruit Juice, Canned Apricots, Peaches, or Pineapple.** Bring to a boil and let simmer with a lid on the frying pan until ham is tender, from 20 to 40 minutes. Let cook uncovered the last 5 minutes or so.

99 Ham Steak Cooked in Milk
Cooking time 45 minutes

Trim the fat from the edges of **1 Slice of Ham** 1½ inches thick. Rub ham with **2 Tablespoons Prepared Mustard** and cover both sides with **Brown Sugar.** Place in frying pan and pour in **Fresh or Diluted Evaporated Milk,** about 2 cups, to the depth of ½ inch. Bring milk to a boil, then reduce fire so that milk will simmer (use asbestos pad if flame cannot be reduced). Simmer until ham is tender, about 40 minutes, covered. If the milk gets too low during the cooking add more. **Potatoes** cut in ½-inch cubes can be cooked in the milk along with the ham, but you will need more milk—enough to cover the potatoes.

100   Ham Butts, Ham Rolls, College Roll, Daisy Roll

Preparation time 6 hours
Cooking time 2½ to 3½ hours

All these names apply to a compact boneless ham about the size of a small beef tongue. Ham butts can be treated exactly like a whole ham. They can be boiled, baked, or sliced for frying or broiling. They are easy to store and have practically no waste. A **Ham Butt** should be soaked for at least 6 hours and then simmered in **Water, Cider, Ginger Ale, or Fruit Juice** about 30 minutes to the pound. It should be allowed to cool in the liquid it is cooked in. It can then be baked if you have an oven, about 10 minutes to the pound.

101   Ham Butt or Daisy Roll, Pressure-cooked

Preparation time 6 hours
Cooking time 1 hour 15 minutes to 1 hour 35 minutes

Cover a 5-pound **Daisy Roll Ham** with **Water** and soak for 6 hours. Pour off water, cover with fresh water and bring to a boil. Pour off water. Place rack in cooker and place ham on it. Pour in 2 cups **Water, Cider, or Ginger Ale.** Cover cooker and place over flame. When steam comes from vent put indicator in place. Cook for 60 minutes (12 minutes to the pound) after indicator reaches fifteen pounds or "cook" position. Cool cooker in cold water for a minute and remove cover.

If galley has an oven, cover ham with mixture of ½ **cup Brown Sugar, 3 Tablespoons Bread Crumbs,** and **2 Tablespoons Vinegar.** Stick **Cloves** in ham if you have them. Put ham in a pan and brown in a 350° oven about 20 minutes.

102   Fried Sausage
Cooking time 20 minutes

Put 1 pound of **Sausage** in a heavy frying pan and cover with **Water.** Let water come to a boil and simmer for 5 minutes. Pour off water, prick sausages with a fork and fry slowly, turning frequently until nicely browned. Drain on brown paper for a minute and serve.

CHICKEN

Chicken is a good food for sailors. It is compact to carry. It has plenty of energy units. It keeps well for several days if refrigerated. It is easy to prepare. It can be served in dozens of different ways. Most people like it. Remember this in ordering chicken: you buy it uncleaned. What is delivered to you by the butcher is a third less weight than you order or pay for. Take this into account when ordering for hungry men, so that you will have something under 1 pound net per person to be served when you start to prepare it. When you get your chicken on board, wash it thoroughly and wrap it in fresh paper, preferably waxed paper. Put it on the ice. An hour or so before you are going to serve it, take it off the ice and let it stay at galley temperature. This will improve the flavor. Remember, chickens are graded as to tenderness. The broiler, fryer, or squab chicken (usually up to about a year old) is the most tender. Next come roasting chickens, and then fowl which are usually largest but are old and suitable only for fricasseeing or stews.

103   Braised Chicken

Cooking time 2 hours

This takes a little time and trouble, but it is well worth the effort if you want a chicken cooked whole for some special occasion. In a heavy pot (a Dutch oven does nicely) melt **4 Tablespoons Butter or Margarine.** When it is very hot put in **a 3- or 4-pound Roasting Chicken** which has been wiped with a damp cloth and rubbed well with **Salt** inside as well as outside. Brown chicken nicely, turning on all sides. Remove chicken from pot. Into pot put a bed made up of **4 Medium Onions,** chopped fine, **3 Carrots,** sliced, **1 clove of Garlic, 4 Slices Bacon or Salt Pork** cut into small pieces, and **3 Stalks of Celery** cut up small with the leaves left on (optional). Add **1½ cups (1 can) Chicken Soup or Consommé.** Return the chicken to the pot. Put over flame. As soon as liquids simmer, put asbestos pad between flame and pot. Cover tightly. Baste carefully every 15 minutes. Cook until chicken is tender, about 1½ hours if the chicken is a year or so old, longer if the chicken is older. During the last half hour of cooking leave lid off pot. If the liquid seems to be used up, add more consommé or hot water. The object is to have the chicken beautifully browned and shining with a thick glaze.

104   Chicken Cacciatore

Cooking time 2 hours

Have **2 Very Plump Broilers** about 2½ to 3 pounds each cut up as for frying. Wipe the pieces with a damp cloth. Shake chicken in a paper bag with **3 Tablespoons Flour, 1 teaspoon Salt,** and ⅛ teaspoon **Pepper.** In a heavy frying pan for which

you have a cover, or a heavy pot (a Dutch oven is ideal) heat
½ cup Olive or other Cooking Oil to the smoking point. Put
in the chicken and cook, turning frequently until it is nicely
browned, about 10 minutes. Then add 1 cup Small White
Onions peeled, 1 cup Green Peppers cut into strips, and 2
Tablespoons Canned Pimientos cut up in small pieces. Let
cook covered for 5 minutes and then add 1 clove of Garlic, ½
Bay Leaf, ¼ teaspoon Marjoram, 1 can Peeled Italian Tomatoes (2 pounds 3 ounces), and 1 cup Dry White Wine. If
you do not have the wine add ½ cup Water with 1 teaspoon
Vinegar in it. Cover and simmer gently (put asbestos pad between flame and pot if you cannot turn down flame) until
chicken is tender, about 1½ hours. Then add 1 6-ounce can
Mushrooms, bring to a boil, and serve very hot. Spaghetti,
either freshly cooked or canned, is the thing to serve with this.

105   Chicken Cacciatore, Pressure-cooked

Cooking time 40 minutes

Prepare 2 2½-pound Broilers as in chicken cacciatore (No.
104). In cooker heat ½ cup Olive Oil. When it is smoking hot,
put in the chicken, turning it frequently until it is a golden
brown. Then add 1 cup Small White Onions, peeled. When
they begin to yellow, add 1 cup Chopped Green Peppers, 2 Tablespoons Canned Pimientos, 1 clove of Garlic, 1 No. 2 can
Peeled Italian Tomatoes, 1 6-oz. can Mushrooms, 1 cup Dry
White Wine, ¼ teaspoon Marjoram, and ½ Bay Leaf. Cover
the cooker, and when steam comes out of the vent put the
indicator in place. Cook for 15 minutes after indicator reaches
fifteen pounds or the "cook" position. Cool cooker in cold
water for a minute, remove cover, and check to see if seasoning
is right. It may require a little salt. Serve very hot with spaghetti, freshly cooked or canned.

106 Chicken Fricassee

Cooking time 2 hours

Have a 4-pound **Fowl** cut in pieces as for frying. Wipe them
with a damp cloth and then rub pieces with **Salt.** In a heavy
pot (a Dutch oven is ideal) melt 1½ **Tablespoons Butter or
Margarine** and 1½ **Tablespoons Bacon Grease.** In this cook
until soft **3 Medium-sized Onions** minced fine (12 minutes),
3 Peppercorns or ½ teaspoon **Pepper,** and **1 Tablespoon
Paprika.** Add **1 can Chicken Soup or Broth** (1½ cups). When
this is simmering, add the chicken. Simmer covered until tender, about 1½ hours. When tender remove chicken and brown
in a frying pan in **2 Tablespoons Bacon Grease.** This step may
be skipped, but it improves the flavor and appearance of the
final product. Meanwhile let materials in which the chicken
was cooked boil down to about 2 cups. Beat **2 Egg Yolks** in ¼
cup **Cream or Undiluted Evaporated Milk.** Take pot off the
stove and add, stirring in well. Place chicken on slices of toast,
zwieback or Holland rusk. Pour sauce over this and serve.

107 Chicken Fricassee, Pressure-cooked

Cooking time 1 hour

Have a 4-pound **Fowl** cut up as for frying. In a paper bag mix
3 Tablespoons Flour, 1 teaspoon Salt, and ¼ **Teaspoon Pepper.** Shake chicken in it until well covered. Melt **4 Tablespoons Butter, Margarine, or Bacon Grease** in the cooker and
brown chicken pieces in it, turning carefully to get them brown
on all sides evenly. Remove chicken and put rack in cooker.
Place chicken on the rack, add ½ **Lemon, 1 Onion** peeled and
sliced, **1 cup Chopped Celery,** and **1 cup Chicken Broth, Soup,
or Water.** Close cooker, and when steam comes out of the
vent put indicator in place. Cook for 30 minutes after indicator
reaches fifteen pounds or "cook" position. Cool cooker in cold
154

water for a minute and remove cover. Mix 1 Tablespoon Flour with ½ cup Cream or Undiluted Evaporated Milk. Pour this mixture slowly into the sauce, which should be simmering on the stove. Let simmer for 5 minutes, check to see whether seasoning is all right, and serve.

108 Chicken Pot Pie
Cooking time 3 hours

Have a 4-pound Fowl cut up as for frying. Put in a heavy pot and cover with water and bring to a boil. Turn down flame or put an asbestos pad between pot and flame if you cannot control flame. Cover pot and let simmer until chicken is tender, about 2½ hours. After chicken has cooked for 1 hour, add ½ teaspoon Salt and ¼ teaspoon Pepper. When chicken has cooked 2 hours 15 minutes and is quite tender, put in dumplings made as follows: Mix 2 cups Flour, 4 teaspoons Baking Powder, and ½ teaspoon Salt and sift together. Stir in slowly 1 cup Milk or Diluted Evaporated Milk. Drop dough into pot where chicken is stewing, a kitchen spoonful at a time. Cook 15 to 20 minutes or until dumplings are cooked through. Thicken stock that chicken has been cooked in by mixing 3 Tablespoons Flour with enough Cold Water so that the mixture will run. Pour this slowly into the stock, stirring all the while. Cook for 6 minutes more.

109 Cream Chicken Stew
Cooking time 1 hour 20 minutes

Have 2 3-pound Chickens cut up as for frying. Wipe with a damp cloth and shake up in a paper bag with 4 Tablespoons Flour, 1 teaspoon Salt, ½ teaspoon Pepper, and ¼ teaspoon Nutmeg, if you have it on board. Melt 5 Tablespoons Butter, Margarine, or Bacon Grease in a heavy pot (a Dutch oven does

155

beautifully). Brown the chicken thoroughly, then add **1 cup Boiling Water,** stirring it slowly into the pot. Add ½ cup **Chopped Onions, 1 Tablespoon Worcestershire Sauce, 1 Bay Leaf, 1 clove of Garlic** (wrap these last two in a small piece of cheesecloth for easy removal later), and **a few sprigs of Parsley,** if you have it. Cook tightly covered until chicken is tender, about 50 minutes. Remove bag with garlic and bay leaf. You will need about 2 cups of liquid, so estimate carefully what is in the pot and add enough chicken soup or boiling water to equal that amount. Mix **3 Tablespoons Flour** with ½ cup **Fresh Cream or Undiluted Evaporated Milk** and stir slowly into pot. Now add **1 6-oz. can of Mushrooms,** if you have it. Add additional seasoning, if you think it needs it, and serve very hot over toast, zwieback, Holland rusk, or rice.

110   Chicken Stew, Pressure-cooked

Cooking time 50 minutes

Have a **4-pound Fowl** cut up as for frying. Wipe the pieces with a damp cloth. Into pressure cooker put **4 Tablespoons Butter, Margarine, or Bacon Grease,** in which the chicken pieces should be browned, about 10 minutes. Add ½ cup **Chicken Broth or Soup or Water,** ½ teaspoon **Salt,** ¼ teaspoon **Pepper,** ¼ cup **Chopped Onions,** 1 teaspoon **Paprika,** 1 **Chicken Bouillon Cube.** Cover the cooker. When steam comes out of the vent, put indicator in place. After indicator reaches fifteen pounds or "cook" position, cook for 20 minutes. Cool cooker in cold water for a minute and remove cover. Add to chicken in cooker 4 **Medium-sized Potatoes** cut into quarters, 1 bunch **Small Carrots** cut into small pieces, and 2 **Tablespoons Parsley,** if you have it. Close cooker and cook for 10 minutes after indicator reaches fifteen pounds or "cook" position. Cool cooker in cold water for a minute and remove cover. Thicken sauce with **1 Tablespoon Flour** mixed smooth in ½ cup **Heavy Cream** or **Undiluted Evaporated Milk.** Simmer for about 5 minutes, stirring all the while. Serve with toast, zwieback, or Holland rusk.

111 Chicken Curry
Cooking time 1 hour

Have **2 2½-pound Chickens,** plump and tender, cut up as for frying. Wipe the pieces with a damp cloth and dry carefully. In a heavy frying pan melt **5 Tablespoons Butter, Margarine, or Bacon Grease.** Cook until soft, about 6 minutes, **1 Apple** peeled, cored, and cut into thin slices, and **3 Small Onions** cut up fine. Add and brown the chicken pieces carefully. This should take about 15 minutes. Now add **1 can Chicken Soup, 1 can Undiluted Tomato Soup, 1 teaspoon Salt, ⅛ teaspoon Pepper, 3 heaping Tablespoons Curry Powder.** Soak **1 can Grated Coconut,** if you have it, in **1 cup Fresh** or **Diluted Evaporated Milk** 20 minutes and add this. If you have no coconut, add **1 cup Diluted Evaporated Milk.** Add ¾ cup **Seedless Raisins** and **3 Tablespoons Chutney,** if you have it (it is a useful thing to have on board, as it does wonders to sandwiches, rice dishes, etc.). Let this combination simmer for 20 to 30 minutes more, or until the chicken is very tender. Then thicken the sauce with **2 Tablespoons Flour** mixed with an equal amount of **Butter or Margarine.** Stir this in carefully and let simmer 5 minutes. Finally add **1 9-oz. can Cut-up Pineapple.** Let come to a boil and serve with lots of well-cooked rice.

112 Smothered Chicken
Cooking time 1 hour

Have a **4-pound Chicken** cut into pieces as for frying. Wipe with a damp cloth. Shake up in a paper bag with **3 Table-**

spoons Flour, 1 teaspoon Salt, ¼ teaspoon Pepper. In a heavy pot heat 3 Tablespoons Butter, Margarine, or Bacon Grease. In this fry 1 Medium-sized Onion chopped fine, about 5 minutes. Then brown the chicken in the fat. Heat 1 can Chicken Soup to the boiling point and pour over the chicken. Add ½ cup Cream, sweet or sour (or ½ cup Undiluted Evaporated Milk). Let chicken simmer in this until tender (about 30 minutes). Remove chicken. Strain liquid in which it has been cooked. Thicken liquid with 2 Tablespoons Flour mixed with an equal amount of Butter or Margarine. Let simmer a moment or so, stirring all the while, and pour over the chicken and serve.

113   Fried Chicken
Cooking time 1 hour

The techniques of frying chicken range all the way from dropping a hacked-up hen into a frying pan with grease in it and cooking until the bird is tender enough to chew, to complicated processes which require time in the oven, special batters, and lots and lots of time and attention. If your boat has an oven the chicken will always be improved for a little time in it, after the frying process has been completed. However, as many boats do not have ovens, we are leaving that step out of our recipes. First be sure that you have a chicken suitable for frying—a fryer or broiler cut up for frying. Don't let the butcher sell you a fowl or older chicken. It just won't be worth the time and trouble of cooking it.

Have a Young 3½-pound Chicken cut up as for frying. Wipe pieces with a damp cloth and shake up in a paper bag with 4 Tablespoons Flour, ½ teaspoon Salt, ½ teaspoon Pepper, ¼ teaspoon Paprika. Dip chicken in 1 Egg beaten up with 2 Tablespoons Water and roll in Dried Bread Crumbs, Cracker Crumbs, or Crushed Corn Flakes. Put ¼ pound plus 2 Tablespoons Butter or 10 Tablespoons Margarine or Bacon Grease in a heavy frying pan. Bring the fat to a sizzling heat (but not enough to smoke) and quickly brown the chicken pieces in it, turning frequently to prevent burning and to get the right golden coat all over (about 12 minutes). When chicken is nicely browned, turn heat way down or put 2 asbestos pads between flame and bottom of pan. Cover chicken and let cook, basting and turning occasionally until chicken is very tender —about 35 minutes, depending somewhat on the size of the chicken and the heat of the pan. When chicken is tender, re-move from the pan. Pour off all but **3 Tablespoons Fat**, then add and cook **3 Tablespoons Flour** in the pan, **½ teaspoon Salt** and **a few grains of Cayenne (Red) Pepper** for 4 minutes, stirring. Pour into this **¾ cup Sweet or Sour Cream or ¾ cup Undiluted Evaporated Milk**. Scrape the pan well, loosening all of the flavorful pieces of chicken stuck to it. Strain sauce and serve with the chicken. Sweet potatoes seem to go par-ticularly well with chicken fried this way.

114   Roast Chicken

Cooking time 2 hours to 2 hours 15 minutes

(For boats with ovens.) Wipe a **4-pound Chicken** with a damp cloth inside and out and then rub entire chicken inside and out with salt. Stuff it lightly with the following mixture: soak **2 cups Bread Crumbs** in Milk; 2 minutes will do. Chop fine and fry **1 cup Onions** in **3 Tablespoons Butter or Margarine**. When onions are soft (about 8 minutes), squeeze the milk out of the bread crumbs and add bread crumbs to onions in the frying pan. Cook for 5 minutes, stirring all the while. Add **1 teaspoon Salt**, **½ teaspoon Pepper**, **½ teaspoon Marjoram, Sage, or Summer Savory** if you have it. Now add enough **Chicken Soup** to moisten but not wet the crumb mixture. Sew up or skewer with a sail needle the opening in the chicken. If you do not want to be bothered with stuffing, just leave it out.

Rub chicken with **3 Tablespoons Butter or Margarine** and put into a 500° oven until chicken begins to brown, about 15 minutes, then turn heat down to 350°. Baste chicken every 15 minutes from ¼ **cup Butter, Margarine, or Bacon Grease** mixed with ¾ **cup Boiling Water.** A roasting chicken is done when the meat on breast and second joint is tender and when the joints of the legs are not stiff when the drumsticks are moved. This usually takes about 2 hours.

115 Roast Chicken, Pressure-cooked
Cooking time 1 hour

Prepare a 4-pound **Chicken** as in recipe for roast chicken (No. 114), but do not stuff. In a heavy frying pan bring 4 **Tablespoons Bacon Grease or Other Cooking Fat** to the sizzling point and carefully brown the chicken all over in it. Place chicken with giblets on rack in cooker and add ½ **cup Chicken Soup or Broth** or the water in which vegetables have been cooked. Put cover on cooker. Place over flame. When steam comes out of the vent put indicator in place. Cook for 30 minutes after indicator reaches fifteen pounds or "cook" position. Cool cooker in cold water for a minute and remove cover. Take out chicken and thicken liquid with **3 Tablespoons Flour** mixed smooth with 3 **Tablespoons Heavy Cream or Undiluted Evaporated Milk.** Cut up giblets fine, simmer in sauce, check seasoning, and serve with the chicken.

116 Chicken Cromwell
Cooking time 1 hour 45 minutes

Have **2 Broilers or Young Chickens**, about 2½ to 3 pounds each, trussed as for roasting. Wipe with a damp cloth and rub well inside and out with salt. Stuff with a mixture described in the recipe for Roast Chicken (No. 114), or your own stuffing, or leave it out. There are good easy-to-use commercial stuffings available. In a heavy pot (preferably a Dutch oven) melt **4 Tablespoons Butter or Margarine** and **4 Tablespoons Olive Oil** (other cooking oil can be used, but it is not as good). Cut a round of brown paper (a paper bag does nicely), slightly larger than the lid of the pot. Oil this well with cooking oil or bacon grease. Put the chickens in the pot, put paper on top and lid on top of that, and press lid down to make as tight a seal as possible. If your boat has an oven, put the pot in at 500° for 1 hour. If you must rely on the top of the stove, turn flame down or put an asbestos pad between pot and flame and cook for 1 hour, looking at chickens occasionally to see that they are not too brown. At the end of 1 hour, take chickens out of pot and set aside while you put ¼ **cup Brandy** in the pot and set it afire. Keep stirring the mixture vigorously as the flame burns out. Then add 1½ **cups Madeira** and stir well. Pour off ¾ cup of this liquid and set it to cool on a pan of cold water so that all the fat can be skimmed off. Put the chickens back into the pot, put the paper ring and lid back on, and let chicken simmer very gently for 20 minutes or until you are ready to serve it. Skim the cooled sauce. In a small saucepan thicken it with **1 Tablespoon Flour** mixed with **1 Tablespoon Butter** and ⅛ **teaspoon Pepper** and let it simmer gently for a few minutes. Keep hot and serve in a side dish with the chicken. Serve the chicken. Give half the breast, second joint, and leg to each person. If there is any chicken left over, it can be served as a wonderful dish cut up in a cream sauce (No. 241) flavored with whatever sauce is left from the chicken. This is a party dish and is excellent served with wild rice. Takes a lot of trouble, but worth it.

MEATS

WAYS OF USING AND IMPROVING CANNED MEATS

There are many brands of most of the canned meats listed below, and not all the suggestions for improvement apply to all of them. That is where the creative ability of the cook can come into full play. Use your taste and judgment to determine which suggestions can best be applied to which canned meat.

The following list of canned meats is usually available in the larger stores. Many of them are available even in country general stores.

Bacon, sliced
Beef and gravy
Beef, corned
Beef, dried
Beef roast
Beef stew
Brains
Chicken, boned
Chicken, deviled
Chicken, mock
Chicken, whole, halved, sliced
Chili con carne with beans
Chile con carne without beans
Frankfurters
Frankfurters with sauerkraut
Ham, chopped
Ham, deviled
Ham, spiced
Ham, whole, half, quarter
Hash, corned beef
Liver, spread or loaf
Meat and beans
Meat, luncheon
Meat, potted
Meat loaf
Meat spread
Mutton, roast
Pigs' feet
Pork
Pork and gravy
Pork, corned
Sausage, bulk, pork
Sausage, cocktail
Sausage, link, pork
Sausage, Vienna
Sausage in oil
Scrapple
Squab
Tamales
Tongue, lamb
Tongue, lunch
Tongue, ox
Tongue, pork
Tripe
Turkey, boned
Tushonka
Veal

MEAT SPECIALTIES

Chop suey
Chow mein
Hors-d'oeuvres paste:
  Ham and tongue
  Liver, beef

Noodles with chicken
Noodles with veal
Poultry spreads
Ravioli
Spaghetti with meat balls

READY-MADE MEAT ENTRÉES

Beef à la mode
Beefsteak and onions
Chicken à la king
Chicken curry
Goulash
Ham and eggs
Hamburg steak

Hamburg steak and onions
Stew, beef
Stew, Brunswick
Stew, Irish
Stew, kidney
Stew, lamb

117   Canned Beef Stew
Cooking time under 20 minutes

If the gravy in the canned beef stew is too thin, it can be given more substance in either of the following ways: With the fingers roll 1 teaspoon or so of Butter or Margarine in an equal amount of Flour until all the flour is taken up in the butter. Drop this into the stew, which should be simmering, until the butter and flour are well absorbed and have simmered in the stew a few minutes. You can then tell whether the stew has body enough. Another way, better when the gravy is not well flavored, is to cook together 1 Tablespoon or so of Butter or Margarine with an equal amount of Flour as for cream sauce (see No. 241). Then add ½ cup Consommé, either canned or from bouillon cubes, to the stew, stirring well.

A great variety of seasonings gives varied results—salt, pepper or cayenne, a pinch of mustard, a pinch of brown sugar, a pinch of curry powder, a pinch of such herbs as thyme, sage, marjoram, or summer savory, a spoonful of Worcestershire or Escoffier sauce, or catsup. With each of these sauces an equal amount of butter should be added.

The appearance of a stew is very important. To give a stew a freshly made look, carefully place a spoonful or so of green peas on top of each serving. If the stew seems lacking in potatoes, open a can of small boiled potatoes and add them. Plenty of onions are a great addition to any stew. If fresh onions are to be used, fry them or boil them until soft in a little water and add them to the stew. Canned onions can, of course, be added directly from the can. Croutons made of little squares or triangles of bread fried until crisp and golden brown add appetite appeal and interest. If nothing else is done to the stew, sprinkle it with paprika just before serving. Not only does this help the flavor but its bright color gives the stew more eye appeal.

118   Norton & Jones Fast, Fancy Beef Stew
Cooking time 25 minutes or 45 minutes

For a really high-speed job this requires a pressure cooker, but it can be made without one. Peel and cut into ¾-inch dice 3 **Medium-sized Potatoes** and 1 **Medium-sized Turnip**. Scrub and cut into ¾-inch pieces 3 **Large Carrots** or 1 **bunch of Small Ones**. Wash and peel 15 **Small Onions**. Cook them all together 7 minutes in a pressure cooker with ½ **cup of Water** or boil 25 minutes with **Water to cover** in a pan with a lid on it. Meanwhile, in a heavy frying pan over a low flame, brown 5 **Tablespoons Flour** until a nice pale brown. Flour should be stirred to keep it from burning on the bottom. Add 5 **Tablespoons Butter** and blend well together. Pour in 1½ **cups Red Wine**, stirring slowly. Dump in a 3-oz. can of **Mushrooms**, juice and all, and let simmer until sauce is good and thick.

Take the top off **1 1-pound can Roast Beef** (Swift's is best) and heat in the can in boiling water. Pour the juice into the sauce. Add vegetables to the sauce and add meat. If sauce is too thick, add a little more red wine. If it appears to be too thin, let it simmer down until it thickens, or thicken with **1 Table-spoon Flour** mixed with **1 Tablespoon Butter or Margarine**. Put in **1 Bouillon Cube or ½ teaspoon Extract of Beef**, 1 **Tablespoon Escoffier Sauce**, if you have it, and **2 heaping tea-spoons Prepared Mustard**. Let simmer until ready to serve. This will adequately serve four people. This is a delicious stew, and if you are reasonably adroit you can prepare it in 25 minutes with a pressure cooker and in about 45 minutes without the pressure cooker.

119 Canned Beef with Gravy

Cooking time under 20 minutes

Frequently the addition of a bouillon cube dissolved in a little hot water, a few drops of kitchen bouquet, a pinch of herbs, nutmeg, or curry powder will turn a flat-tasting gravy into something to be well remembered. A pinch of mustard can be a great addition, as can be a spoonful of Escoffier sauce, Wor-cestershire, catsup, or any of the other good commercial sauces or seasonings. An amount of butter equal to the amount of sauce added and mixed well with it will make the gravy richer and better bring out the flavor of the added sauce. The gravy can be thickened by the addition of **1 teaspoon or so of Butter** rolled in an equal amount of **Flour** until the flour is all ab-sorbed. This latter should be stirred well into the gravy and simmered until it is well absorbed, about 6 minutes. By achiev-ing a variety in the gravies it is possible to eat the same kind of canned meat day after day with enjoyment.

120 Boned Canned Chicken
Cooking time under 20 minutes

This meat can be eaten as it comes from the can either hot or cold. It can be creamed Newburg (see No. 49), or it can be cut up with celery and mixed with mayonnaise to make a good chicken salad. It can be mixed with cream sauce (No. 241) and served on toast, with rice, or rolled up in pancakes. It can be mixed with an equal amount of cooked potatoes cut into ½-inch dice and enough cream or undiluted evaporated milk to moisten, seasoned with salt, pepper or cayenne, curry powder, nutmeg or herbs, and slowly fried in 2 or 3 tablespoons of butter or bacon fat to make a delicious chicken hash. When well browned on the bottom, one half should be turned over the other as with an omelet and served all brown and crisp.

121 Canned Whole Chicken
Cooking time under 20 minutes

This good food can be heated by immersing the unopened can in hot water. It can be removed from the can and heated in a saucepan over hot water. In either case the melted jelly and juices make a delicious gravy. It can be thickened to the desired degree by adding small amounts of butter rolled in equal amounts of flour. These should simmer in the juices until the correct thickness is arrived at. This mixture can be seasoned by adding a small amount of curry powder, a pinch or so of marjoram or summer savory, a little onion or garlic salt or a little Escoffier, Worcestershire, or soy bean sauce.

122 Canned Chicken à la King
Cooking time under 20 minutes

Chicken à la king can usually be improved by the addition of a small can of mushrooms. If the juice of the mushrooms thins the sauce too much, thicken it by the addition of small amounts of butter rolled in equal amounts of flour and simmered until the desired thickness is attained. A tablespoon or so of sherry or Madeira just before serving heightens the taste. A little soy bean sauce gives an interesting flavor. If you have them, cut into slivers a tablespoon or so of bleached almonds (almonds soaked in boiling water, the skins removed, and the almonds dried) and sprinkle them on top just before serving, to give an added touch.

123   Canned Chicken Fricassee

Cooking time under 20 minutes

If the sauce is too thin, it can easily be thickened by the addition of a teaspoon or so of butter rolled in the same amount of flour until both are blended. This should be stirred into the heated fricassee and simmered with it for about 6 minutes. If the chicken flavor is weak, it can be strengthened by the addition of a chicken bouillon cube or so. Soy bean sauce makes an interesting addition, as does a tablespoon or so of sherry or Madeira. A small can of mushrooms adds to the flavor. A pinch of onion or garlic salt adds variety. Other interesting flavors can be obtained by adding a pinch of curry powder or mustard, a pinch of thyme, marjoram, summer savory, or tarragon. A judicious drop of Worcestershire, soy bean, or Escoffier sauce can add interest. The addition of chopped blanched almonds (almonds soaked in boiling water, the skins removed and the almonds dried) and diced celery give an Oriental aspect. The many combinations of the above can give enough delicious variations to the chicken to gain great recognition and acclaim for the cook.

124 Canned Corned Beef

Cooking time under 20 minutes or 1 hour 15 minutes

Good by itself, this basic canned product can be made into a truly wonderful hash. Bake **4 Medium Potatoes** (see No. 181). Cut up equal amounts of corned beef and baked potatoes into ½-inch dice. Chop up **3 Large Onions** and fry until soft in **Butter, Margarine, or Bacon Grease,** about 12 minutes. Mix meat, onion, and potato well. Season with 1½ teaspoons **Salt,** ¼ teaspoon **Pepper,** and ½ teaspoon **Nutmeg.** Moisten with ½ cup **Cream or Undiluted Evaporated Milk** and mix well. If galley has an oven, bake in a shallow pan 20 minutes in a 350° oven. If there is no oven, melt **2 Tablespoons Butter, Bacon, or Other Fat** in a heavy frying pan and fry hash until brown on the bottom, about 10 minutes. Then turn one half over the other, as with an omelet, and serve.

Corned beef sliced and heated in the top of a double boiler over boiling water can be very good served with any of the following sauces: horseradish (No. 246), mustard (No. 249), mushroom (No. 250), or Madeira (No. 247). The dish can be further improved by the addition of a small can of mushrooms. Canned corned beef makes a hearty dish served on a platter of boiled cabbage (see No. 154). When cabbage is nearly cooked, slice corned beef on top of it and keep on fire until corned beef is hot.

125 Canned Corned Beef Hash

Cooking time under 20 minutes

This good solid all-around food can be taken from the can, heated in a double boiler or frying pan, and it is ready to eat. However, it is improved by the addition of **3 or 4 Onions** chopped fine and fried until soft, about 6 minutes, and mixed well into the hash. The hash can be made more interesting if 3 Tablespoons of Butter, Margarine, or Bacon Grease are heated to the sizzling point and then the hash is browned in this. As soon as it is lightly browned on the bottom it should be stirred up to mix the crisp part all through the hash and then, with a little more fat added, browned again. It should then be turned one half over the other as with an omelet, slid out of the frying pan, and served. Sometimes it is more convenient to make the hash into little patties or balls. A raw egg mixed well with the hash before it is made into balls will keep it from falling apart while cooking. These can then be served in any of the good sauces listed (see Nos. 242, 246, 249, 253, 256). Corned beef hash is also good mixed with an equal amount of cream sauce (No. 241), mushrooms, chopped parsley, bits of celery root, or pieces of other leftover vegetable. If the galley stove has an oven, this mixture can be sprinkled with cheese and nicely browned in the oven, about 20 minutes at 350°.

126 Dried Beef

Cooking time under 20 minutes

Dried beef or chipped beef is usually served in a cream sauce (No. 241). In amount there should be 2 cups of cream sauce for each ½ pound of chipped beef. You can have variety by mixing the beef with 2 cups of the following sauces: Brown sauce (No. 242) with 1 tablespoon of sherry or Madeira, a little Worcestershire or Escoffier sauce (about 1 teaspoonful), or a few drops of soy bean sauce or Angostura bitters. Curry sauce (No. 243) or egg sauce (No. 244) is good. If you have a few anchovies, they may be added to the egg sauce for greater flavor. Onion sauce (No. 253) or mushroom sauce (No. 250) is good and gives variety to this inexpensive, easy-to-keep meat. Dried beef is very good heated up in a can of cream of mushroom soup. Make soup using half as much water or milk to dilute.

127 Canned Frankfurters

Cooking time under 20 minutes

Canned frankfurters need not necessarily end up as hot dogs. Cut into small sections, ½ inch or so long, they are a very substantial addition to heavy soups such as bean, black bean, lentil, or split pea. Frankfurters can be slit in one side and filled with apple sauce, mashed white or sweet potatoes, sauerkraut, or various kinds of pickle relish. If you have an oven, place the filled frankfurters in a baking dish and place in a moderate oven for 20 minutes or so. They can be heated in the same way in a Connolly oven. Lacking either kind of oven, put them in a tightly closed pan which should be set for 20 minutes in boiling water.

128 Canned Hamburgers

Cooking time under 30 minutes

Canned hamburgers can be cooked as is or improved by the addition of chopped onions fried until soft (about 3 large onions to a can of hamburger). Chopped parsley mixed in well is an additional flavor. Curry sauce (No. 243), onion sauce (No. 253), mustard sauce (No. 249), or Madeira sauce (No. 247), can be served over them to make a delicious dish. Cream sauce (No. 241) to which has been added sour cream (half and half) plus a pinch or so of dill and nutmeg, will give a reasonably good facsimile of Swedish meat balls.

129 Canned Deviled Ham
Cooking time under 20 minutes

This is one of the most useful of canned meats in that it can be used in so many ways. First off, it is a marvelous sandwich spread either alone or with chopped boiled eggs or pickles. Second, spread on toast it is wonderful under poached eggs or under either sliced chicken or chicken cooked in any of the various sauces suggested. It can be mixed with boiled rice and tomatoes. It is good mixed in scrambled eggs, and turned into an omelet it makes a really fine ham omelet (No. 262). A tablespoon or so of deviled ham adds greatly to the flavor of black bean, split pea, asparagus, or potato soup.

130 Canned Lamb Stew
Cooking time under 20 minutes

All of the suggestions for improving canned beef stew (No. 117) apply to lamb stew. A pinch of dried mint is an additional and good variant.

131 Canned Roast Beef Hash
Cooking time under 20 minutes

Roast beef hash is susceptible to all the improvements suggested for corned beef hash (No. 125).

132 Canned Sausages

Canned Sausages may be prepared in the same ways as fresh sausage (see No. 102).

133 Canned Tongue

Cooking time under 20 minutes

Cold sliced tongue is delicious in sandwiches or salads. It is very good served hot with Madeira sauce (No. 247). Cut up and mixed with an equal amount of boiled potatoes cut into ½-inch dice (canned if you like) and about half as much chopped onions gently fried until soft, about 6 minutes, seasoned well with salt and plenty of pepper, and browned well in a frying pan in which 4 tablespoons of bacon or other fat are sizzling, it makes a delicious hash.

134 Corned Beef and Chicken Succotash

Cooking time 35 minutes

Drain off and save the liquid from **1 can Lima Beans** and from **1 can Corn.** In this liquid (adding water to cover if needed) boil **4 Medium-sized Potatoes** cut into quarters, and **8 Small Peeled Onions.** When potatoes are soft, about 20 minutes, add the lima beans and corn. Let simmer a minute or two and add **1 12-ounce can Corned Beef** cut into 1-inch cubes and **1 can Boned Chicken.** Season with **1 teaspoon Salt,** ⅛ teaspoon Pepper and ¼ teaspoon Mustard and simmer about 5 minutes more or until ready to serve.

135 Canned Corned Beef Boiled Dinner

Cooking time 45 minutes

Boil together in **Salted Water** (1 teaspoon per quart) until soft (about ½ hour) **1 cup Turnips** cut into ½-inch dice, **2 Parsnips** sliced, **8 Small Carrots** cut into ½-inch pieces, **4 Medium-sized Potatoes** cut into ½-inch dice. Then add **1 Small Cabbage,** quartered, and **1 can Corned Beef** cut into

1-inch cubes. Simmer until cabbage is soft, about 10 minutes. Season with ½ teaspoon **Mustard** and ⅛ teaspoon **Pepper**. This is a very good dish even if you do not have all of the vegetables listed.

VEGETABLES

There is no good excuse for not serving interesting and appetizing vegetables on a boat, no matter how small it is. They can be prepared in so many different ways and are so very good for you. And there are so many kinds usually available. Escoffier, in *The Guide to Modern Cookery*, lists 250 different ways of preparing vegetables. Most cookbooks tell how to prepare, cook, and serve a great number. There is little excuse for serving the same old vegetables in the same old way day after day.

In preparing vegetables wash them carefully, but unless otherwise directed do not let them soak. If vegetables seem wilted, dampen them and put them in the icebox for a short time to freshen them. Most vegetables, to be at their best, should be cooked in as little water as possible and for as short a time as possible. There are exceptions, of course. Brussels sprouts, cabbages, cauliflower, potatoes, and onions should be cooked in a great deal of water, as should green corn. Once cooked, they should be immediately drained and kept warm in a double boiler. Do not use baking soda. True, it helps vegetables to keep their color, but it completely ruins their vitamin content. Do not overlook the pressure cookers when thinking of vegetable preparation. They cut the cooking time. They use very little water. They preserve the flavor of really good vegetables. Instructions for using pressure cookers are included with the vegetable recipes.

When you use canned vegetables, think twice before you

throw away the liquid in the cans with them. It is full of vitamins and mineral salts. We recommend that you boil down the juices to reduce the quantity and increase the flavor and then heat the vegetables up in them with the correct seasoning to suit you. When the vegetables are served, think again before you throw away the juices in which they were cooked. Put juices into a jar or can and use them for making sauces, diluting condensed soups, or providing a liquid for stews or dehydrated soups.

If small boats had low-temperature refrigerators, frozen foods would be perfect for short or long cruises, as there is no waste and they stow easily. As it is, they are excellent if they can be used in the first two days. They do not keep well after they thaw. If they are packed in one of the several kinds of insulated bags or boxes (discussed in the chapter on stowage), frozen foods can be brought on board and will stay in good condition even after the second day. However, it is best to plan on using them up during the first two days. We are not including any special recipes for them, as most of them have adequate recipes on or in the boxes they come in. Frozen vegetables can be used in all recipes for fresh vegetables.

(Each recipe serves 4.)

136 Artichokes

Preparation time 30 minutes—optional
Cooking time 45 minutes

Pick out **Artichokes** that are fresh and plump, 1 to a person. Tear off outside leaves if they appear to be wilted. Cut off stem close to the bottom of the artichoke and cut 1 inch off the top of each. They will be better if you soak them ½ hour or so (upside down) in fresh water. Place them in a heavy pot over the direct flame and cover them with boiling water salted, **1 teaspoon Salt** to the quart plus **1 teaspoon Vinegar** per quart.

Boil until artichokes are tender and leaves will pull out easily.
This will take from 30 minutes to 1 hour, depending upon the
size and age of the artichokes. Serve with plenty of **Melted
Butter.**

137   Artichokes, Pressure-cooked
Preparation time 30 minutes—optional
Cooking time 12 minutes

Prepare **Artichokes** as in No. 136. Place them in pressure
cooker on rack. Add ½ cup **Water.** Put cover on cooker and
cook for 10 minutes after indicator reaches fifteen pounds pressure or "cook" position. Cool cooker in cold water for a minute
and remove top.

138   Artichokes Provençale
Preparation time 30 minutes—optional
Cooking time 45 minutes

Pull off outside leaves of **Artichoke** until very fresh leaves are
reached. Cut off stem close to the bottom of the artichoke.
Cut ¾ inch off the top. Spread leaves a little. Artichokes are
better if soaked upside down in fresh water for ½ hour. Shake
out all the water, place in the bottom of a heavy pot, tops up,
and sprinkle gently with **Pepper** and **Salt.** A Dutch oven serves
nicely. Add 4 **Tablespoons Olive or Other Cooking Oil.** Put
on cover very tightly, using a round of brown paper between
pot and lid. A paper bag which has been oiled with cooking
oil or greased with bacon grease, will do. Place an asbestos pad
between pot and flame or turn down flame. Cook for 15 minutes. Then add about 1 quart **Lettuce Leaves** cut up in small
pieces. Wilted lettuce that you could not use otherwise will
do. Cook for ½ hour more or until leaves can be pulled from

artichoke easily. The lettuce and oil provide the necessary moisture. Serve with **Melted Butter**.

139   Asparagus

Cooking time 25 minutes

Cut or break the bottom ends off **2 pounds Asparagus**. Wash the asparagus carefully, using a brush if necessary to get out all of the sand. Tie asparagus into as many bunches as there are people to be served and stand up in the bottom of a double boiler in boiling water almost up to the top. Water should be salted, 1½ teaspoons **Salt** to the quart of water. Cover bottom pot with the inverted top part of the double boiler and boil until asparagus is tender, about 15 minutes. Place each bunch on a piece of toast or a Holland rusk, remove string, pour a little **Melted Butter** over asparagus, pepper lightly, and serve.

140   Asparagus, Pressure-cooked

Cooking time 7 minutes

Prepare **Asparagus** as in No. 139. Place asparagus on rack with ½ **cup Water**. Place cover on cooker. When steam begins to come out, close vent with pressure indicator. Cook for 2 minutes when indicator reaches fifteen pounds or is at "cook" position. Cool cooker in cold water for a minute, remove top, season asparagus with ½ **teaspoon Salt**. Place asparagus bunches on pieces of toast or Holland rusk. Remove binding, pour **2 Tablespoons Melted Butter** over each bunch, and serve.

141   Green Beans

Cooking time 25 to 45 minutes

Remove ends and strings from **1 pound Green Beans**. Wash carefully in cold water. Cut across with knife or scissors in small pieces or split lengthwise in the French manner. Cover with boiling water and cook until soft, 20 to 40 minutes, depending upon the age and freshness of the beans. After beans have cooked for 15 minutes add **Salt, 1½ teaspoons** to the quart of water. When beans are soft, drain, saving the water for soup or sauces. Toss in pot a moment or so over the fire to dry beans. Dot **Butter** over beans, **Salt** if necessary, and add a little **Pepper.** Shake up and serve. If beans are not to be served at once, pour in **3 Tablespoons Cream or Undiluted Evaporated Milk** and keep hot over hot water. As a change add ⅛ teaspoon **Nutmeg** after beans have been cooked.

142 Green Beans Spencer

Cooking time 35 minutes
Additional cooking time 15 minutes—optional

In a small saucepan melt **2 Tablespoons Butter.** Into this put **1 pound Washed, Stringed, and Cut-up Beans.** Fry gently for a few minutes, shaking pan to be sure that all beans have been covered with the hot butter. Cover with **Heavy Cream or Undiluted Evaporated Milk** and simmer with asbestos pad between pot and flame until cream is about ½ its original quantity, and beans are tender. This will take about 25 minutes. Take off stove, add ½ teaspoon **Salt, a pinch of Nutmeg,** and a few grains **Cayenne (Red) Pepper.** Then stir in the yolks of **2 Eggs** beaten up with a little **Fresh Cream or Undiluted Evaporated Milk,** about **2 Tablespoons.** Cook for a moment or so until cream begins to thicken and serve. Do not let this boil again after the egg is added, or it will separate.

If your galley has an oven the creamed beans can be put into an oven dish without adding the egg yolks. A little **Cheese** can be grated on the top. Put in the oven and brown about 15 minutes.

142A   Green Beans in the Chinese Manner, see pg. 289.

143 Green Beans, Pressure-cooked

Cooking time 15 minutes

Wash, string, and cut up **1 pound Green Beans**. Place beans on rack in pressure cooker. Add ½ **cup Water** and ½ **teaspoon Salt**. Put lid on cooker, and when steam is coming out of the vent close it with pressure indicator. Cook for 4 minutes after indicator reaches fifteen pounds pressure or "cook" position. Cool cooker by placing in cold water for a minute. Pour off excess water. Shake pot over fire to dry beans and add **2 Table-spoons Butter or Margarine, Salt** if needed, and about ¼ **tea-spoon Pepper**.

144 Lima Beans

Cooking time 45 minutes plus

Shell enough **Lima Beans** to make **2 cups**, or buy them shelled. Place in a pot or saucepan and cover with **Boiling Water**. Add **1 teaspoon Salt** after they have cooked for 15 minutes. Cook until the beans are tender and most of the water has evaporated, at least ½ hour. When beans are tender, pour off the little remaining water, which should be saved for soup or making sauces, and add **3 Tablespoons Cream or Undiluted Evap-orated Milk** and ⅛ **teaspoon Pepper**. Shake well over fire and keep hot over boiling water until you are ready to serve. Beans actually improve if kept this way for ½ hour or so.

145 Lima Beans, Pressure-cooked

Cooking time 10 minutes

Shell (or buy shelled) enough **Lima Beans** to make **2 cups**. Place on rack of pressure cooker with ½ **cup of Water**. Close cooker, and when steam comes out of the vent put pressure indicator in place. Cook for 3 minutes after indicator reaches
178

"cook" position or fifteen pounds pressure. Cool cooker, re-move top, and pour off water, which should be saved for soups or sauces. To beans in cooker add **1 Tablespoon Butter or Margarine**, ½ teaspoon **Salt**, ⅛ teaspoon **Pepper**, and **3 Tablespoons Cream or Undiluted Evaporated Milk**. Shake well over the fire until butter is melted and mixed with the other ingredients, then serve.

BEETS

When you buy beets select those with fresh, crisp leaves. The roots should not be ridged or rough. Try to get beets that are approximately the same size. Beets should not be cut up or scraped before boiling, as that causes them to "bleed" and lose their color.

146   Boiled Beets

Cooking time 45 minutes to 1¾ hours

Wash **12 Medium-sized Beets**, cutting off the tops and leaving 1 inch of stem. Do not cut off roots. Cover with cold water with **1 teaspoon Salt** and **1 Tablespoon Sugar** in it and bring to a boil. Cook until tender—about 40 minutes if the beets are young, or up to 1½ hours if the beets are old. When beets are tender enough to slide off a fork that has been poked into them, take off fire. Pour water off, cool with cold water, slip off skins and remaining tops and roots with the fingers. Put beets back in pot with **1 Tablespoon Butter or Margarine** and ⅛ teaspoon **Pepper**. Shake in pot over the fire until beets are hot and well covered with butter and serve.

147   Beets, Pressure-cooked

Cooking time 15 to 25 minutes

Cut off tops, leaving only 1 inch of stem, from **12 Medium-sized Beets**. Do not cut off roots. If beets are young, cook in ⅓ cup Water and ½ teaspoon Salt for 10 minutes at fifteen pounds pressure after indicator shows "cook." If beets are old use ¾ cup Water and ½ teaspoon Salt and cook for 20 minutes at fifteen pounds pressure after indicator shows "cook." Cool cooker by standing in cold water for a minute. Remove skin and roots from beets, slipping them off with your fingers. Serve beets either cut up or whole, shaking up with 1 Tablespoon Butter or Margarine, ½ teaspoon Salt, and ⅛ teaspoon Pepper.

148 Fried Beets

Cooking time 10 minutes

In a heavy frying pan melt 4 Tablespoons Butter or Margarine and add 2 cups Cooked Beets cut into ½-inch dice. Season with 1 teaspoon Sugar and 1 Tablespoon Lemon Juice. Cook until beets are well covered with butter, about 6 minutes.

149 Beet Greens

Cooking time 12 minutes

A very delicious and healthful form of greens. Put Greens, carefully washed in several waters, but whole, into a pot which can be tightly covered. Add ¼ cup Boiling Water, ½ teaspoon Salt, and 2 teaspoons Sugar. Put over flame and cook until stems of greens are tender, about 8 minutes. Cool and chop as fine as you can on a chopping board or in a bowl. Return to pot and add 1 Tablespoon Butter or Margarine and ¼ teaspoon Pepper. Shake up well in pot over flame and serve.

150 Beet Greens, Pressure-cooked

Cooking time 7 minutes

Prepare Greens as in No. 149. Place in pressure cooker with ½ teaspoon Salt and ½ cup Water. Be sure that greens are

pushed far enough down in pot so that they cannot inter-
fere with vent. Cover cooker. As soon as steam starts coming
out of the vent, put indicator on and cook for 3 minutes after
indicator reaches fifteen pounds or indicates "cook." Cool
cooker, remove top, pour off water, and chop greens fine. Shake
up over flame with **2 Tablespoons Butter or Margarine** and
¼ teaspoon **Pepper** and serve.

151   Boiled Brussels Sprouts
Preparation time 15 minutes—optional
Cooking time 20 minutes

Remove the wilted leaves from **3 cups Brussels Sprouts** (about
1 box as they are sold now), selecting the light green, compact heads. It is best to let them soak for 15 minutes in cold
water. Place in a pot and cover with **1 quart Boiling Water** in
which there is **1 teaspoon Salt**. Cook until tender enough to
pierce with a fork, 12 to 20 minutes. Pour off the water in
which they have been cooked and add **2 Tablespoons Butter
or Margarine**. Shake well in the butter and serve.

152   Brussels Sprouts, Pressure-cooked
Preparation time 15 minutes—optional
Cooking time 5 minutes

Prepare **Brussels Sprouts** as in No. 151. Place on rack in
cooker with ½ cup **Water** and ½ teaspoon **Salt**. Close cooker,
and when steam comes out of the vent put indicator in place.
Cook for 3 minutes after indicator reaches fifteen pounds or
"cook" position. Cool cooker quickly by placing it in cold
water for a minute. Remove top, pour off water, and add **2
Tablespoons Butter**. Shake up well and serve.

153   Creamed Brussels Sprouts
Cooking time 35 minutes

Cook as in the recipe for boiled **Brussels Sprouts** (No. 151). Pour off water in which sprouts have been cooked and add **3 Tablespoons Butter or Margarine.** Let cook in the butter, turning frequently for 3 minutes. Then chop fine. Add ½ **cup Cream or Undiluted Evaporated Milk** and simmer gently until cream has been reduced to about ½ its original quantity (about 12 minutes) and serve.

154   Boiled Cabbage
Preparation time 30 minutes—optional
Cooking time 8 minutes

Remove the outside leaves from **1 head of Cabbage.** Cut into quarters and remove all of the central stem if very tough. It is better if soaked for 20 minutes in cold water, salted 1 teaspoon to the quart. Shake water from cabbage and cut up fine. Place in a pot that can be covered. Add ½ **cup Boiling Water** with ½ **teaspoon Salt** added to it. Cover pot and cook until cabbage is tender, about 8 minutes. Drain off water and shake cabbage up over flame until dry. Add **3 Tablespoons Butter or Margarine** and ⅛ **teaspoon Pepper** and serve.

155   Cabbage, Pressure-cooked
Preparation time 30 minutes—optional
Cooking time 5 minutes

Prepare **Cabbage** as for boiled cabbage (No. 154). Place in rack of pressure cooker with ½ **cup Water** and ½ **teaspoon Salt.** Put top on cooker and put over flame. When steam comes out of the vent put indicator in place. When indicator reaches

fifteen pounds pressure or "cook" position, cook for 3 minutes.
Cool cooker by placing in cold water for a minute. Take off
top, drain off water, add **3 Tablespoons Butter or Margarine,**
⅛ **teaspoon Pepper,** and shake up well. Serve while good and
hot.

156   Red Cabbage and Apples
Cooking time 40 minutes

Remove the outside leaves from **1 head of Red Cabbage.** Cut
cabbage into quarters and remove all of the inner stem. Cut
cabbage up into strips ½ inch or so wide. Put into pot and
add **1 cup Boiling Water.** Cook covered until stems of cabbage can be easily pierced with a fork, about 10 minutes. Add
4 Apples peeled and cored and cut into thin slices, ½ **teaspoon
Salt, 1 teaspoon Sugar.** Cook until apples are soft, about 25
minutes. Stir up well and let simmer gently until ready to
serve. During this latter period an asbestos pad should be
placed between pot and flame.

157   Boiled Carrots
Cooking time 35 minutes

Wash **1 bunch of Carrots** carefully. Cut off the tops and the
root ends, but do not scrape. Put in a pot and cover with **Cold
Water Salted,** 1 teaspoon salt to the quart. Cook until tender,
20 to 30 minutes. Add **2 teaspoons Sugar** and cook 5 minutes
more. Pour off the water, saving it for soups or sauces. Cool
carrots and squeeze off skins with fingers. Cut carrots up and
return to pot. Add **1 Tablespoon Butter or Margarine** and ⅛
teaspoon Pepper, shake over flame until carrots are hot, and
serve.

158 Carrots, Pressure-cooked

Cooking time 7 minutes

Wash 1 bunch of **Carrots** carefully. Cut off tops and roots and place in the pressure cooker on the rack. Add ½ cup **Water** and ½ teaspoon **Salt**. Close cooker. When steam comes out of the vent put indicator in place. Cook for 3 minutes after indicator reaches fifteen pounds or "cook" position. Cool cooker in cold water for a minute, take off top, pour off water which should be saved for soups or sauces, and remove carrots. With fingers slip off skins. Cut carrots either across or in long slices. Put back in cooker with **2 Tablespoons Butter** and ⅛ teaspoon **Pepper**. Add more salt if your taste requires it and shake up in cooker over the flame.

159 Carrots Burgundy

Cooking time 50 minutes or 25 minutes

Cook 1 bunch of **Young Carrots** as indicated in recipe for boiled carrots or carrots pressure-cooked (Nos. 157, 158). Meanwhile in a small frying pan melt **2 Tablespoons Butter or Margarine**. In it gently fry **4 Medium-sized Onions** cut up in very small pieces. When onions are soft, not browned (about 8 minutes), add the carrots cut across in small pieces. Sprinkle with **1 Tablespoon Flour**, browning it well. Add **1 cup Consommé**, ½ teaspoon **Salt**, and ⅛ teaspoon **Pepper** and simmer for 15 minutes.

160 Boiled Cauliflower

Preparation time 30 minutes
Cooking time 25 minutes

Select a **Cauliflower**, the head of which is very white and the leaves fresh and green. Remove the leaves and cut off the

184

stem. Soak it upside down in **Water Salted** 1 teaspoon to the quart for ½ hour. Shake well and put into a pot, head side up. Pour over it **2 quarts Boiling Water** with 2 teaspoons Salt in it. Cover and cook until cauliflower is tender, about 20 minutes. Place in the dish in which it is to be served and pour over it **3 Tablespoons Melted Butter.** A very good way to finish this dish is to fry **3 Tablespoons Bread Crumbs** in **3 Tablespoons Butter or Margarine** and pour this over the top of the cauliflower just before it is to be served.

161 Cauliflower, Pressure-cooked
Preparation time 30 minutes
Cooking time 7 minutes

Prepare 1 head of Cauliflower as for boiled cauliflower. Place on rack in cooker, head up. Add **½ cup Water** and ½ teaspoon **Salt.** Place top on cooker, and when steam comes out of the vent put indicator in place. Cook 5 minutes after indicator reaches fifteen pounds or "cook" position. Cool cooker in cold water for a minute. Remove top. Pour off water. Pour **3 Tablespoons Butter or Margarine** over cauliflower and serve. You may wish to fry slightly **3 Tablespoons Bread Crumbs** in **3 Tablespoons Butter or Margarine** and salt with ¼ teaspoon **Salt.** Pour over the cauliflower and serve.

162 Corn on the Cob
Cooking time 15 minutes

Select **8 ears of Corn,** the silk of which is still moist and fresh. Keep corn in the husks until you are ready to prepare it. Have **3 quarts Water Boiling.** Do not put salt in it, as that will toughen the corn. Add **3 Tablespoons Sugar.** Remove all but the inner husk and put into boiling water one ear at a time so as not to stop the boil. Cook corn until tender, about 6 minutes—seldom any more, as longer cooking makes corn tough. Remove corn from pot, strip off inner husk, wrap in a napkin or other cloth, and serve with salt and plenty of butter.

163   Corn on the Cob, Pressure-cooked

Cooking time 7 minutes

Remove silk and all but the inner husks from **8 small ears of Corn.** Place in pressure cooker on the rack. Add ¾ **cup Water.** Be sure that none of the corn is near the vent, as it might close it. Put top on cooker. When steam comes out of the vent put indicator in place. When indicator reaches fifteen pounds or "cook" position, cook for 3 to 5 minutes, depending on the age of the corn. Cool cooker in cold water for a minute, remove cover, and pour off water. Strip off husks and sprinkle corn with **1 teaspoon Salt.** Wrap in a napkin or other cloth and serve very hot with salt and plenty of butter or margarine.

164   Boiled Cucumbers

Cooking time 15 minutes

Peel and cut into slices 2 **Large Cucumbers.** Place in a saucepan and cover with **Chicken Soup,** about 1 can, or **Boiling Water, Salted** 1 teaspoon to the quart. Cook until the cucumbers are tender, about 10 minutes. Drain off the liquid, add **1 Tablespoon Butter or Margarine,** and ¼ **teaspoon Pepper.** Toss in the pan over the fire until cucumbers are well covered with butter or margarine, and pepper, and serve.

165   Boiled Eggplant

Cooking time 20 minutes

Select 1 **Eggplant** which is firm and sound. Peel it and cut it into slices ¾ inch thick and about 1 inch square. Sprinkle with

¾ teaspoon Salt, add 1½ cups Water, bring to a boil and let simmer covered until very soft, about 15 minutes. If you cannot control the flame, put an asbestos pad between pot and flame. Pour off water. Season with 1 teaspoon Sugar, ⅛ teaspoon Pepper, ¼ teaspoon Cinnamon. Add 2 Tablespoons Butter or Margarine and stir. If you have lamb broth, either homemade or canned, use it instead of water. This is the Near East method.

166 Eggplant, Pressure-cooked

Cooking time 10 minutes

Peel 1 Eggplant and cut into 1-inch cubes. Place on rack of pressure cooker and add ½ cup Tomato Juice and ½ teaspoon Salt. Put cover on cooker. When steam comes out of the vent put indicator in place. When pressure reaches fifteen pounds or indicator shows "cook," cook for ½ minute. Cool cooker in cold water. Remove top, add 1 Tablespoon Butter or Margarine, ⅛ teaspoon Pepper, and ½ teaspoon Onion or Garlic Salt if you have it. Shake well in the cooker over the flame and serve hot.

167 Eggplant, Fried

Cooking time 50 minutes

Select 1 Heavy Eggplant, the skin of which is whole. Wash it and cut it into slices ¾ inch thick. Roll each slice in flour and dip in a mixture of 1 Egg beaten up with 1 Tablespoon Water and ½ teaspoon Salt, and then roll in Cracker or Dry Bread Crumbs. In a frying pan heat 3 Tablespoons Olive or Other Cooking Oil to the smoking point and put in the eggplant slices, enough to fill the pan; brown, about 10 minutes, on each side. When browned, slices should be well drained on brown paper. A paper bag or a paper towel does very nicely.

168 Eggplant Provençale

Cooking time 47 minutes

Peel 1 **Eggplant** and cut into pieces 1 inch or so square. Sprinkle with **8 teaspoons Salt.** Let set 20 minutes. Then wash off Salt and green juice. Remove the skins from 4 **Firm Tomatoes.** Peel and cut into thin slices **6 Small Onions.** In a heavy frying pan heat **3 Tablespoons Olive or Other Cooking Oil** until it begins to smoke. In it put the eggplant. 5 minutes later add the onions and tomatoes. Cook covered over a low flame. If you cannot control the flame, put an asbestos pad between flame and pan. Cook until the vegetables are soft, about 18 minutes. Season with ½ **teaspoon Salt,** ¼ **teaspoon Pepper,** and **a pinch of Cinnamon,** if you have it.

169 Greens

Cooking time 17 minutes

Greens include **Spinach, Chard, and Beet Tops.** Wash greens carefully in three waters (sea water will do), as they tend to be very sandy and will taste gritty if not well washed. Lift from pot while water is still in it, so that sand will remain in the bottom. Push greens well down in a pot or kettle that can be tightly sealed. Add ½ **cup Boiling Water** and cook tightly covered over a low flame or with an asbestos pad between pot and flame, until stems of greens are soft, about 8 minutes. Drain off water. Save it for soup or sauces if you have space to keep an extra jar. Chop greens fine and add ½ **teaspoon Salt,** ⅛ **teaspoon Pepper,** and **2 Tablespoons Butter.** Shake well over the fire and serve. An addition appreciated by many is ⅛ **teaspoon Nutmeg.**

170 Greens, Pressure-cooked

Cooking time 10 minutes

Prepare **Greens** as indicated above in the recipe for greens (No. 169). Place in pressure cooker, pressing down well so that none of the leaves will be near the vent. Add ½ cup **Water** and ½ teaspoon **Salt**. Cover cooker, and when steam comes out of the vent put indicator in place. When indicator points to "cook" or fifteen pounds, cook for 2 minutes. Cool cooker in cold water, remove top, and pour off water. Add **2 Tablespoons Butter or Margarine** and ⅛ teaspoon **Pepper**. Chop greens up as fine as possible. Heat and serve.

171 Mushrooms Fried in Butter

Cooking time 20 minutes

Remove stems and peel the caps of **1 pound Fresh Mushrooms**. Cut the dried bottom ends off the stems and cut stems into ½-inch pieces. Caps can be cooked either whole or sliced thin. Put stems in a small saucepan and cover with boiling water in which there is ½ teaspoon **Salt**. Boil until tender, about 10 minutes. Meanwhile in a small frying pan melt **2 Table-spoons Butter or Margarine** and in it gently fry the caps of the mushrooms. When they are tender, about 6 minutes, sprinkle them with **2 Tablespoons Flour**. Cook well, stirring into but-ter. Brown flour, add cooked pieces of the stems, and slowly pour in water in which stems were cooked. If this is too thick, thin it with a little **Cream or Undiluted Evaporated Milk**. Add **2 Tablespoons Lemon Juice** and ⅛ teaspoon **Pepper**. Serve on toast, Holland rusk, or zwieback. Marvelous on steak.

172 Creamed Mushrooms

Cooking time 25 minutes

Peel caps of **1 pound Mushrooms**. Slice mushrooms from top straight down through stems. Melt **2 Tablespoons Butter or Margarine** in a frying pan. In it gently fry the mushrooms until they begin to soften, about 6 minutes. Sprinkle with ½ teaspoon **Salt**, ⅛ teaspoon **Pepper**, and **1 teaspoon Lemon Juice**. Cover mushrooms with **Heavy Cream or Undiluted Evaporated Milk, about 1 cup,** and simmer gently until cream has reduced ⅓, about 10 minutes. Serve on toast, Holland rusk, or zwieback. Mushrooms creamed this way are very good over rice or spaghetti.

173 Boiled Onions

Cooking time 40 minutes

Remove the outer skins from **1 pound Onions**. These can be taken off with a knife, but the easiest way is to cover the onions with boiling water for 5 minutes. Pour off the water and the outer skins can be removed with the fingers. Incidentally, if this is done under cold water there will be no smell of onions on the hands. Put onions in a large pot and cover with **Boiling Water, Salted** 1 teaspoon to the quart. There should be twice as much water as there are onions. Boil until onions are tender, about 25 to 35 minutes. Pour water from pan. Put in **3 Tablespoons Butter**. Shake onions well in butter and serve. Some good cooks add **1 teaspoon Sugar** and ¼ **teaspoon Powdered Cloves**.

174 Onions, Pressure-cooked

Cooking time 17 minutes

Wash and remove the outer skins from **1 pound Medium-sized Onions**. Place onions on the rack in the cooker and add

½ cup Water and ½ teaspoon Salt. Cover cooker and put over flame. When steam begins to issue from the vent, close indicator. When indicator reaches fifteen pounds or "cook" position, cook for 7 minutes. Cool cooker in cold water, remove top, and pour off water, which should be saved for soups or sauces. Add 1 Tablespoon Butter and ⅛ teaspoon Pepper. Shake well and serve.

175 Creamed Onions

Cooking time 55 minutes or 35 minutes

Cook **Onions** as in boiled onions (No. 173 or No. 174), but take off fire before onions get really soft. In a small frying pan or saucepan melt **2 Tablespoons Butter or Margarine.** Fry the onions gently in this, stirring until all are coated with butter. Then pour over the onions 1 cup **Heavy Cream or Undiluted Evaporated Milk.** Simmer gently until the cream is reduced to half its quantity (about 20 minutes). Add ½ teaspoon Salt, a few grains of Cayenne (Red) Pepper, ⅛ teaspoon Nutmeg, and the yolk of 1 Egg beaten in 2 Tablespoons Cream or Milk. Let simmer for 5 minutes and serve.

176 Green Peas, Boiled

Preparation time 40 minutes (30 minutes optional)
Cooking time 15 to 45 minutes

Select **2 pounds Plump Unshelled Peas.** They should feel crisp to the touch. Shelled they will yield about 2 cups or 4 portions. It is good to soak shelled peas in cold water for ½ hour, throwing away all that float to the top. Place the peas in a saucepan and add 1½ **cups Boiling Water.** Cook until the peas are tender, anywhere from 15 to 45 minutes, depending upon the age of the peas. Add ½ teaspoon Salt and 1 teaspoon **Sugar** after peas have cooked 10 minutes. If the water gets low, add a little more. There should be almost none left when you finish cooking. Pour off the water and dry peas by shaking in the pot over the flame. Take off fire and add **1 Tablespoon Butter or Margarine** and ⅛ teaspoon **Pepper,** shaking well to get butter on all of the peas. If peas must be kept a few minutes, put **2 Tablespoons Cream or Undiluted Evaporated Milk** in pot and cover.

177   Green Peas, Pressure-cooked
Preparation time 40 minutes (30 minutes optional)
Cooking time 5 minutes

Shell **2 pounds Green Peas.** Soak shelled peas ½ hour in cold water. Place peas on rack in pressure cooker with ½ teaspoon **Salt, 1 teaspoon Sugar,** and **1 Tablespoon Butter or Margarine.** Add ½ cup **Water** and put on cover. Place over the flame, and when steam comes out of the vent put indicator in place. When indicator shows fifteen pounds pressure or "cook," cook for 5 minutes. Cool cooker in cold water for a minute, remove cover, and pour off water, saving it for soups or sauces. Add **1 Tablespoon Butter** and ⅛ teaspoon **Pepper.** Shake well together in cooker and serve.

178   Green Peas, Country Style
Cooking time 40 minutes to 1 hour

Cut up **5 slices Lean Bacon** into very small pieces (easy if you use scissors). Put in a heavy frying pan over low fire and cook until bacon bits are crisp; then take them out of the fat and keep on brown paper or paper towel. Pour off all but 2 tablespoons of the fat and in it fry **1 cup Onions** chopped up fine. When onions begin to brown, sprinkle over them **2 Tablespoons Flour.** Cook for 5 minutes, stirring, and then add **1 can Undiluted Consommé.** Return bacon bits to the pan and add

2 cups Shelled Peas. Simmer gently until the peas are tender, usually from 15 to 40 minutes, depending on the age of the peas.

POTATOES

Potatoes are an ideal food at sea. They have valuable food elements, bulk, and are easy to prepare. Hot potatoes seem to counteract seasickness. They come in cans ready for instant use. They are canned whole, small, and julienne (which means cut up small). The last is ideal for chowders, creamed potatoes, omelets, or to serve hashed brown.

179   Boiled Potatoes

Cooking time 30 minutes

Wash and scrub **8 Medium-sized Potatoes.** If they are new potatoes, they can be boiled in their jackets or skins. If they are potatoes that have been kept for a while, they should be peeled and soaked in cold water for at least 10 minutes. Put potatoes in the pot with enough water to cover. Add **1 teaspoon Salt for each 4 cups Water.** Bring pot to a boil and let boil until potatoes are soft when poked with a fork. Pour off the water and shake potatoes in the pot over the fire until they are well dried. Shake them up with **a little Butter** and **Chopped Parsley or Chives,** if you have them.

180   Potatoes, Pressure-cooked

Cooking time 16 minutes

Wash and scrub **8 Medium-sized Potatoes.** Place on rack in cooker and add **½ cup Water** and **1 teaspoon Salt.** Cover cooker and put over flame. When steam begins to come out of the vent put indicator in place. Cook for 12 minutes after indicator reaches fifteen pounds or "cook" position. Cool cooker in cold water for a minute and remove cover. Pour off water, saving it for soups or sauces, and serve potatoes while good and hot.

181   Baked Potatoes

Cooking time 45 minutes to 1¼ hours

Stove-top potato bakers such as the Connolly oven make it possible to have baked potatoes even on boats with no ovens in their galleys. The process of preparing the potatoes is the same. Wash the **Potato** carefully and dry it. Rub the surface over with a little **Olive or Other Cooking Oil or a little Butter** if you expect to eat the skins (optional). With a fork poke several holes in the potato. Place in a hot oven, about 380° if you have an oven thermometer, and bake until potato is tender. It will take from 40 minutes to 1¼ hours. The skin will be wrinkled, and the potato will squeeze when held in a pot holder. If potatoes are not to be used at once, pierce with a fork to let steam out; otherwise potato may be soggy.

182   Salt-Glazed Potatoes

Cooking time 30 minutes

This is best done with small new potatoes. Wash and scrub **2 pounds Small New Potatoes**. Put in pot and cover with water. Into water pour **Salt** until potatoes float; it will take at least 2 cups. Put potatoes over flame and cook until tender, about 25 minutes. Lift potatoes from pot with a spoon and serve. The potatoes will have a thin glaze of salt. Serve plenty of **Butter** to be eaten with them. They are delicious. Boil most of the water off the salt remaining in the pot and save the salt for another use. This way of cooking potatoes originated in the salt factories in Syracuse, N.Y., where workmen brought potatoes to work with them and cooked them in the salt being refined.

183 Creamed Potatoes

Cooking time 40 minutes

Peel and cut into ½-inch dice 4 Medium-sized Potatoes. Soak in cold water for 10 minutes, then drain and put in a shallow pan. Pour ½ cup Cream or Undiluted Evaporated Milk, ½ cup Milk, ½ teaspoon Salt, and ¼ teaspoon Pepper and simmer until potatoes are soft and liquid is reduced about ½ (about 20 minutes). Shake a little Paprika on the top and serve.

184 Potatoes in Cream Sauce

Cooking time 40 minutes

Peel and cut into ½-inch dice 4 Medium-sized Potatoes. Soak for 10 minutes in cold water; drain. Put in pot and cover with Cold Water Salted, 1 teaspoon salt to the quart. Simmer until the potatoes are tender, about 20 minutes. Pour off water. Mix with 1 cup Cream Sauce (No. 241). Heat, being careful not to burn, and serve.

185 Creamed Potatoes, Pressure-cooked

Preparation time 25 minutes
Cooking time 25 minutes

Peel and cut into ½-inch dice 4 Medium-sized Potatoes. Soak for 10 minutes, drain, and place in cooker with ½ cup Water. Cover cooker and put over flame. When steam comes out of the vent put indicator in place. When indicator reaches "cook" position or fifteen pounds, cook for 10 minutes. Cool cooker in cold water, remove top, and pour off water, saving it for soups or sauces. Add 1 cup Heavy Cream or Undiluted Evaporated Milk, 1 teaspoon Salt, ¼ teaspoon Pepper, and ½ teaspoon Nutmeg. Simmer with an asbestos pad between pot and flame if you cannot control flame, until cream is reduced to ½ its original volume, about 12 minutes. Potatoes should be stirred occasionally. Sprinkle with **Paprika** and serve.

186 Fried Potatoes

Preparation time 35 minutes
Cooking time 30 minutes

Cut into thin slices 4 **Cold Boiled Potatoes.** In a heavy frying pan melt 3 Tablespoons **Butter, Margarine, or Bacon Grease.** Cook potatoes over a medium flame (if flame cannot be controlled use an asbestos pad between flame and pan). Cook until they are light brown, about 7 minutes, on each side. During cooking sprinkle generously with **Salt** and **Pepper.** New potatoes can be cooked without boiling. Slice 4 **Medium-sized New Potatoes** without peeling. Soak them for 30 minutes in cold water. Remove from water and dry carefully. Melt 4 **Tablespoons Butter, Margarine, or Bacon Grease** in a heavy frying pan and fry potatoes as above, about 10 minutes on each side.

187 Hashed Brown Potatoes

Cooking time 20 minutes

Stir 4 **Medium-sized Boiled Potatoes** cut into very small pieces with 1 teaspoon **Salt,** ¼ teaspoon **Pepper,** 1 Tablespoon **Flour,** and 4 Tablespoons **Cream or Undiluted Evaporated Milk.** In a small frying pan melt a good 4 Tablespoons **Butter, Margarine, or Bacon Grease.** When it is sizzling hot, pour in the potatoes and press well down in the pan. Cook over a medium flame (use an asbestos pad if you cannot control flame) until potatoes are brown on the bottom, about 10 minutes. That will be indicated by the little puffs of steam that will come up from the potatoes. Fold one side over the other as with an omelet and slide out on the plate upon which it is to be served.

188   Mashed Potatoes

Preparation time 30 minutes
Cooking time 30 minutes

Peel, cut into quarters, and soak for at least 20 minutes 4 **Medium-sized Potatoes**. Boil them until soft in **Water Salted** 1 teaspoon of salt to the quart, about 20 minutes. Pour off all the water, saving it for soups or sauces. Shake potatoes in pot over fire until they are quite dry. Heat ½ **cup Milk or Diluted Evaporated Milk, 3 Tablespoons Butter, 1 teaspoon Salt and** ¼ **teaspoon Pepper**. With a rotary egg beater or a whip mash the potatoes, slowly pouring the hot milk mixture over them. Then beat them with the rotary beater until they are light and fluffy. Add more milk if they seem too stiff. Dot top with 1 **teaspoon Butter**. Sprinkle with ½ **teaspoon Paprika** and serve. Easier by far and almost as good are the **Instant Mashed Potatoes** on the market. (Borden's is our favorite.) Follow directions on box.

189   Mashed Potatoes, Pressure-cooked

Preparation time 30 minutes
Cooking time 15 minutes

Peel, cut into quarters, and soak for 20 minutes **4 Medium-sized Potatoes**. Drain and place in cooker with ½ **cup Water** and ½ **teaspoon Salt**. Cover cooker and place on the flame. When steam comes out of the vent put indicator in place and cook for 10 minutes after indicator shows fifteen pounds or "cook." Cool cooker in cold water for a minute and remove cover. Pour off water, which should be saved for soups or sauces. Shake potatoes over flame in pot to dry. Heat ½ **cup Milk with 3 Tablespoons Butter and** ⅛ **teaspoon Pepper**. With a rotary egg beater mash potatoes, slowly adding the hot milk. When potatoes begin to be soft, whip with the rotary beater until they are fluffy. Sprinkle with **Paprika and serve**.

190 Mashed Sweet Potatoes

Cooking time 35 minutes

Wash and boil in their skins **6 Medium-sized Sweet Potatoes.**
When soft (about 25 minutes), peel potatoes and place in bowl.
With an egg-beater if you have one, if not, a heavy bottle does
almost as well, mash potatoes until they are without lumps.
Add **3 Tablespoons Butter,** ½ teaspoon **Salt,** and ⅓ cup **Hot
Fresh or Diluted Evaporated Milk** (for a change you can sub-
stitute **Hot Orange Juice**). Beat with the egg-beater, or whip,
until potatoes are fluffy.

191 Sweet Potatoes, Pressure-cooked

Cooking time 15 minutes

Wash **8 Medium-sized Sweet Potatoes or Yams.** Place in cooker
and add ½ cup **Water.** Cover, and when steam comes out of the
vent put indicator in place. Cook 10 minutes after indicator
reaches fifteen pounds or "cook" position. Cool cooker in cold
water and remove top. Potatoes can be served with jackets on
or peeled. If they are peeled, put back in the pot and sprinkle
with ½ teaspoon **Salt,** 1 teaspoon **Brown Sugar,** and **2 Tablespoons Butter or Margarine.** Shake up well in pot and serve.

192 Mashed Sweet Potatoes, Pressure-cooked

Cooking time 20 minutes

Cook **Potatoes** as indicated in recipe for sweet potatoes, pressure-cooked (No. 191). Pour off water, peel potatoes. Mash with
a rotary egg beater. Add ½ cup **Hot Milk or Orange Juice** and
½ teaspoon **Salt.** Whip well and serve.

193 Baked Sweet Potatoes

Cooking time 40 minutes

Wash 4 Medium-sized Sweet Potatoes, rub the surfaces with Olive or Other Cooking Oil or Butter. In galleys with an oven, place in 385° oven and bake until tender, about 40 minutes. In galleys without an oven put potatoes in a Connolly oven, place over flame, and bake until soft, turning occasionally to make sure all sides are cooked.

194 Candied Sweet Potatoes

Cooking time 45 minutes

Boil until soft (about 25 minutes), peel, and cut into thin slices 6 Medium-sized Sweet Potatoes. Melt 4 Tablespoons Butter or Margarine in a heavy frying pan. Add ½ cup Brown Sugar. Add potatoes and turn until each is brown on both sides, about 8 minutes. Add ¼ cup Boiling Water. Cover closely and cook until potatoes are very tender, about 10 minutes. Drain on brown paper and sprinkle lightly with salt.

195 Potato Cakes

Cooking time 25 minutes

Take 2 cups Cold or Hot Mashed Potatoes. Mix with them the Yolks of 2 Eggs. Make into 2-inch balls. Do not press them too hard, as this makes the cakes heavy. Dip balls into 1 Egg beaten with 1 Tablespoon Cold Water. Roll in Flour and flatten at top and bottom. Melt 3 Tablespoons Butter, Margarine, or Bacon Grease in a heavy frying pan. Over a medium flame or with an asbestos pad under pan, fry until cakes are brown, about 10 minutes on each side.

196 Boiled Spinach
Cooking time 15 minutes

Cut off roots and remove yellow leaves from **2 pounds Spinach** (**½ peck**). Wash carefully, shaking in water to loosen and remove all sand. Wash in 3 waters (sea water will do), then lift from water (if you pour water off, sand remains in spinach). Put spinach, all wet and dripping, in a pot. Cover closely and put over flame for 6 minutes or until spinach is tender. If spinach is old, a small amount of additional water may be needed to cook it until tender. When tender, pour off water and chop fine. Add **2 Tablespoons Butter, 1 teaspoon Salt** and **¼ teaspoon Pepper.** Toss spinach in the pot and serve.

197 Spinach, Pressure-cooked
Cooking time 10 minutes

Cut off roots and yellow leaves from **2 pounds Fresh Spinach.** Wash carefully in 3 waters (sea water will do), lifting spinach from pot each time to leave sand in the bottom. Place spinach in cooker, press well down and add **½ cup Water,** and cover cooker. Place over flame. When steam comes from the vent put indicator in place. Cook 1 minute after indicator reaches fifteen pounds pressure or "cook" position. Cool cooker for a minute in cold water. Chop spinach very fine and add **2 Tablespoons Butter** and **1 teaspoon Salt.** Toss together in pot and serve.

198 Creamed Spinach
Cooking time 30 minutes

Cook **2 pounds Spinach** as for boiled spinach (No. 196). In heavy frying pan melt **3 Tablespoons Butter** and **2 Tablespoons Finely Chopped Onions.** Cook until onions are soft,

about 3 minutes, and sprinkle with **2 Tablespoons Flour.**
Blend well and add **1 teaspoon Salt, ¼ teaspoon Pepper,** and
½ cup Hot Fresh or Diluted Evaporated Milk. Blend well until smooth. Stir in chopped spinach and let simmer for 5 minutes. Serve hot.

199 Boiled Summer Squash

Cooking time 25 minutes

Cut into 1-inch cubes **2 Small Summer Squash** with the skins
left on. Place in a pot with **2½ cups Boiling Water, ½ teaspoon Salt** and cook until squash is tender, from 15 to 20
minutes. Pour off any water that remains, add **½ cup Cream
or Undiluted Evaporated Milk** and **¼ teaspoon Pepper.** Let
simmer for 5 minutes, stirring all the time.

200 Summer Squash, Pressure-cooked

Cooking time 12 minutes

Peel and cut into 1-inch cubes **2 Summer Squash** with the
skins left on. Place in cooker and add **½ cup Water and ½
teaspoon Salt.** Cover cooker and place over flame. When
steam comes out of the vent put indicator in place. When indicator reaches fifteen pounds pressure or "cook" position,
cook for 6 minutes. Cool cooker in cold water for a minute,
remove cover and pour off water. Add **2 Tablespoons Butter
or Margarine, 2 teaspoons Brown Sugar** and more **Salt** if
needed. Shake well over the fire and serve.

201 Fried Squash

Cooking time 20 minutes

Peel and cut into ¾-inch cubes **2 Small Squash.** Shake the
squash in a paper bag with **4 Tablespoons Flour, 1 teaspoon**

Salt and ⅛ teaspoon **Pepper**. In a heavy frying pan heat **3 Tablespoons Butter**. Put squash cubes in the frying pan and cook covered until they are crisp and brown, about 18 minutes.

202 Stewed Tomatoes

Cooking time 25 minutes

Wash **6 Large Tomatoes**. Hold each tomato over the direct flame on the end of a fork for a minute or so, turning the tomato so that the flame reaches all sides, and peel off the skin of each. Quarter tomatoes and place in a stew pan. Sprinkle with ½ teaspoon **Salt**, ¼ teaspoon **Pepper**, and **2 Tablespoons Brown Sugar**. Cook slowly with an asbestos pad between pan and flame until tomatoes are soft, 10 to 20 minutes, stirring occasionally to prevent scorching. Thicken with **4 Tablespoons Bread Crumbs**. Cook 2 minutes more and serve.

203 Tomatoes, Pressure-cooked

Cooking time 10 minutes

Prepare **6 Large Tomatoes** as in recipe for stewed tomatoes (No. 202). Place in the cooker and add ½ **cup Water**. Put cover in place and put on flame. When steam comes out of the vent put indicator in place. Cook for 1 minute after indicator reaches fifteen pounds or "cook" position. Cool cooker in cold water for a minute and remove cover. Add ½ **teaspoon Salt**, ¼ teaspoon **Pepper**, **2 Tablespoons Butter**, and **4 Tablespoons Dry Bread Crumbs**. Stir well over flame and serve.

204 Fried Tomatoes

Cooking time 15 minutes

Wash **4 Large Tomatoes** and cut into halves crosswise. Wipe each half with **Melted Butter** and sprinkle with **Salt, Pepper,** and **Brown Sugar.** Dip in **1 Egg** beaten with **1 Tablespoon Water** and roll in **Bread Crumbs.** In a heavy frying pan melt **3 Tablespoons Butter.** With an asbestos pad between pan and flame fry tomatoes until soft and well browned, about 8 minutes. Tomatoes cooked this way are a fine garnish for meat or may be served on toast, Holland rusk, or French toast.

WAYS OF IMPROVING CANNED VEGETABLES

Canned vegetables are very good just as they come out of the can. Follow the directions and you can't go wrong. However, they do get monotonous, if you have the misfortune to have aboard too many cans of the same kind. This section is to help you keep your reputation as an ingenious sea cook under such conditions.

Nutmeg is used in vegetable cooking by most French chefs. A pinch of it gives a subtle difference to most vegetables. In the Middle East, cinnamon is used with eggplant, squash, cooked cucumbers, tomatoes, and rice. Sugar, used for flavoring and *not* for sweetening, finds a place in many French vegetable recipes. Polish and Russian cooking favor sour cream. Mustard and the dried herbs such as marjoram, dill, summer savory, basil, sage, and thyme can give a most pleasing variety to the same old canned stuff. Use them to get variety. Experiment with your own ideas.

A most common mistake in the use of canned vegetables is to drain off and throw away the liquid in which the vegetables are packed. Not only does this fluid add to the flavor of most vegetables, if properly used, but it contains a very large proportion of the vitamins and mineral salts originally in the vegetables. You should drain the liquid from the can, and in the pan in which the vegetables are to be cooked boil it down until it is reduced to about ⅓ of its bulk. Then heat the vegetables in it. We find that an onion sliced into the liquid to be reduced often gives it a grand new flavor. If you do not need the juice for heating the vegetables, save it for soups or sauces. For rough weather and where time or space is at a premium, several cans can be heated at same time in hot water in large pot or pail.

As the following list shows, there is a great variety of canned vegetables available. It is surprising how easy it is to get most of them in even tiny stores.

Artichokes
Asparagus, green
Asparagus, white
Bamboo sprouts
Bean sprouts
Beans, asparagus pack
Beans, baked, plain
Beans, baked with pork
Beans, cut
Beans, French style
Beans, green
Beans, kosher
Beans, lima
Beans, red
Beans, red kidney
Beans, red kidney with pork
  and tomato sauce
Beans, soya, green
Beans, with tomato sauce
Beans, wax
Beet greens
Beets, diced
Beets, julienne or shoestring
Beets, sliced
Beets, whole
Broccoli
Brussels sprouts
Cabbage
Carrots and peas

Carrots, diced
Carrots, julienne or shoestring
Carrots, whole
Cauliflower
Celery
Cereal, strained
Chard
Collard greens
Corn, cream style
Corn, whole grain
Corn on the cob
Corn-meal mush
Dandelion greens
Hominy
Kale
Lentils
Mushroom caps
Mushrooms, chopped
Mushrooms, sliced
Mustard greens
Okra
Onions
Parsnips
Peas
Peas, black-eye
Peppers, green
Peppers, sweet
Pickles
Pimientos

Poke greens
Potatoes, French fried
Potatoes, sweet, dry pack
Potatoes, sweet, syrup pack
Potatoes, sweet, vacuum pack
Potatoes, white, julienne
Potatoes, white, whole
Pumpkin
Rice
Sauerkraut
Spinach
Squash
Succotash, plain
Succotash with tomato

Tomatoes
Tomatoes, whole peeled Italian
Tomatoes and okra
Tomato paste
Tomato pulp
Tomato purée
Tomato sauce
Truffles
Turnip greens
Turnips
Vegetables for salad
Vegetables, mixed
Vegetables, strained

Dress up vegetables when you serve them. A lump of butter melting on the top makes the dish more appetizing. Chopped parsley is a great help to boiled potatoes. A hard-boiled egg sliced thin and placed around a dish of spinach has saved many a meal from looking too dreary.

205 Canned Artichoke Hearts Newburg

Cooking time 20 minutes

Wash carefully in 3 separate waters the **Artichoke Hearts from 1 can Artichokes**. This vegetable is packed in citric acid and unless carefully washed will carry the flavor of the packing in the finished dish. Dry the artichokes and put them in a small frying pan in which **2 Tablespoons Butter** have been melted. Over gentle heat cook the artichokes, turning over all the time until each has been covered with hot butter. Then pour into the pan **1 cup Heavy Cream or Undiluted Evaporated Milk**. Let this simmer until it is reduced to about ½ its bulk. You can tell when by the position of the cream on the edge of the pan. Then add **a few grains of Cayenne (Red) Pepper, 3 Table-spoons Sherry**, and the **Yolks of 2 Eggs** stirred up in **4 Table-**

spoons Cream or Undiluted Evaporated Milk. Heat, but do not bring to a boil or it will separate, and serve.

206 Creamed Asparagus Tips with Croutons
Cooking time 10 minutes

In a small saucepan blend 3 Tablespoons Butter or Margarine and 3 Tablespoons Flour. When they have cooked together for a couple of minutes, slowly stir in the Liquid from 1 can Asparagus Tips. Add enough Milk or Cream or Undiluted Evaporated Milk to make a smooth sauce a little heavier in consistency than heavy cream. Add the Asparagus Tips and season with ½ teaspoon Salt and a few grains Cayenne (Red) Pepper and let simmer for 5 minutes. Meanwhile remove the crusts from 4 slices Bread, cut the bread into ½-inch squares and fry it until it begins to brown in 3 Tablespoons Butter. Let fried squares drain on a paper towel or piece of brown paper bag. Serve croutons on top of asparagus tips.

207 Canned Beets Sauté
Cooking time 7 minutes to 10 minutes

Melt 2 Tablespoons Butter or Margarine in a frying pan. Drain liquid from 1 can Diced Beets, or dice 1 can of whole beets. Dry beets with a paper towel and add to butter in frying pan. Shake 1 teaspoon Sugar and 1 Tablespoon Lemon Juice over the beets and fry them gently until each is covered with the hot butter. If flame cannot be controlled, put asbestos pad between flame and pot. After beets have cooked for 5 minutes remove from fire, shake ⅛ teaspoon Pepper over them, and serve.

208 Canned Beet Greens
Cooking time 10 minutes

Pour liquid from 1 can Beet Greens in a saucepan. Boil to reduce it to ⅓ of its original bulk. Meanwhile chop up the
greens as fine as you can get them. Put them in the saucepan
with the reduced liquid and ½ teaspoon Salt, 2 teaspoons
Sugar, and ⅛ teaspoon Pepper. Add 1 Tablespoon Butter or
Margarine. Toss well in pan over fire and serve.

209 Canned Brussels Sprouts, Creamed
Cooking time 15 minutes or 7 minutes

Melt 2 Tablespoons Butter or Margarine in a small saucepan.
Pour the liquid off 1 can Brussels Sprouts. Put the sprouts in
the pan with the butter and toss them well until all the sprouts
are covered with butter. Then add 1 cup Cream or Undiluted
Evaporated Milk and simmer gently until cream is thick,
about 12 minutes. Another method is to heat 1 cup Thin
White Sauce (No. 241) and let the sprouts simmer in it for 5
minutes. Then add ¼ teaspoon Pepper and ⅛ teaspoon Nutmeg. Stir well and serve.

210 Canned Cabbage and Apples
Cooking time 20 minutes

Drain the liquid from 1 can Sliced Apples into a saucepan.
In another saucepan melt 1 Tablespoon Butter. Toss the
apple slices in this. Add the liquid from 1 can Cabbage to the
apple liquid and add cabbage to apples in saucepan. Boil
down liquid from apples and cabbage until it is about ⅕ its
original bulk and add to the apples and cabbage in the saucepan. Season with 1 teaspoon Salt, stir well, and let simmer
until you are ready to serve. This goes wonderfully with braised
meats, particularly pork chops.

211 Canned Carrots Burgundy

Cooking time 30 minutes

Peel and mince 4 **Medium-sized Onions** and put them in a
frying pan in which **2 Tablespoons Butter or Margarine** has
been melted. When onions are soft and beginning to brown,
about 12 minutes, add the contents of **1 can Diced Carrots**
from which the liquid has been drained. Sprinkle vegetables
with **1 Tablespoon Flour** and brown. Add ⅛ teaspoon **Pepper** and **1 cup Consommé.** Simmer for 15 minutes and serve.

212 Canned Carrots, Glazed

Cooking time 15 minutes

In a small frying pan melt **2 Tablespoons Butter or Margarine.** Into this put **1 can Diced Carrots,** drained, and shake
up well. Add ½ cup **Corn Syrup or Honey,** or ½ cup **Sugar**
and **4 Tablespoons Water.** Add ½ teaspoon **Salt** and simmer
gently, basting and turning over the carrots from time to time.
When carrots have a good glaze (about 12 minutes), serve. Carrots cooked in a glaze are usually used to decorate some important dish, but we assure you that they are very good by
themselves.

213 Canned Corn-meal Mush, Fried

Cooking time 15 minutes

Take the end off **1 can Corn-Meal Mush** and slide the contents
out in one piece. Slice the mush crosswise into rounds about
¾ inch thick. Melt **3 Tablespoons Butter, Margarine, or
Bacon Grease** in a heavy frying pan and, with an asbestos pad
between pot and flame, slowly fry the mush until it is nicely
brown, about 6 minutes, on each side. Drain on brown paper
or a paper towel. This is very good served with ham, bacon, or

sausages for breakfast, or it is a fine addition to roast or fried chicken.

214 Canned Mushrooms in Cream Sauce

Cooking time 17 minutes or 10 minutes

This can be prepared in two ways. The easiest, and we think the best, is to drain and save the juice from 1 6-oz. can Mushrooms. In a small saucepan melt 2 Tablespoons Butter or Margarine. In it gently fry the mushrooms for 3 minutes. Then sprinkle them with 2 Tablespoons Flour. Let the flour brown, about 4 minutes, and then slowly add, stirring all the while, the juice from the mushrooms. To this add ½ cup Cream or Undiluted Evaporated Milk and let simmer, about 5 minutes. Season with ½ teaspoon Salt, add a few grains Cayenne (Red) Pepper. Just before taking off the fire to serve, add 1 Tablespoon Lemon Juice, which should be well stirred in.

The other way, which requires less watching, is to melt 2 Tablespoons Butter or Margarine and blend with 2 Tablespoons Flour, ½ teaspoon Salt, and a few grains Cayenne (Red) Pepper. Let cook 2 minutes and add slowly, stirring all the while, the juice of the mushrooms. Add ½ cup Cream or Undiluted Evaporated Milk. Add the mushrooms, let simmer for 5 minutes, stirring, and then add 1 Tablespoon Lemon Juice. Stir and serve on toast, zwieback, or Holland rusk.

215 Canned Onions, Creamed

Cooking time 10 minutes

Melt 1 Tablespoon Butter or Margarine in a small saucepan. Drain and save liquid from 1 can Small Onions. Shake the onions well in the butter. Sprinkle them with 1 Tablespoon Flour and slowly add the liquid from the can. Let simmer until sauce thickens to consistency of cream, about 5 minutes. Add a few grains Cayenne (Red) Pepper and serve.

216 Canned Onions, Glazed

Cooking time 12 minutes

Like glazed carrots, these are usually used to decorate some important dish. They can be so used, but they are very good in their own right. In a small saucepan melt **2 Tablespoons Butter or Margarine**. Drain the liquid from **1 can Small Boiled Onions** and place the onions in the pan. Shake them well in the butter until each is well covered. Then add **½ cup Corn Syrup or Honey**, or **½ cup Sugar** mixed with **4 Tablespoons Water**. Let the onions simmer in this, turning frequently to glaze all sides until each has a slightly brown glaze all over it, about 12 minutes. Serve while very hot.

217 Canned Peas, Country Style

Cooking time 30 minutes

Cut **5 slices Bacon** into small pieces. This is done most easily with a pair of scissors. Put bacon in a heavy frying pan and fry until bacon bits are crisp. Then take them out of the fat and pour off all but about 2 tablespoons of the fat. In it fry **1 cup Onions** chopped fine. When onions are soft and begin to brown (about 12 minutes), sprinkle them with **2 Tablespoons Flour**. Cook until flour browns, stirring well, about 5 minutes, then add **1 cup Undiluted Consommé**. Return bacon bits to the pan and add **1 can Peas**. Simmer for 5 minutes, stirring occasionally. Add **⅛ teaspoon Pepper** and serve.

218 Canned Potatoes, Creamed

Cooking time 12 minutes

Pour and save liquid from **1 can Boiled Potatoes**. Cut potatoes up into ½-inch cubes. Melt **3 Tablespoons Butter or**

Margarine in a heavy frying pan. In it place the cut-up potatoes. Cook for 5 minutes, and then sprinkle with 3 Tablespoons Flour, ½ teaspoon Salt and a few grains Cayenne
(Red) Pepper. Stir well and then add 1 cup Hot Milk or
Diluted Evaporated Milk, stirring all the while. If cream
seems too thick, thin it with some of the liquid poured from
the potatoes. If this is not to be served at once, keep warm over
hot water, as it will burn easily. Another way to make this dish
is to take a cup of thin cream sauce (No. 241) and simmer potatoes in it, mixing them well with the sauce. Many think ¼
teaspoon Nutmeg helps potatoes served this way.

219 Canned Potatoes, Fried

Cooking time 15 or 20 minutes

Melt 2 Tablespoons Butter, Margarine, or Bacon Grease in a
heavy frying pan. Drain the water from 1 can Boiled Potatoes
and dry the potatoes in a paper towel. Cut potatoes in slices
and put into the frying pan. Sprinkle generously with Salt and
Pepper. As soon as potatoes are brown on one side (about 6
minutes), turn and brown the other side, again sprinkling with
salt and pepper. Drain cooked potatoes on a paper towel or
brown paper and serve hot.

If ½ cup Chopped Onions are cooked in the fat before the
potatoes are put in, this is potatoes lyonnaise, a very tasty
dish.

220 Canned Potatoes, Hashed Brown

Cooking time 15 minutes

Remove the liquid from 1 can Boiled Potatoes. Dry the potatoes and cut them or chop them into very small pieces, or use
canned potatoes julienne. Mix them well with 1 teaspoon
Salt, ⅛ teaspoon Pepper, 1 Tablespoon Flour, and 4 Table-

spoons **Cream** or **Undiluted Evaporated Milk.** In a small frying pan melt **4 Tablespoons Butter, Margarine, or Bacon Grease.** Press the potatoes down in this to make a tight cake. With an asbestos pad between flame and pan, cook until potatoes are brown on the bottom, about 10 minutes. That will be indicated by little puffs of steam that will come up from the potatoes. Tilting pan toward you with one hand, fold one side of the potatoes over the other side as with an omelet (No. 260). Slide out of the pan and serve.

221 Canned Sweet Potatoes, Fried
Cooking time 12 to 25 minutes

The sweet potatoes in dry pack are best for this, but if you have them packed only in syrup, drain off the syrup from **1 can Sweet Potatoes.** Slice potatoes about ½ inch thick. Sprinkle with **1 teaspoon Salt** and **2 teaspoons Brown Sugar.** In a heavy frying pan melt **3 Tablespoons Butter, Margarine, or Bacon Grease.** When it is hot, place as many potatoes in the pan as it will hold. Fry potatoes until they are brown on one side, about 5 minutes, and then turn and brown the other side. Drain on brown paper or a paper towel and serve hot. Very good with any kind of chicken.

222 Canned Sweet Potatoes, Candied
Cooking time 20 or 25 minutes

Sweet potatoes in syrup are best for this, but sweet potatoes dry-packed can of course be used. They require a little more butter and sugar than the other pack, so increase the quantities given here. Slice into ½-inch pieces the contents of **1 can Sweet Potatoes.** In a heavy frying pan melt **4 Tablespoons Butter or Margarine.** Shake the potato slices in this until each is well covered with butter. Sprinkle ½ **cup Brown Sugar** over the potatoes, add ½ cup **Boiling Water**. Cover tightly and let simmer, turning often until potatoes are well candied, about 12 minutes.

If your galley has an oven, slice a layer of sweet potatoes into an oven dish, smear layer with **Butter or Margarine**, sprinkle with **1 Tablespoon Brown Sugar**, add another layer, butter and sprinkle with sugar, and so on until dish is filled or all the potatoes are used up. Pour over it ½ cup **Corn Syrup, Molasses, or Water**. Place in a 350° oven until brown, about 20 minutes. Very good this way.

223 Canned Spinach, Creamed
Cooking time 15 minutes

Pour the liquid from **1 can Spinach**. Chop the spinach fine. Melt **1 Tablespoon Butter or Margarine** in a saucepan and put the spinach in it. Pour ½ cup **Heavy Cream or Undiluted Evaporated Milk** over it and let simmer until the cream is reduced to ½ its bulk, about 10 minutes. Season with ½ teaspoon **Salt**, ¼ teaspoon **Pepper**, and ¼ teaspoon **Nutmeg**. Stir well and serve.

224 Canned Tomatoes, Scalloped
Cooking time 30 minutes

Remove the crusts from **5 slices Bread**. Break them into pieces approximately 1 inch square. In a heavy frying pan melt **2 Tablespoons Butter or Margarine**. Fry the pieces of bread in this until they begin to brown. In a heavy saucepan (a Dutch oven does nicely) make a layer ¾ inch thick of **Canned Tomatoes**. Cover tomatoes with a layer of the bread pieces. Sprinkle with **1 Tablespoon Brown Sugar**, ¼ teaspoon **Salt**, and ⅛ teaspoon **Pepper**. Put in another layer of tomatoes, bread, and sugar, and continue until pan is full or all the tomatoes are used up. Cover saucepan tightly and let simmer with an asbestos pad between flame and pan for 15 minutes. Serve in pan.

SALADS

Salads served to hungry men at sea should be easy to prepare, should be nourishing, and should taste good. As an accessory to a meal a green salad, either plain or mixed, is grand. For a main dish at lunch, however, it does not contain enough food energy to last to the next meal. For such uses a mixed salad is called for. Fabricate such a dish generously and with imagination. There are hundreds of known combinations. We list only a few. Use them as a point of departure and let your imagination develop dozens of new ones. Remember, tomorrow's salad is a splendid place for today's cold meats and vegetables.

A large wooden bowl and a wooden spoon and fork are almost essential for a proper tossed salad. The bowl does not have to be costly or elaborate. It will be much better if it is not finished with a hard finish. Plain rough birch bowls seem best to us, and they are the least expensive. We prefer those with fairly high sides. Care of the bowl is easy. Never wash it. When you are through, wipe it out carefully with paper towels, paper napkins, or pieces of newspaper, and put it away. Occasionally it can be wiped with a damp cloth, but never with soap and water. Eventually the bowl will take on a fragrance and character of its own. We believe that each time the bowl is used it should first be rubbed well with a cut clove of garlic. Salads that require mayonnaise or cream dressings should not be served in a wooden bowl used for mixed green salads to be made with French-type dressings. Use a china or stainless steel bowl for the combination salads and those that use the thick dressings. If you want garlic flavor in salads served in china bowls, rub a small crust of bread with a cut clove of garlic on which salt has been generously sprinkled. Rub until the garlic is well worn down. Put the bread in the salad when it is mixed. You can dig it out and put it aside when the salad is being served.

Don't always make your green salads production-line jobs. Vary them by using different greens, and use the greens in different proportions. There are several kinds of lettuces, including the white iceberg, tightly rolled Boston, and the open green kind. Then there is escarole, slightly bitter-tasting, but delicious and crisp. Romaine or cos is the most generally used in fine restaurants. Chicory and watercress are usually used in combination with some of the others. Endive, which is imported from Belgium, is the most expensive, but it is a great addition, as it has a unique flavor and texture. A little fresh parsley is a great addition to a salad, as are the fine inner leaves of spinach. When you shop for a cruise or a week end, get several kinds of greens. They can brighten up all meals. When you get your lettuce on board, go over it and throw away all broken or wilted leaves. Wash the heads carefully and wrap in a damp cloth. Dish towels will do, but it is much better to have cheesecloth or loosely woven cloth bags. Put the lettuce in the icebox, if there is room. If not, hang it in a cool place where there is plenty of ventilation.

Vegetables that are particularly good in salads are scallions, young onions, celery, cucumbers, beets, potatoes, and tomatoes. Peas, string beans, carrots, lima beans, cauliflower, and cabbage are also very good. When you cook any of them for dinner, cook up enough extra so that some can be set aside for tomorrow's lunch salad. Most fruits are good in salads, though they seem a little on the lightish side. Salads can be dressed up with garnishes such as hard-boiled eggs sliced or deviled, olives and pickles sliced or whole, or little balls made of cream cheese and ground-up nut meats. Strips of cheese and small strips of ham and tongue are used to make chef's salad.

As to dressing, there are two main divisions with many modifications: for plain green salads a mixture of pepper, salt, oil, and vinegar—French dressing, in other words; for mixed salads, fish and meat, and fowl, mayonnaise. French dressing takes on all sorts of new aspects. It is mixed with lemon or lime juice. Chutney, curry, and horseradish are mixed with it. It is found mixed with chopped hard-boiled egg, cheese, green peppers, or olives. Mustard, chives, and mint give it new twists. Mayonnaise, too, goes through many transformations. Chopped spinach, capers, onion, and watercress are added to make ravigote. Pimientos, chives, hard-boiled egg, and chili sauce make it Russian dressing. Mixed with chopped or canned ham it takes on a new hue and direction. While all of our salad dressings call for olive oil, other salad oils can be substituted, though they are not as good nor anywhere near as nourishing. There is really no limit to what can be done to a salad with the use of a good imagination. Why not try yours?

(Each recipe serves 4.)

225 Lobster Salad

Preparation time 45 minutes

Cut 2 cups Fresh or Canned Lobster into ½-inch pieces. Mix with it 2 teaspoons Onion chopped very fine. Let soak for ½ hour or so in the icebox, in enough French Dressing to cover. Just before serving, drain the French dressing in which the lobster has been soaked and toss in it the Lettuce to be served, about ½ bowlful. Put lettuce leaves in bowl. Mound lobster on the lettuce and put ½ cup Mayonnaise on the lobster. Decorate with slices of hard-boiled eggs, olives, or pickles if you care to.

This same method can be followed for salads made of crabmeat, fish flakes, frogs' legs, salmon, shrimp, or tuna.

226   Wintertime Salad
Preparation time 5 minutes

Wash carefully **2 bunches Watercress,** using only the leaf tops
and not the stems. Put the cress in a wooden or china bowl.
Slice and then cut into thin stick-like strips **4 Cold Cooked
Beets** and the **Hearts of 2 bunches of Celery.** Arrange these
vegetables on the cress and dress with **3 Tablespoons Olive Oil,**
1 Tablespoon Vinegar, ½ **teaspoon Salt,** and ¼ **teaspoon
Pepper.** Toss all well together.

227   River Salad
Preparation time 30 minutes

Remove the outside leaves and wash **2 small tight heads of
Iceberg or Boston Lettuce.** Cut each head in half and arrange
on the plate upon which it is to be served. Peel and slice **2 Ripe
Tomatoes** (whole peeled canned Italian tomatoes will do) and
place slices on the halves of lettuce. Peel and chop fine **6 Small
Onions** with the **Whites of 2 Hard-boiled Eggs** and sprinkle
on the tomato slices. Stir the **2 Yolks of the Eggs** smooth with
1 Tablespoon Olive Oil and mix with **2 Tablespoons Olive
Oil, 1 Tablespoon Vinegar,** ½ **teaspoon Salt,** and ¼ **teaspoon
Pepper.** Beat until mixture is smooth and divide on decorated
lettuce halves.

228   Chicken Salad
Preparation time 45 minutes

Mix **2 cups Canned Chicken, or Cold Cooked Chicken** with
the skin and bones removed, with **1 cup Finely Cut-up Celery**
and soak for ½ hour in enough French dressing (No. 235) to
cover. Wash, shake dry, and cut in strips enough **Lettuce** to
half fill a bowl (not your wooden salad bowl). Drain the French

dressing from the chicken-celery mixture onto the lettuce and toss. Mound the chicken and celery on the lettuce and on top of it place ½ cup (8 Tablespoons) **Mayonnaise.**

229 Green Salad

Preparation time 7 minutes

Rub your wooden salad bowl with **1 cut clove of Garlic,** or if you plan to use a china, glass, or metal bowl, rub a small crust of bread sprinkled with salt with 1 cut clove of garlic until the garlic is almost used up and place the bread crust in the salad bowl. Break off the stem, wash, and shake dry enough **Lettuce, Escarole, Chicory, or Romaine,** or a combination of them, to fill the salad bowl. Cut into strips with a knife or scissors and arrange in the bowl. Put bowl in the refrigerator or in a cool place until you are ready to serve. You can then pour **2 Tablespoons Prepared French Dressing** over the salad and toss it well with the salad fork and spoon. Or you can mix in the following way: Shake ½ **teaspoon Salt,** ¼ teaspoon **Pepper,** and ⅛ teaspoon **Paprika** over the salad. Fill the salad spoon with **Olive Oil,** about **2 Tablespoons,** and sprinkle it over the salad. Sprinkle over the salad ⅓ as much **Tarragon Vinegar,** if you have it. Toss salad well with fork and spoon until it is well mixed and each leaf is coated with dressing. Serve at once. After salad has been tossed or "fatigued," as the French call it, it wilts very quickly. To such a salad celery, cut in small pieces, slices of cucumber, peeled scallions and small onions, or radishes can be added and tossed with the salad. All these vegetable additions will be much improved if they are allowed to soak for 1 hour in a mixture of **3 parts Olive Oil, 1 part Vinegar,** ½ **teaspoon Salt,** and ¼ **teaspoon Pepper.**

230   Tomato Salad

Preparation time 30 minutes

Peel 4 **Good-sized Ripe Tomatoes** (or 4 tomatoes from a can
of Italian peeled tomatoes). To peel a fresh tomato easily, hold
on a fork over the flame or put into boiling water for a couple
of minutes; the skin will then slip off easily. Slice them across.
It is best if you can put the slices in a bowl with ½ **clove of
Garlic** and cover them with French dressing (No. 235) and let
soak for 1 hour in the icebox or a cool place. Wash, shake dry,
and cut up into strips enough **Lettuce** to half fill a bowl. Just
before serving, drain the French dressing off the tomatoes onto
the lettuce. Toss lettuce well. Arrange tomato slices on it and
serve. This can be attractively decorated with slices of hard-
boiled egg, olives, pickles, or radishes.

231   Potato Salad

Cooking and preparation time 1½ hours

Boil 4 **Medium-sized Potatoes** in their skins in well-salted
water, about 20 minutes. Let them get cold, peel them, and
cut them into ½-inch dice. Shell and chop fine **2 Hard-boiled
Eggs**, peel and chop fine **4 Medium-sized Onions**. Soak all the
above in French dressing (No. 235) for ½ hour. Wash and
shake dry enough lettuce leaves to decorate the sides of a bowl
(not your wooden salad bowl). Pour the French dressing off
the potato mixture onto the lettuce leaves and toss together.
Mix ½ cup Mayonnaise with the potato mixture and put it in
the bowl on the lettuce leaves so that the lettuce leaves show
around the edges. Sprinkle with **Paprika** and serve. Incidentally, a very good potato salad comes in cans. It is good as
is, or it can be doctored up to suit your taste.

232 Fruit Salad

Preparation time 30 minutes

This can be served on individual plates or in a salad bowl. Cut
up 2 cups **Fresh Fruit** or take 2 cups **Canned Fruits** or **Canned
Fruit Salad** from a can. Soak in French dressing (No. 235) for
15 minutes or more. Wash and shake dry enough **Lettuce
Leaves** to go around the sides of a bowl. Put the lettuce in
place and put the fruit in the middle of it, or place lettuce on
the individual plates and pile ¼ of the fruit on each. In either
case top with **Mayonnaise.**

233 Vegetable Salad

Preparation time 1 hour

Almost any combination of cooked or raw vegetables will make
a good vegetable salad. Canned mixed vegetables such as carrots and peas combined with any cold vegetables left from
previous meals will marry and make a satisfactory salad. Make
enough French dressing (No. 235), about 1½ cups, so that the
vegetables can soak in it for at least 1 hour before they are to be
served. You can put leftover vegetables to soak in the French
dressing when the evening meal is finished, and they will be
fine for lunch the next day. For raw vegetable salad you can
chop fine or put through the meat grinder, using the coarse
blade, any or all of the following, blending them as your
imagination dictates: young spinach, carrots, onions, scallions,
celery, cabbage, or cauliflower. Vegetables should soak in
French dressing for 1 hour or more. They should be drained
and served on lettuce, either plain or decorated with mayonnaise. The vegetables can, of course, be combined with canned
or raw fruits, nuts, raisins, or olives. Raw and cooked vegetables go well together, as they offer different textures. Any
of these salad combinations are improved in appearance if

decorated with hard-boiled eggs, stuffed olives, nut meats, or slices of orange or grapefruit.

234 Waldorf Salad

Preparation time 20 minutes

Peel, core, and cut into fine dice **3 Apples** or enough to make **2 cups.** Wash and cut up fine enough **Celery** to make **2 cups.** Add, if you have them, ¼ **cup Walnut or Other Nut Meats** chopped fine. Mix with **1 Tablespoon Powdered or Granu-lated Sugar, Juice of 1 Lemon,** and ½ **cup Mayonnaise.** Stir well and serve on lettuce leaves on individual plates.

235 French Dressing

Preparation time 5 minutes

In a bottle which can be corked, mix ¾ **cup Olive Oil** (you can use other salad oil, but it just is not as good), ¼ **cup Vine-gar** (white wine or white wine and tarragon is best), ½ **tea-spoon Salt,** ¼ **teaspoon Pepper, 1 teaspoon Sugar.** Shake vio-lently and keep in icebox. Shake before using each time.

236 Mayonnaise Dressing

Preparation time 20 minutes

In a bowl that has been chilled on the ice put ¼ **teaspoon Dry Mustard,** ½ **teaspoon Salt,** a few grains **Cayenne (Red) Pep-per,** ½ **teaspoon Granulated Sugar,** and the **Yolk of 1 Egg.** Stir until all are well mixed; while still stirring, add **1 Table-spoon Vinegar.** Stirring evenly all the while, pour in very slowly, in a thin stream, ¾ **cup Chilled Olive Oil** (other salad oil can be used, but it is not as good). Beat constantly and thoroughly until mixture is very stiff. It will take about 12 minutes from the time you start pouring in the oil. If mayon-naise should separate, beat it slowly into a fresh egg yolk in a cold bowl. Add slowly, just as you would with oil being added. Mayonnaise can be kept for more than ten days if kept in the icebox in a screw-top jar.

237 Deviled Eggs

Preparation time 20 minutes

Cut 6 Hard-boiled Eggs in two and separate the yolks from the whites. Mash the Yolks and mix with 3 Tablespoons Mayonnaise. Add to the mixture ½ teaspoon Salt, ½ teaspoon Mustard, ⅛ teaspoon Pepper, a few grains Cayenne (Red) Pepper, and ½ teaspoon Lemon Juice. With a fork mix these ingredients together until they make a smooth, workable paste. With the paste fill up the whites, rounding the mixture on the top. Sprinkle generously with Paprika. If eggs are not to be eaten at once, chill in the icebox. Anchovy paste or other fish or meat pastes can be added or substituted for the mustard. In this dish again you can bring your imagination into play and fill the egg whites with many different combinations of yolk seasoning.

SANDWICHES

For a noontime meal when under way there is probably no food that can compare in popularity with sandwiches. Their virtues are that they are easy and quick to prepare; they create no cleaning-up problem; they are generally what people expect. Their disadvantages are that they are too largely starch; they are filling but not sustaining; and unless someone is especially vigilant the maker gets in a rut and the crew and guests get the same kind of sandwiches day after day. We do not approve of sandwiches for lunch, but we have them more than any other food. We do try to vary them. For this we depend on the many kinds of prepared pastes that are available, and intelligent use of leftovers, particularly meats. Among the spreads that will be found in most first-rate stores are anchovy paste, chicken spread, chicken liver spread, corned beef spread, finnan haddie spread, smoked halibut spread, ham spreads galore, herring spread, olive spread, paste spreads (including paté de foie gras), paté de foie, smoked rainbow trout, rattlesnake meat, salmon spreads, sardine spreads, turkey spreads, and smoked turkey spreads. Then there are various sorts of processed cheeses, cream cheese, peanut butter, jellies, jams, and marmalades. A number of these are now available in tubes, which greatly facilitates storing. These can be spread on white, graham, whole wheat, raisin, or rye bread, zwieback, Holland rusk, buns, cold baking powder biscuits, and various species of crackers. They can be made into open or closed sandwiches either decorated or unadorned, plain or fancy. We strongly recommend spreading them with lots of butter. Butter is the highest in energy per pound of the most easily digested foods. If you must serve sandwiches, and we know you will, try to serve something hot with them. If you do not want to start the stove, put some hot soup or coffee in the thermos when you are cleaning up after breakfast. Finish off the sandwich meal with all the fruit you can get your crew to eat. That will help to offset the clogging effect of too much starch in the system. If you have a box or dresser-top tray (see Galley Layout, p. 18) which will hold all your sandwich gear, you can take it up into the cockpit and make lunch there instead of being cooped up in the galley. Following are a few of the hundreds of combinations that can be arrived at with the multiplicity of fillings and a good imagination.

238   Sandwich Fillings

Mix **1 package Philadelphia Cream Cheese** with **1 cup Dried Beef** cut (with scissors) into small pieces. Flavor with **a dash of Worcestershire Sauce** and spread.

Mix 1 package **Cream Cheese** with ½ **cup Almonds** chopped fine. Spread.

Mix 1 **package Cream Cheese** with **6** crisp slices **Bacon** broken up into small pieces. Spread.

Place a piece of **Swiss Cheese** on a **Well-Buttered slice of Rye Bread**. Spread the cheese with **Prepared Mustard**. Cover cheese with a **slice of Ham (or Spam)**. Cover with a slice of **Rye Bread** and serve.

Mash up some **Liverwurst or Other Liver Sausage** with some **Soft Butter** until it will spread easily. Spread on rye or whole wheat bread. This makes a good open sandwich.

Mash up **a can of Chicken** with some **Soft Butter** until it will spread easily. Spread some of it on a slice of bread. Cover with **bits of Broken-up Bacon** and a slice of **Tomato**. Put a dab of **Mayonnaise** on the top, cover and serve.

A variation of the above is to add to it a slice of tongue. Very nourishing.

Chop fine **2 Hard-boiled Eggs**, mix with **2 Tablespoons Mustard** and **1 can Crabmeat**. Spread on bread. Decorate with **Sliced Olives** and serve as an open sandwich.

Mix well **8 Tablespoons Peanut Butter** with **6 slices Very Crisp Bacon** broken into small pieces. Very good spread on zwieback or Holland rusk.

Mash ¼ **pound Roquefort Cheese** with **1 Tablespoon Mayonnaise,** spread on thin bread, and cover.

There are any number of good hot sandwich combinations. Among them are hot bacon with tomatoes fried along with them. Spread bacon on buttered bread and place tomato on top of bacon, cover with a slice of bread and serve.

Fried eggs, either alone or with bacon or ham, make wonderful sandwiches. Fry the eggs with yolks broken, until they are firm. Sprinkle with salt and pepper and place on a slice of well-buttered white bread. Cover, cut in two and serve. Many like a little catsup on the egg. When ham or bacon is used, put whichever is used on top of the egg and cover.

When hamburgers are used for sandwiches, press the cakes quite flat, fry them until they are done to your preference, put them on buttered slices of bread, cover with the other slice, and serve. Many like a slice of onion. Some like catsup or some sort of relish. Chutney is very good if you have it aboard.

A package of cream cheese mixed with 3 tablespoons of chutney is an interesting sandwich filling. It is pretty rich, so don't use it alone for the complete meal.

Hard-boiled eggs, stuffed (No. 237), or plain, are a very good accompaniment for sandwiches. Hard-boiled egg slices are a help to almost any filling.

SAUCES

Charles Ranhofer, chef of Delmonico's, listed 264 separate sauces in *The Epicurean* in 1894. This was one of the most ambitious cookbooks of the times and for years a bible of chefs. The famous Escoffier of the Carlton Hotel in London, whose *A Guide to Modern Cooking,* published first in 1907, and periodically brought up to date to be the standard handbook for chefs, listed but 163 sauces. This cookbook lists only 16. However, they are all highly useful, and they are simple enough to be made in a small boat's galley. With them the cook can build himself a reputation by experimenting and adding to them different wines, liquors, herbs, spices, prepared commercial sauces, anchovy and other fish pastes, pickles, olives, and condiments until as an originator he can rival his great predecessors in the number and variety of his sauces.

Most hot sauces depend on flour or egg yolks for their basic thickening element. In the flour sauces this element is called a roux. Simply stated, a roux is a combination, usually in even parts, of flour and butter (margarine or bacon grease will serve) cooked together. Roux can be made as needed, or for convenience roux can be made in advance, put in a can or jar, and kept in a cool place until used. For use in galleys it can be made at home and brought on board with the other supplies. It should be kept in the icebox.

To make a sauce the roux is mixed with meat, fowl, or fish stock, or court bouillon (No. 20). The roux can also very conveniently be mixed with white wine, canned consommé, canned chicken soup, milk, cream, or evaporated milk diluted or undiluted.

(Each recipe serves 4.)

239   White Roux (Base for White Sauces)
Cooking time 10 minutes

For future use—to be made at home and taken aboard: Cook together in a heavy frying pan equal quantities of **Butter, Margarine, or Bacon Grease** and **Flour,** stirring all the while over the flame until it just begins to brown, about 5 minutes. ¼ **pound Butter (8 Tablespoons),** and **8 Table-spoons Flour** will make 1 cup of roux. When mixed later with liquid, this will make about 1 quart of thin cream sauce or enough for 4 separate cream dishes each for 4 persons. Roux should be put in a screw-top or pressure-top container or jar and kept in a cool place until needed.

Cooking time 5 minutes

For immediate use: Take **1, 2 or 3 Tablespoons** each of **Flour** and **Butter, Margarine, or Bacon Grease,** depending on whether you want a thin, medium or thick sauce, cook together in a heavy frying pan over the flame, stirring all the while, until it just begins to brown, 3 to 5 minutes. Mixed with a cup of liquid this will make a little more than 1 cup of sauce.

240 Brown Roux (Base for Brown Sauces or Gravies)
Cooking time 15 minutes

For future use—to be made at home and taken aboard: Cook **8 Tablespoons Flour** in a heavy frying pan over a bright flame, stirring all the while, until it is about the color of cocoa (about 10 minutes, depending on the degree of heat). Then add ¼ **Pound Butter (8 Tablespoons)** and cook, stirring all the while until mixture is well blended, about 4 minutes after butter is melted. This will make 1 cup of roux. When mixed later with liquid this will make about 1 quart of sauce, or enough for 4 separate dishes each for 4 people. Roux should then be put in a screw-top or pressure-top can or jar and stored in a cool place until needed.

Cooking time 10 minutes

For immediate use: Take **1, 2 or 3 Tablespoons Flour**, depending on whether you want a thin, medium, or thick sauce. Cook over a bright flame in a heavy frying pan until a cocoa brown, about 5 minutes. Add an equal quantity of **Butter, Margarine, or Bacon Grease** and cook, stirring all the while until mixture is well blended, about 4 minutes after the butter is melted. Mixed with a cup of liquid this will make a little more than 1 cup of sauce.

241 Cream (White) Sauce
Cooking time 15 minutes

Excellent for eggs, poultry, boiled or canned fish, macaroni, rice, or vegetables. For thin sauce take 2 tablespoons of white roux (No. 239); for medium sauce heat to the bubbling stage

4 tablespoons of white roux; for thick sauce take 6 tablespoons
of white roux. If roux is not available already cooked, use half
of these quantities each of **Flour** and **Butter, Margarine, or
Bacon Grease** cooked together, stirring all the while, in the
top of a double boiler over the direct flame. Meantime heat
1⅛ cups **Rich Milk or Cream (Undiluted Evaporated Milk)**
in which has been put **1 Bay Leaf, 1 teaspoon Lemon Juice, a
few grains Cayenne (Red) Pepper, ½ teaspoon Salt.** Let this
simmer about 6 minutes, and then add this seasoned milk
through strainer slowly into the butter and flour mixture.
Sauce should then be cooked until it thickens, about 4 minutes, stirring all the while, over the direct flame; or it can be
cooked 10 minutes in the top of a double boiler over boiling
water.

When liquid used to make this sauce is part meat stock, it
is **Béchamel Sauce;** when fowl or fish stock, it is **Velouté Sauce.**

242 Brown Sauce

Cooking time 15 minutes

This sauce is most generally used for making an appetizing
dish of leftover meats. Meats are usually cut in small pieces
and put to heat in a double boiler top with sauce. Where
quantity of meat seems insufficient it can be stretched by adding slices of boiled eggs, leftover vegetables, or broken bits of
toast. Canned meats such as tongue, corned beef, or roast beef
can be made most appetizing by serving in this sauce with any
of the seasoning suggested below.

For thin sauce take 2 tablespoons of brown roux (No. 240);
for medium sauce take 4 tablespoons of brown roux; for thick
sauce take 6 tablespoons of brown roux. If roux is not available already cooked, use half of these quantities each of **Flour
and Butter, Margarine, or Bacon Grease,** cooked as in **No.
240.** Put in top of double boiler over fire. Add gradually **1 can**

Undiluted Consommé, stirring all the while. Season with ⅛ teaspoon **Pepper, Salt** if needed. Cook in top of double boiler over boiling water for 15 minutes.

This sauce can be further seasoned with such herbs as marjoram, thyme, and rosemary; onion, lemon juice, Worcestershire sauce, catsup, curry, or wines such as sherry or Madeira.

243 Curry Sauce
Cooking time 20 minutes

Not a real curry (see No. 52), but a good sauce for canned lobster, shrimp, crabmeat, or leftover fish, boiled eggs, rice, macaroni, or vegetables. To each cup of **Cream Sauce** (No. 241) add 2 teaspoons or more, according to taste, of **Curry Powder** moistened in a little cold water to make a paste. Cook 8 minutes in double boiler over boiling water.

244 Egg Sauce #1
Cooking time 15 minutes

Particularly good over boiled or baked fish. Also good with fish leftovers. To each cup of **Cream Sauce** (No. 241) add 2 **Hard-boiled Eggs,** chopped fine. Add ⅛ teaspoon **Salt.** Cook 4 minutes in double boiler over boiling water.

245 Egg Sauce #2
Cooking time 10 minutes

Heat 1 cup **Cream** or **Undiluted Evaporated Milk** to which 2 **Chopped Hard-boiled Eggs** have been added, to the boiling point. Add 2 **Tablespoons Court Bouillon** (No. 20) or water in which fish has been cooked. Take off flame. Pour into 1 **Well-beaten Egg Yolk,** stirring well. Add 2 **Tablespoons**

Finely Chopped Parsley if you have it, and serve either over fish or in separate sauce dish.

246 Horseradish Sauce

Cooking time 15 minutes

Good with boiled beef, pot roast, or boiled mutton. To each cup of **Cream Sauce** (No. 241) add 1 teaspoon Sugar, 2 Tablespoons Grated (Prepared) Horseradish, and ⅛ teaspoon **Nutmeg** (optional). Add ½ cup of **White Wine** (optional). Cook in top of double boiler over boiling water until sauce is of desired consistency—about 12 minutes if wine is included, less if not.

247 Madeira Sauce

Cooking time 20 minutes

Two Madeira sauces follow. Both are good. The second is perhaps a bit easier, though it takes a little longer to cook. Madeira sauce adds a great deal to hot tongue. It is very good with beef or pieces of leftover steak cut in small pieces, for instance.

1. Cook 1½ cups **Brown Sauce** (No. 242) in top of double boiler, over flame, stirring all the while, until sauce is reduced to 1 cup—about 10 minutes. Add ¼ cup Madeira. Cook in top of double boiler over boiling water for 6 minutes, stirring occasionally.

2. Simmer 1 can **Condensed Consommé** undiluted until volume is reduced by half, about 10 minutes. Add ¼ **cup Brown Sugar** (white if you haven't brown), ¼ teaspoon **Pepper**, and ¼ **cup Madeira**. Cook in top of double boiler over boiling water until sauce is thick enough to coat the back of a spoon—about 10 minutes.

248 Mornay Sauce
Cooking time 15 minutes

Famous with fish—also excellent for macaroni, chicken, potatoes or other vegetables. To each cup of **Cream Sauce** (No.
241) add ¾ **cup White Wine** (optional) and ⅓ **cup Grated
Cheese.** Traditionally this should be at least 2 kinds of cheese.
Cook until thick, about 12 minutes, in top of double boiler
over boiling water.

249 Mustard Sauce
Cooking time 10 minutes

Excellent with ham, boiled beef, or mutton. To each cup of
Cream Sauce (No. 241) add 1 teaspoon **Sugar,** 1 teaspoon
Lemon Juice or Vinegar, and 1 Tablespoon **English Mustard**
(dry mustard mixed with enough water to make a thick paste).
Prepared mustard can be used, about 2½ **Tablespoons.** Cook
6 minutes in top of double boiler over boiling water.

250 Mushroom Sauce
Cooking time 20 minutes

Another good sauce with leftover meats. Good also on macaroni and rice. Cook ⅔ **cup Brown Sauce** (No. 242) with ⅔ **cup
Juice of Canned Mushrooms** until sauce is thick, about 12
minutes. Add ¼ teaspoon **Nutmeg,** a few grains **Cayenne
(Red) Pepper,** ¼ teaspoon **Salt,** and ½ **can Canned Mushrooms.** Cook in top of double boiler over boiling water for
8 minutes. Just before serving stir in 1 Tablespoon **Butter**
(optional).

251 Newburg Sauce

Cooking time 12 minutes

This sauce was invented for lobster Newburg, but it is excellent with shrimp, crabmeat, artichoke hearts, or mushrooms. Into a small frying pan put 1 **Tablespoon Butter.** In it gently fry whatever food the sauce is to be served with. When the food is warmed through and coated with butter, add 1 **cup Heavy Cream.** Let simmer until cream is reduced about ½, about 6 minutes. This can be estimated by noting the position of the cream on the edge of the pan when you pour it in. Take pot off flame. Add a **few grains Cayenne (Red) Pepper,** ¼ **teaspoon Salt,** ⅛ **teaspoon Nutmeg.** Beat up the **Yolks of 2 Eggs** in a little **Cold Fresh Cream** and stir into the hot cream. Add 3 **Tablespoons Sherry.** Heat but *do not boil,* as it will separate. (If it *should* separate, beat the yolk of 1 egg in a bowl and pour sauce slowly into it, stirring all the while. Return to pan and heat, carefully this time.)

252 Olive Sauce

Cooking time 6 minutes

Good with leftover duck, vegetables, or rice. To each cup of **Cream Sauce** (No. 241) add ⅓ **cup Finely Chopped Olives** and 1 **Tablespoon Chopped Parsley.** Cook in double boiler over boiling water for 4 minutes.

253 Onion Sauce (Soubise)

Cooking time 15 minutes

Excellent with lamb, chicken leftovers, or canned tuna fish. To each cup of **Cream Sauce** (No. 241) add ½ **cup Finely Chopped Onions** which have been boiled 6 minutes and carefully drained, ½ **teaspoon Nutmeg,** and ½ **teaspoon Salt.** Cook in top of double boiler over boiling water 6 minutes.

254 Parsley Sauce
Cooking time 20 minutes

This can be made with dried or fresh parsley. It is good with leftover fish, chicken, boiled potatoes, and other vegetables. To each cup of Cream Sauce (No. 241) add **3 Tablespoons Parsley Tea**. This is made by pouring **½ cup Boiling Water** over **3 Tablespoons Fresh or 1½ Tablespoons Dried Parsley** and letting it steep for 6 minutes and then straining it slowly into the sauce. Add **⅓ cup White Wine** (optional) and **1 Tablespoon Fresh Chopped Parsley** if it is available. Cook 12 minutes in double boiler over boiling water. Just before serving, beat in **1 Tablespoon Butter**.

255 Poulette Sauce
Cooking time 10 minutes

Good with leftover chicken, fish, canned asparagus, or canned or fresh shellfish. To each cup of Cream Sauce (No. 241) add separately, beating each in by itself, **3 Egg Yolks**. Add **2 Tablespoons Lemon Juice**, **¼ teaspoon Salt**, and **1 Tablespoon Chopped Parsley** if you have it. Keep warm in top of double boiler over hot, *not* boiling, water.

256 Tomato Sauce
Cooking time 20 minutes

In **1 cup Canned Tomato Soup** (undiluted) cook for 15 minutes **1 Bay Leaf**, **2 Tablespoons Chopped Celery Leaf**, **2 Small Onions** chopped fine, **1 clove of Garlic**, sliced, **2 Cloves**, and **2 Peppercorns**. Strain through a wire sieve. Combine with **1 cup Hot Cream Sauce** (No. 241) and **½ cup Rich Cream or Undiluted Evaporated Milk**.

233

257   Velouté Sauce

Cooking time 15 minutes

This is the primary sauce to be used with cut-up leftover chicken, fish, or mushrooms. It is the sauce generally used when food is to be mixed and put in patty shells or served on toast. This sauce is made exactly as cream sauce is made (No. 241), except that strong chicken stock or fish stock (see No. 20) is used instead of milk. Undiluted condensed chicken soup, strained, serves very well if you have no chicken stock.

EGGS

As there are basically only eight ways of cooking eggs, an egg cook has a great opportunity to show his ingenuity and creative imagination. The accepted methods of cooking eggs are to boil, to poach, to fry, to scramble, to make into an omelet, to prepare en cocotte, or to coddle, and, if you have an oven, to bake or to make into soufflés. Yet there are dozens of ways of dressing up any of these methods. This book will touch on only a few. The dishes you can make in which eggs cooked in several ways are combined with leftovers, sauces, wines, smoked fish, anchovy, or other fish pastes can surprise and delight the crew you cook for and give you a deserved reputation as a marine chef.

(Each recipe serves 4.)

258   Boiled Eggs

Cooking time less than 10 minutes

Anyone can boil an egg, but paradoxically an egg should never be cooked in boiling water unless the end product is to be hard-boiled eggs. For soft- and medium-boiled eggs, put in a

large saucepan over the fire enough water, say 2 quarts, for 4
eggs. (This is a lot of water, but use it for making your coffee
and for washing the dishes.) When it comes to a boil, put the
eggs carefully in it, one at a time. When pot again comes to a
boil put lid on. Turn out flame or take pan off stove. Lightly
boiled eggs will be done in 4 minutes. In 6 minutes the white
will be set. In 8 minutes the yolk will begin to stiffen. If this
seems fussy, remember that it leaves a burner free for other
cooking.

259   Boiled Eggs Cinderella
Cooking time 10 minutes

A good lunch dish can be made by boiling eggs (No. 258) for
4 minutes, plunging them into cold water, and removing the
shells, keeping eggs whole. Eggs can be kept hot by carefully
placing them in hot, not boiling, water, salted 1 teaspoon salt
to the quart of water. Now prepare a deep dish in which they
are to be served by covering the bottom with heated canned
sweet corn (whole kernel). Cover this with heated canned
chicken, tuna fish, crab flakes, or lobster, broken into small
pieces. The eggs are put on this bed and then covered with a
cream sauce (No. 241), Mornay sauce (No. 248), or curry sauce
(No. 243). It should be served immediately. Many combinations of this dish will suggest themselves, adding to the fame
of the cook.

259A   Eggs Marlou, see p. 289.

OMELETS

Omelets are quick and easy to prepare. They offer variety
limited only by the foods combined with them. They can be
used for the principle item of a meal or can be made into a
very satisfactory dessert. A plain omelet is good. A parsley
omelet is better. A filled omelet is still better. All are easy to

cook. Even if they do not turn out perfectly, they are still mighty edible.

260 Plain Omelet for Four
Cooking time 20 minutes

Step I. Break **8 Eggs** into a bowl. Add **6 Tablespoons Cream, Undiluted Evaporated Milk, or Water,** 1 teaspoon Salt, ¼ teaspoon Pepper. Beat with a rotary beater or a fork until all are well beaten—about 2 minutes. Let eggs "rest" for 5 minutes. (This is the time to light the stove and do any chores to be done.)

Step II. Beat eggs again for about 1 minute. Put frying pan with **4 Tablespoons Butter, Margarine, or Bacon Grease** in it over the flame. When butter is sizzling and beginning to brown, tilt pan so that butter runs well up on the sides of the pan. Stir eggs in bowl with a wooden spoon, if you have it, and pour into frying pan all at once. Grasp handle of pan in left hand (you will probably need a hot-plate holder to keep from being burned) and wooden spoon in right hand. As egg begins to coagulate along edges of pan, with wooden spoon push it gently toward the center, tipping pan so that uncooked egg flows in to take the place of egg that is hardening. Continue to do this on both sides of the pan until the entire omelet is beginning to become firm. It should be soft and creamy (wet) on top.

Step III. Push pan off flame. Tilting pan slightly, slide omelet away from first one edge and then the other to be sure it is not stuck to the pan. Then tilt pan toward you and at the same time, with pancake turner or spoon, turn (flip) the half of the omelet farthest away over the near half. Bring pan back over flame. Put ½ **Tablespoon Butter, Margarine, or Bacon Grease** in empty side of pan. As it melts, tilt pan so that it will run under omelet and brown it beautifully, helping to distribute butter by lifting omelet slightly with pancake turner or spoon. When omelet has browned nicely, about 1 minute, be sure it is loose in the pan and then turn out on platter (hot if possible) with browned bottom up.

261 Mushroom Omelet
Cooking time 25 minutes

Before omelet, to be cooked as in No. 260, is put into pan, right after Step I, open 1 6-oz. can Mushrooms. Into a saucepan put 2 Tablespoons Flour. Stirring over flame all the while, brown flour slightly, about 2 minutes. Add 2 Tablespoons Butter, Margarine, or Bacon Grease, ¼ teaspoon Salt, and a few grains Cayenne (Red) Pepper. Cook together until well mixed, about 1½ minutes, and then slowly add the liquid in which the mushrooms are packed, stirring all the while. When this is well mixed and beginning to thicken, add the mushrooms. Continue to stir over the flame until sauce is about the consistency of thick cream. Keep hot. Now proceed with Step II of the omelet. Between Step II and Step III, pour mushrooms and sauce along the edge of pan nearest you. Proceed with Step III of the omelet.

262 Ham Omelet
Cooking time 20 minutes

If you have any leftover boiled or baked ham, either with the meat grinder or with a knife on a board cut up enough Ham to make 1½ cups. Mix ½ cup into eggs when omelet is first beaten. (No. 260, Step I.) Heat rest of ham. Now proceed with Step II of the omelet. Between Step II and Step III put ham along edge of pan nearest you. Proceed with Step III of the omelet. If you have no leftover cooked ham, use 2 2¼-ounce cans of Underwood's (or other brand) Deviled Ham, heated.

263 Cheese Omelet

Cooking time 25 minutes.

Grate 1½ cups Stale Cheese. Mix with eggs when omelet is first beaten in Step I (No. 260). Then proceed with Step II and Step III of omelet.

264 Crab Omelet

Cooking time 20 minutes

Drain the liquid from 1 6½-ounce can Crabmeat and heat. Now proceed with Step I and Step II of omelet (No. 260). Between Step II and Step III, put the crabmeat along the edge of pan nearest you. Proceed with Step III of omelet.

265 Jelly Omelet

Cooking time 20 minutes

Add to omelet (No. 260) 1 Tablespoon Sugar. Cook as in Step I and Step II. Between Step II and Step III add 6 Tablespoons Currant, Blackberry, Apple, or Other Jelly. Cook as in Step III. Sprinkle with sugar, powdered if you have it, and serve.

266 Omelet Savoyard

Cooking time 35 minutes

At breakfast time fry 6 extra slices Bacon until crisp, and save. Cut up potatoes from 1 #2 can (1½ lb.) Boiled Potatoes into ½-inch dice. Cut up 1 can Pre-cooked Onions into small pieces, or chop fine 1 cup Raw Onions. Fry onions in 2 Tablespoons Bacon Grease or Butter. Just before onions begin to brown (about 6 minutes), add potatoes and bacon you have saved, broken into very small pieces. Fry mixture, stirring occasionally until potatoes begin to brown—about 5 minutes. Take off flame and keep warm until needed. Make omelet as in No. 260. Between Step II and Step III add ⅓ of bacon, onion, and potato mixture and continue cooking omelet through Step III. When omelet is on platter, neatly arrange remaining bacon and rest of mixture beside it.

267 Shad Roe Omelet
Cooking time 35 minutes

Open and drain 1 can (7¾ ounces) Shad Roe. (Other, less expensive, canned roe can be substituted. Brillat Savarin made a famous omelet with carp's roe.) Dry roe very carefully with paper towel, as wet roe sputters and breaks up when in the hot frying pan. Slowly pan-fry roe in 1 Tablespoon Butter, with an asbestos pad between frying pan and flame. If roe sputters and spits over edge of pan, cover pan with an inverted colander. This allows air in and does not soften roe as cooking under lid would. When roe is nicely browned on each side (about 4 minutes to the side) season with ½ teaspoon Salt and ⅛ teaspoon Pepper and add ¾ cup Cream or Undiluted Evaporated Milk. Let thicken slightly by allowing to cook about 4 minutes more. Place mixture in omelet between Step II and Step III (No. 260) and continue to cook omelet as in Step III.

268 Sausage Omelet
Cooking time 30 minutes or 45 minutes

This can be made with frankfurters or pork sausage. Cook 4 Frankfurters 6 minutes in boiling water, remove skin, and break meat into small pieces. With pork sausages, cook 6 in frying pan with water to cover and let boil for 5 minutes. Remove sausages, empty water from pan, and put sausages back in pan. Fry, pricking each with fork, until nicely browned— about 10 minutes. Drain on paper and cut into small pieces.

Place sausage meat in omelet between Step II and Step III
(No. 260). Continue to cook as in Step III.

269 Leftovers Omelet

Cooking time 30 minutes

Warm up 1 cup of **Leftover Meat, Fish, or Vegetable** cut up
in small pieces. Add ½ cup **Cream or Undiluted Evaporated
Milk.** Season with 1 **teaspoon Curry Powder** (optional) and
let cook until thick, about 6 minutes. Place in omelet (No.
260) between Step II and Step III and cook as in Step III.

270 Scrambled Eggs

Cooking time 6 minutes or 10 minutes

Scrambled eggs can be cooked in at least two ways.
   A. The most usual is in a frying pan. When so cooked the
flame should be very low, which is sometimes difficult with a
galley pressure stove, although a couple of asbestos pads between flame and frying pan are a great help. Pour 8 **Eggs**
beaten with 4 **Tablespoons Water or Milk lightly Salted** and
sprinkled with **Pepper** into frying pan over a low flame. Stir
eggs with spoon, preferably wooden, until eggs are all of a
creamy consistency (about 4 minutes) and serve at once.

Cooking time 10 minutes

   B. The other way to scramble eggs is in a double boiler over
boiling water. This takes slightly longer, but the eggs are
creamier, stay creamy longer, and can be kept hot until needed
—which means that the cook can enjoy the first part of breakfast with the rest of the crew and still serve hot eggs. You can
vary the method with the menu. When hot cereal monopolizes
the double boiler at breakfast, use the frying pan. When cold
cereal or none is served, use the double boiler.

Unless your crew is particularly hungry, break **2 Eggs per Person** into a bowl. Add ½ **Tablespoon Milk or Cold Water for Each Egg, Salt,** and **Pepper.** Beat thoroughly with a fork, about 1 minute. In top of double boiler put **1 Tablespoon Butter for Each 2 Eggs.** Melt over boiling water and add eggs. Stir with wooden spoon if you have one. When eggs begin to thicken, turn off flame. Keep stirring eggs until they are firm. Eggs cooked this way will keep moist and soft for 10 minutes. When eggs are to be mixed, as in some of the following recipes, the added foods should be put in while the eggs are still very moist, to insure complete blending.

271 Scrambled Eggs with Kippers (Kippered Herring)
Cooking time 10 minutes

A 14-ounce can Imported Kippered Herring (we like Marshall's best) mixed with an appropriate amount of scrambled eggs will serve 4 to 8 people. (On occasion, two of us have finished off an entire can ourselves.) Take herring from can and drain on paper towels or newspaper. Remove skin and bones and break all but 4 of the fish into small bits about the size of olives. When the eggs begin to get firm but are still moist (No. 270) add the broken bits of fish, stirring well into the eggs. Serve garnished with the unbroken pieces of fish.

Other canned or smoked fish that can be cooked in the same manner are sardines, tuna, smoked salmon, and anchovies.

272 Scrambled Eggs with Cheese
Cooking time 6 to 10 minutes

Proceed as in No. 270, but add ½ **cup Grated American Cheese** before eggs have started to cook.

273   Scrambled Eggs with Tomato Paste
Cooking time 6 to 10 minutes

Mix 2 Tablespoons Tomato Paste with each 8 Eggs, stirring in
before eggs have started to cook. See No. 270.

274   Scrambled Eggs with Creamed Onions
Cooking time 20 minutes

In a saucepan put 1 Tablespoon Butter, 1 Tablespoon Flour,
½ teaspoon Salt, and a grain or so of Paprika. After cooking this about 2 minutes, stirring all the while, add slowly the
Liquid from 1 can Boiled Onions. Continue to cook for about
2 minutes, still stirring. The mixture should be about the consistency of thick cream. If it gets too thick, add a little milk.
Into this pour the entire can of boiled onions. Heat thoroughly. When eggs, cooked as in No. 270, have reached the
stage when they begin to get firm, add the onions and sauce
and mix well. A few mushrooms, if you have them, served with
this make a very interesting dish.

275   Eggs en Cocotte
Cooking time 5 to 10 minutes

These are usually prepared in a glazed pottery casserole, but
any kind of cup will do—a custard cup, a tea cup, or the little
glass jars chicken comes in. Place the cups in a pan in which
there is 1 inch of very hot water. Put 1 teaspoon Butter in
each cup. Break into each cup 1 or more Eggs, depending on
whether or not this is to be a main course. Add enough Salt
and Pepper to season. Keep water hot, but do not boil. Eggs
are ready when white has solidified, at least 5 minutes.

There are many delicious variations of this basic dish. A
tablespoon cream or undiluted evaporated milk can be added.

Sometimes broken-up bits of cooked bacon, minced ham, chopped-up canned mushrooms are used together or in combinations—put in the cup and break the egg on top. For a lunch dish minced canned chicken with 1 tablespoon of cream and 1 tablespoon or so of sherry added makes a dish your crew will remember.

276 Poached Eggs

Cooking time 5 minutes

Poaching eggs is not hard. All the equipment you need is a heavy frying pan and a slotted spoon. Have 1½ inches of water barely boiling in a heavy frying pan. Break an egg into a small saucer and sprinkle a little salt on the yolk. Then start the water in the pan whirling around with your spoon. Slide the egg off the saucer into the center of the little whirlpool you have created. The whirling water will help to keep the egg from spreading out. In a moment move it carefully to the side and repeat with another egg until the desired number are cooking. *Do not let the water come to a boil.* It takes about 5 minutes to cook 4 eggs this way. Remove the eggs carefully with the slotted spoon. They may be served on toast, Holland rusk, or zwieback.

277 Fried Eggs

Cooking time 4 minutes

Many real cooking enormities are committed in the name of fried eggs. Scaly, dry, and tough on the bottom, the yolk staring out of the partly liquid white like a Cyclops in agony— these are not really fried eggs.

To make the perfect fried egg, melt 1 **Tablespoon Butter** in a small frying pan over a very low flame, or with an asbestos pad or two between flame and pan. Break a single egg into a saucer and slide it from the saucer into the gently seething butter. Let it cook very slowly. Tilt the pan to catch up the excess butter in a teaspoon and spoon it over the egg. Sprinkle a very little Salt over the yolk of the egg, and when yolk and white are firm, serve at once.

The further away you get from this ideal procedure, the less good your fried eggs will be. Under all circumstances, remember to use plenty of butter or bacon grease and never let the pan get too hot. Baste the eggs with the hot grease.

BREADS, CEREALS, PANCAKES, SPAGHETTI, AND RICE DISHES

BREAD

In addition to white, graham, whole wheat, rye, raisin, and other specialty breads, suggestions for the stowage of which will be found under the heading of Stowage, the following breads come in cans and are very good: brown bread, date and nut bread, prune bread, and pumpernickel. Canned white bread is now also on the market. When you want any of these canned breads hot, put the whole can in boiling water for at least 20 minutes, as the heavy texture of the bread takes a long time to heat through. Crackers, or biscuit as they seem to be called at sea, have been long-time favorites, with very good reason. Biscuits such as Bent's and pilot last indefinitely and for some reason or other seem to keep their crispness. Crackers with less enduring shortening, such as saltines and the butter-covered Ritz or Hi-Ho's, are good for a week or so, longer if they are kept in airtight containers. After that they seem to lose something of their crispness and flavor, even if kept in unopened packages. Some of the crispness can be restored by heating in an oven if you have one. For boats which have ovens we are including a few hot bread recipes to take care of the emergencies when you either get tired of bread and biscuits or run out of them.

The easiest way to make oven-baked hot breads is to carry on board one or more of the commercial mixes such as Bisquick. These prepared mixes come ready to use for biscuits, muffins, corn bread, gingerbread, and popovers, among others. Most of them require only the addition of water or milk. A few of them require the addition of an egg or two. By carefully following the directions on the packages you can hardly go wrong. One item of equipment which is inexpensive and which will help you always to get good results is an oven thermometer. Some ovens come equipped with one. For those ovens that do not, this handy little gadget either hangs from the shelf or sits on it. If your oven is one of those that sits on the burners an adjustment of asbestos pads can give you almost any oven temperature your recipe calls for.

(Each recipe serves 4 unless otherwise noted.)

278 Steamed Corn Bread
Cooking time 2 hours

Here is one hot bread that can be made without an oven. Sift together into a large bowl **2 cups Flour, ½ cup Yellow Corn Meal, 2½ teaspoons Baking Powder, 1 teaspoon Salt, 2 Tablespoons Sugar. Melt 2 Tablespoons Butter** and add it to **1¼ cups Milk.** Pour milk and egg mixture into sifted ingredients, stirring only enough to mix thoroughly. Butter well the top part of a double boiler and pour the batter into it. Cover and cook over boiling water for about 2 hours or until a sharpened matchstick can be inserted into bread and withdrawn clean. Turn out on breadboard, cut bread into slices, and serve hot with plenty of butter.

279 Baking Powder Biscuits
Cooking time 30 minutes

Sift together into a large bowl **2 cups Flour, 3 teaspoons Baking Powder, ½ teaspoon Salt.** Add to them **4 Tablespoons Shortening, Butter, Margarine, Lard, Crisco, Spry, or Other Commercial Shortening.** With a knife held in each hand, cut the flour and shortening together until the mixture resembles coarse corn meal. Then gradually add about **¾ cup Fresh or Diluted Evaporated Milk.** It is impossible to give the exact amount, as flour differs in its dryness. A good rule to follow is to use as little milk as you can after the dough begins to hold together. Spread a piece of wax paper on a board or other surface and place the dough upon it. Knead it for about ½ minute. Then cover it with another piece of wax paper and roll the dough out until it is about ½ inch thick. If you haven't a rolling pin, a bottle serves adequately. Cut into 2-inch rounds with a biscuit cutter if you have one. If not, a small sharp-edged tin can or a glass will do. Flour it to keep dough from sticking. The easy way to do this is to make a small mound of flour and rub the bottom of the cutter in it before each cutting. This will make about 16 biscuits of 2-inch diameter. Arrange them on an ungreased baking sheet or in a shallow pan. Bake in a 450° oven. It will take from 12 to 15 minutes. If you have no oven, 8 biscuits can be cooked at a time in a Connolly oven over the flame. (Half the dough can be wrapped in wax paper and kept in the icebox as much as two days if you do not use it all up in two installments. Do not cut the recipe in half, as it will not work.) When done, if biscuits are not to be eaten at once, to keep them crisp turn biscuits over in the pan, cover with a clean dish towel, and return to the oven, the door of which should be kept slightly open.

Many combinations can be made from this basic recipe. **Wonderful cheese biscuits** can be made with 1 cup of grated cheese added to the flour and sifted with it. They are particularly good with salads. Jam or marmalade biscuits can be made by cutting an incision in each biscuit after it has been rolled and putting a teaspoon of jam or marmalade in it. Ham or peanut butter biscuits can be made by adding 3 tablespoons of chopped-up ham or deviled ham paste or peanut butter to the shortening and mixing as the biscuits are made. A cup of chopped leftover meat can be added just before the milk. The results are delicious. It is unnecessary to go on with the many combinations and the permutations of them. Use your own combination that no one has tried. You may make a few mistakes too. Just pitch them overboard and try again.

280 Corn Bread

Cooking time 40 minutes

Sift together ¾ cup Flour, 1½ cups Yellow Corn Meal, 4 teaspoons Baking Powder, 1 teaspoon Salt, 3 Tablespoons Sugar, into a large bowl. Beat 2 Eggs slightly and combine with 1¼ cups Fresh or Diluted Evaporated Milk. Stir milk and eggs into flour combination, mixing well. Melt 4 Tablespoons Butter, Margarine, or Bacon Grease (use butter if you possibly can) and pour into flour, egg, and milk mixture, stirring well to get thoroughly mixed in. Pour batter into a well-greased 8 x 12-inch pan, bake in a 400° oven for 30 minutes or until a sharpened matchstick stuck into bread comes out without any dough sticking to it. When bread is done, cut into squares and turn each on edge in pan. Cover with a clean cloth and return to the oven, the door of which should be kept open. If you do not have an oven, it can be cooked in the Connolly oven in the Connolly #400 pan.

281   Bacon-Topped Corn Bread
Cooking time 40 minutes

Make corn bread as in No. 280 for corn bread, except that you use **2 Tablespoons Butter** instead of 4. When in the pan cover top of batter with **6 slices Bacon** cut into very small pieces. The easiest way to cut up the bacon is with a pair of scissors. Bake corn bread about 30 minutes. Bacon should be very crisp and nicely browned. This is a swell dish for hungry men on a cold and blustery day. If you do not have an oven, it can be cooked in the Connolly oven in the Connolly #400 pan.

282   Corn Bread Very Damn De Luxe
Cooking time 45 minutes

Sift together 1½ cups **Flour**, 1½ cups **Corn Meal**, **5 teaspoons Baking Powder**, ¼ **teaspoon Salt**, and 1 cup **Sugar**. Beat **2 Eggs**, and mix with them **1 cup Fresh Milk**. Stir the eggs and milk into the other ingredients, stirring only enough to moisten the dry ingredients. Do not beat. Stir in **1 cup Melted Butter** (yes, 1 cup!) and mix it in so that it is well distributed. Pour into a pan approximately 8 x 8 x 2. Bake in a 350° oven for 40 minutes. If you do not have an oven, it can be cooked in the Connolly oven in the Connolly #400 pan.

283   Muffins
Cooking time 30 minutes

Sift together **2 cups Flour**, **3 teaspoons Baking Powder**, ¾ **teaspoon Salt** and **4 Tablespoons Sugar**. Combine **2 Eggs** well beaten, ¾ cup **Fresh or Diluted Evaporated Milk**, and **2 Tablespoons Melted Butter or Margarine**. Pour the liquid quickly into the flour mixture, stirring only enough to be sure that all the flour is dampened. Make no attempt to stir out the lumps. They will take care of themselves. Transfer the batter quickly, a spoonful at a time, to well-greased muffin tins or paper baking cups and bake in a 425° oven for 15 to 23 minutes. You can test to find whether the muffins are done by piercing one with a sharpened matchstick. If it comes free without sticking, the muffins are done. If you do not have an oven, the muffins can be cooked in the Connolly oven in the Connolly muffin pan, #300.

284   Blueberry Muffins
Cooking time 30 minutes

These muffins can be made with fresh blueberries or with canned blueberries with the juice poured off. These are made as in the recipe for muffins, with these exceptions: Keep out ¼ cup **Flour,** sprinkle it over **1 cup Blueberries,** and shake until all are covered. Add blueberries to flour mixture. Use **4 Tablespoons Butter** instead of 2, and use **8 Tablespoons Sugar** instead of 4. Put in pans and bake the same way as muffins (No. 283).

285   Corn Muffins
Cooking time 40 minutes

Make exactly the same as corn bread except that the mixture is put into greased muffin tins instead of a pan. (See No. 280)

CEREALS

No cookbook seems to give very much space to cereals. One reason for this may be that the recipes on the boxes in which cereals come are so explicit that further help is not needed. Most cereals come in quick-cook varieties which does away with the 3- or 4-hour cooking which at one time was necessary. Be sure when you purchase cereals that you are getting the kind that can be cooked in a few minutes. Pressure-cooking of cereals is even quicker, so we are including a number of pressure-cooking recipes.

286   Corn-Meal Mush
Cooking time 1 hour 20 minutes

Mix together 1 cup Corn Meal, 1 cup Cold Water, 1½ teaspoons Salt. Bring to a boil in the top of a double boiler over the direct flame 4 cups Water. Into this boiling water pour slowly, so as not to lose the boil, the corn-meal mixture. Cook, stirring, for 10 minutes. Then put top of double boiler over boiling water and let cook for 1 hour or more. Keep corn-meal mush hot after serving so that what is left can be poured into a glass, clean tin can, or plastic icebox container to be kept on the ice. When it is cold it can be sliced and fried as part of another meal. (See No. 213.)

287   Corn-Meal Mush, Pressure-cooked
Cooking time 20 minutes

Bring 2½ cups Water mixed with ½ teaspoon Salt to a boil in the bottom of the cooker. Slowly stir in ½ cup Corn Meal. Put cover in place, and when steam comes out of the vent put indicator in place. When indicator reaches fifteen pounds pressure or "cook" position, cook for 10 minutes. Cool cooker in cold water for a minute and remove the cover. Stir cereal well before serving.

288   Cream of Wheat, Pressure-cooked
Cooking time 20 minutes

Bring 5½ cups Water to a boil in the bottom of the cooker. When boiling, stir in slowly, so as not to interrupt the boil, 1 cup Cream of Wheat and 1 teaspoon Salt. Cover cooker. When steam comes out of the vent, put indicator in place. Cook for 2 minutes after indicator reaches fifteen pounds pressure or "cook" position. Cool cooker in cold water and take off top. Stir cereal well before serving. Cut-up prunes, dates, raisins, or figs can be added after the cereal is in the cooker and cooked with it. These treatments add variety to your menu. Leftover Cream of Wheat can be saved. When it is cold it can be sliced and fried for part of another meal. (See No. 213.)

289 Oatmeal—Quick Oats, Pressure-cooked
Cooking time 15 minutes

Bring 2 cups Water to a boil in the bottom of the cooker and add ½ teaspoon Salt. Into the boiling water stir 1 cup Oatmeal slowly, so as not to stop the boil. Cover the cooker, and when steam comes out of the vent put indicator in place. Cook 3½ minutes after indicator reaches fifteen pounds or "cook" position. Cool cooker in cold water for a minute and remove cover.

290 Ralston, Pressure-cooked
Cooking time 15 minutes

Bring 3 cups Water to a boil and add 1 teaspoon Salt. Into boiling water slowly pour, so as not to stop the boil, 1 cup Ralston. Cover cooker, and when steam comes out of the vent put indicator in place. Cook for 6 minutes after indicator reaches fifteen pounds pressure or "cook" position. Cool cooker in cold water for a minute and remove cover. Stir well before serving.

291 Wheatena, Pressure-cooked
Cooking time 20 minutes

Bring 3 cups Water and ½ teaspoon Salt to a boil in the cooker. Slowly stir in, so as not to disturb the boil, 1 cup Wheatena.

Cover the cooker. When steam comes out of the vent, put indicator in place. Cook for 5 minutes after the indicator reaches fifteen pounds pressure or "cook" position. Cool cooker in cold water for a minute and remove cover. Stir Wheatena well before serving. As with Cream of Wheat, this cereal can be given variety by adding cut-up dates, figs, prunes, apricots, or raisins. Put in a full cup of any of them when the cereal is added to the boiling water. Leftover Wheatena can be saved. When it is cold it can be sliced and fried for part of another meal. (See No. 213.)

292 Pancakes

Cooking time 25 minutes

A great many pancake mixes are available which will serve adequately. The addition of a beaten egg improves most of them. However, the following recipe will turn out pancakes which in our judgment are far superior.

Sift together twice **1 cup Flour, 4 Tablespoons Sugar, ¾ teaspoon Salt,** and **1 teaspoon Baking Powder.** The easy way to sift things twice is to put the sifter or fine sieve on a large sheet of paper. Pour the dry ingredients into the sifter and sift onto the paper. Put sifter in the bowl batter is to be mixed in, return flour mixture to the sifter by lifting the paper by the edges and pouring flour into the sifter. With a fork lightly beat the **Yolks of 2 Eggs.** To them add **1 cup Fresh or Diluted Evaporated Milk** and stir. Add milk and eggs to the dry ingredients and stir together until smooth. Lightly beat the **Whites of 2 Eggs.** Add them to the batter, turning them in well. Add **3 Tablespoons Melted Butter or Margarine** and stir well. Batter should be the consistency of light cream. Heat heavy frying pan until a drop of water sizzles on it, then grease with a piece of bacon or bacon rind stuck on a fork or with a rag smeared with grease. Pour about a cooking spoonful of batter into each of three places in the pan, being careful that none of the cakes touches another. A large cooking spoon or a small pitcher makes pouring easier. When bubbles form and burst on the top of the cake and it begins to look dry (about 1 minute), turn with a pancake turner. Brown the other side and set cakes on a hot plate to serve. If cakes are too thick, add a little milk to the batter; if too thin, add a little flour. It may be necessary to try different combinations of asbestos pads to get frying pan at the correct temperature where cakes will cook through without burning. They should be a nice golden brown. Serve with lots of butter and some kind of syrup or jelly.

293   Rhode Island Johnnycake

Cooking time 15 minutes

Put 1 cup Water-ground Corn Meal and ½ teaspoon Salt in a bowl. Into it slowly pour **Boiling Water,** stirring well until the mixture will drop from a knife like heavy cereal. Heat a heavy frying pan until a drop of water sizzles on it and grease it with bacon or bacon rind on the end of a fork or with a rag dipped in grease. Pour a cooking spoon of the batter in each of three places in the pan. Cakes should be about 3 inches in diameter and ⅛ inch thick. If cakes are too thick, add a little more boiling water; if too thin, add a bit more corn meal. Cakes should be nicely browned, about 1 minute on each side. Serve with hot sausages or crisp strips of bacon.

SPAGHETTI AND MACARONI

Both spaghetti and macaroni come canned in many excellent brands, both plain and with sauces or meat balls. When heated, they are very good. Fresh-cooked spaghetti gives you another chance to display your inventiveness and creative ability, as almost any combination of tomatoes, green peppers, pimientos, eggplant, onions, meat, shellfish, cheese, and garlic goes well with spaghetti. It does require a lot of fresh water. On the other hand, it is easy to cook. Most American palates like their macaroni and spaghetti soft. The Italians like it *al dente*— that is, a little crackling and a little chewy. You can experiment to get your special degree of softness. Macaroni can be substituted in any recipe for spaghetti.

294 To Cook Spaghetti

Cooking time 35 minutes

Bring 2 quarts Water to a rolling boil and season with 1½ teaspoons Salt. Take ½ pound Spaghetti from the box and wet the ends in the boiling water so that they will curl around in the pot. Let boil hard for 12 to 18 minutes if you like it *al dente*. Boil for 20 minutes if you like it the way most Americans prefer it. Put spaghetti in a strainer or colander and pour over it at least 2 quarts of cold water. Put spaghetti in the top of a double boiler and reheat. Add a little cream or butter if spaghetti is to be served as a vegetable. If it is to be served with a sauce, put hot spaghetti on a platter and pour sauce over it.

295 Spaghetti Sauce Martha

Cooking time 35 minutes

Peel and chop fine 1 Medium-sized Onion. Fry it until soft but not brown in a heavy frying pan in 2 Tablespoons Butter and 2 Tablespoons Olive Oil, about 7 minutes. Peel and cut up into small pieces 4 Large Tomatoes or use 2 cups Canned Tomatoes with very little juice. Wash and dry 6 Anchovy Fillets and chop them very fine. Add them to the pan, together with 1 Tablespoon Chopped Parsley. Sprinkle on the mixture a pinch of Nutmeg and a pinch of Thyme, if you have it. Add 1 clove of Garlic, mashed, and cover with ½ can

BREADS, CEREALS, ETC.

Consommé. Season with ½ teaspoon **Salt** and ⅛ teaspoon **Pepper.** Simmer gently for 25 minutes. If flame cannot be lowered, use asbestos pad between flame and pan. Just before sauce is done mix in 4 **Tablespoons Parmesan or Other Freshly Grated Cheese.** Pour sauce over hot spaghetti and serve with grated cheese on the side.

Use this sauce as a point of departure and invent others of your own. Chopped-up bacon might be a start. Butter, bacon, salt pork or ham and their fat, almost anything that has oil in it, garlic, tomatoes, condensed tomato soup or tomato paste, basil or thyme, grated cheese, meat in one form or another, can be simmered in varied and interesting combinations to make a good sauce for spaghetti.

RICE

It is no wonder that rice is the staple food of the majority of the peoples of the world. It is inexpensive. It is easy to cook. It has little bulk and stores well. It has plenty of energy units. One cup of cooked rice equals, in energy units, a slice of roast beef. Because of its universal prevalence it is small wonder that there have developed so many ways of cooking it. Gen. Frank R. McCoy, a distinguished soldier, told us of one way he learned when he was a young officer on a scouting expedition searching for Aguinaldo in the Philippines. The Filipino guide who was with him cut a section of a growing green bamboo from a tree. He put a large handful of rice into a section of it and plugged up the opened end. This piece of bamboo was then thrown on the fire for a while. When it was well charred on the outside, the log was withdrawn and the plug was removed. Inside was what the General said was the best rice he had ever eaten. It was cooked, of course, in the sap of the bamboo which the heat had driven into the rice.

The three main differences in rice cookery seem to be cooking in a little water, cooking in a large amount of water, and frying the rice in some sort of fat and then adding a little liquid. Whichever way is used, the rice is usually good, though the flavor may be different. Try all methods and perhaps invent some until you get rice the way you like it. The one advantage of cooking the rice in a lot of water is that it can be rinsed with cold water afterward so as to rid it of the sticky starch that sometimes makes a dish of rice a gooey mess.

There are several very good quick-cooking brands of rice on the market. It is hard to go very far wrong with any of them. Follow the rules on the packages and the rice should come out dry and fluffy. The brand that we like best is Minute Rice, made by the General Foods Corporation. This is a precooked rice that tastes good and is certainly the easiest to prepare that we have ever found. Just follow the directions and you will have good rice in a few minutes. The timing on the following recipes is for old-fashioned unprocessed rice.

Rice, either freshly cooked or leftover, can be served in many combinations with a great variety of foods. Among the better-known combinations are kedgerees (see lobster kedgeree, No. 48), risottos (see fried rice, No. 298), jambolayas, and pilaffs. "Jambolaya" is said to be a negro corruption of the French word *jambon,* meaning ham. Probably originating in New Orleans, this dish must at one time have been based on a mixture of rice and ham. Generally nowadays it includes any meat (usually bacon), tomatoes, onions, or peppers mixed in varying quantities with cooked rice. You can work out any combination, depending upon what you have on hand. "Pilaff" is a name derived from an Oriental dish called *pilau.* It is usually a mound of rice containing small bits of meat or fish. In Turkish or Armenian cooking the rice is usually lightly fried in butter cooked in lamb broth with the meat, and finished in the oven. It is usually served in a beautifully rounded mound obtained by pressing the rice and meat into a hot bowl and then unmolding it on a plate. Persian pilaffs are usually served unmolded, loosely piled on a platter.

Any of these rice dishes make wonderful lunch dishes on a boat, particularly now that Minute Rice and the pressure cooker have so reduced the cooking time of the rice. Give the boys something that is a little more sustaining than sandwiches and soup for lunch. They will be a lot better-tempered if they have to wait for dinner because you want to go ashore or want to be on deck to see the sunset.

296 Boiled Rice

Cooking time 45 minutes

Wash 1 cup Rice thoroughly until all starch is removed. On a boat where running water is a problem, the best way is to put the rice in a strainer and shake it well in a pan of water until water comes out of the strainer very clear. Then bring to a boil 8 cups Water seasoned with 1½ teaspoons Salt. Add the washed rice slowly so as not to stop the boil. Let boil without stirring until rice is tender, about 12 minutes. Pour rice into a strainer or colander and slowly pour over it 6 cups of cold water, or put water in a pan and gently shake strainer in it until rice is well washed. Reheat rice in top of double boiler, over boiling water. Put 2 Tablespoons Butter on top. Let it melt and serve.

297 Rice Cooked by Chinese Method

Cooking time 50 minutes

Wash rice as in preceding recipe and put into a small heavy frying pan or saucepan. Use 1 cup Rice well washed. Add 1 teaspoon Salt and 2 cups Cold Water. Bring to a boil and lower heat to the merest simmer. Use 2 asbestos pads between pan and flame if flame cannot be controlled. Cook without stirring until rice is very tender, about 45 minutes. Remove cover and cook for a few minutes more to eliminate any water. Then loosen rice with a fork. It should be fluffy and dry.

298   Fried Rice

Cooking time 50 or 40 minutes

In a small heavy frying pan or a low-sided saucepan, melt **2 Tablespoons Butter.** In it fry **2 Medium-sized Onions** chopped very fine, until the onions are soft but not browned, about 6 minutes. Add **1 cup Well-washed Rice.** Cook until the rice loses its transparency (about 6 minutes), turning the rice over with a fork to keep it from burning and to get all of it cooked. Then pour over it **1 can Condensed Consommé** and 1½ **cups Water.** Let come to a boil. Cover pan with a piece of buttered or oiled brown paper and put lid tightly over it. Let simmer for 25 minutes after liquid comes to a boil. It may be necessary to put an asbestos pad between flame and pot if flame cannot be turned low enough.

If your galley has an oven the rice can be finished in it after the liquid is added. In that case, use **1 can Consommé** and ½ **cup Water.** Cover with buttered paper and lid and cook in a 350° oven for 17 minutes. Liquid should be absorbed and the rice very tender. With a fork stir in **a small piece of Butter,** about ½ tablespoon, and serve.

This dish is the base for many kinds of Spanish or Italian rice. Usually they are called risottos. To the onion add tomatoes, pimientos, green peppers, cucumber bits, garlic, cut-up pieces of meat, fish, or shellfish. You can develop many interesting combinations of your own. Leftovers too small in quantity to serve individually can make a splendid dish when served in fried rice in combination with other foods. When the bulk of the rice is increased by dry materials, use a little more liquid. When chicken or fish is used, chicken soup is better than consommé; or you can use tomato or other vegetable soups. Experiment.

299 Wild Rice Alice
Cooking time 1 hour 40 minutes

This recipe is a little trouble, but the results are marvelous. We have never seen it in any other cookbook. It has never been served without applause. Wash carefully in cold water 1 cup Wild Rice. Put it in a heavy china bowl with 1 teaspoon Salt. Bring to a boil 1 can of Condensed Consommé and 1½ cups Water. Pour consommé and water over the rice in the bowl and let rice soak for 15 minutes. Pour liquid off rice at the end of that time and again bring it to a boil. Pour it over the rice and let it soak for another 15 minutes. Repeat this process twice more, four times in all. Then put rice and the little liquid that has not been absorbed in the top of a double boiler and let it cook over boiling water until all the liquid is absorbed—about 20 minutes or, if your galley has an oven, the rice can be covered with a sheet of buttered or oiled brown paper, the lid put in place, and the rice cooked in a 350° oven for 15 minutes. With a fork stir into the rice about 1 Tablespoon Butter and serve. This is particularly wonderful with chicken, especially chicken Cromwell. It is troublesome but good.

300 Boiled Wild Rice
Cooking time 45 minutes

Wash rice thoroughly in cold water. Add ½ teaspoon Salt to 3 cups Boiling Water. Into this pour the rice slowly, so as not to stop the boil. Boil without stirring until rice is tender, from 40 to 45 minutes, and water is absorbed. Shake pot occasionally to keep rice from sticking. Stir in 1 Tablespoon Butter or Margarine with a fork, mixing well into rice.

301 White or Wild Rice, Pressure-cooked

Cooking time 20 minutes

Wash thoroughly, as described in recipe for boiled rice (No. 296), 1 cup White or Wild Rice. Bring to a boil in the cooker 4 cups Water seasoned with ½ teaspoon Salt. Into boiling water drop the rice slowly, so as not to stop the boil. Close cooker, and when steam comes out of vent put the indicator in place. Cook 10 minutes after the indicator reaches fifteen pounds pressure or "cook" position. Cool cooker in cold water for a minute and remove top. Wash rice in a strainer in cold water. Pour off water in which rice was cooked and return rice to cooker. Shake cooker over a flame until rice is dry, about 4 minutes. Add 1 Tablespoon Butter or Margarine to the rice and mix it in well with a fork. Serve rice very hot.

DESSERTS

Desserts fall into many classes: fruits—fresh, dried, preserved and canned; puddings, custards and blancmanges, mixed or from packages ready mixed for instant use; ice creams, cakes, pies, and pastries. Whole books have been written about them. We list only a few for you to use as points of departure. They may sound complicated, but we leave most of the short desserts to your imagination and give only suggestions for variations you may have forgotten or overlooked.

Desserts should always create a little stir. They should have glamour. As most of the appetite is gone when they arrive, they must have eye and appetite appeal. Dress them up. Give them garnishes. Even if the larder offers only prunes, do something with them to make them even a little spectacular. Give your crew and guests something to remember and to be grateful for.

Gelatin and cornstarch are the basis for most of the package desserts. With a package of each aboard you can go a long way.

If you prefer only to add water or milk, stock up on such favorites as Jello, which comes in a number of fruit flavors, My-T-Fine, which is available in many flavors including a good butterscotch, Royal Gelatins in a number of flavors, Royal Puddings, Royal Tapioca, and Bernsdorf Chocolate Pudding. Then there is Junket of childhood memory and S. S. Pierce's Epicure and Overland brands, which include coffee and wine jellies. That offers enough variety for quite a cruise, and it doesn't begin to exhaust the list of different manufacturers or the kinds of preparations, each of which has some difference or improvement which justifies its wide sale. These and most of the following desserts take little cooking time but require an hour or more to chill. They last for a couple of days.

Canned fruits are available almost anywhere in profusion. Study this list and see if you have missed any bets in the past that might brighten future meals.

Apple butter
Apple sauce
Apples, baked
Apples, sliced or quartered
Apples, whole
Apricots, halved, peeled or unpeeled
Apricots, whole
Bananas
Blackberries
Blueberries
Boysenberries
Cherries, black
Cherries, red
Cherries, white
Citrus peel
Citrus pulp
Coconut
Crabapples
Cranberry jelly
Cranberry sauce
Currants
Dewberries
Elderberries
Figs
Fruit cocktail
Fruits, for salad
Fruits, spiced or pickled
Fruits, strained
Gooseberries
Grapefruit
Grapefruit juice
Grapefruit and oranges
Grape pulp
Grapes
Huckleberries
Lemon juice
Loganberries

Olives, ripe	Pineapple, spears
Orange juice	Pineapple, tidbits
Papayas	Pineapple, sauce
Peaches, halves	Plums
Peaches, sliced	Prunes
Peaches, whole	Prunes, dry
Pears, halves	Quinces
Pears, sliced	Raspberries, black
Pears, whole	Raspberries, red
Pineapple, chunks	Rhubarb
Pineapple, crushed	Strawberries
Pineapple, sliced	Youngberries

Combinations of fresh and canned fruits are highly recommended. For example, try combining canned black cherries with sliced bananas. In addition, there are the many fine dried fruits, most of which are available in small tight packages that will keep indefinitely. Nowadays these dried fruits are treated so that they require no long soaking. They have joined the "quick-cooking" family. They include apples, apricots, dates, figs, peaches, pears, and prunes, not to say currants and raisins, which are such important additions to many puddings. Even if you do not get around to cooking them, these dried fruits are much better for your crew to nibble on than doughnuts or crackers.

Candied fruits and fruit peels come in 3-ounce tins. They keep well and are really wonderful to dress up desserts. They include citron, orange peel, lemon peel, red cherries, mixed fruits, and pineapple. The cherries and pineapples are worth having for old-fashioneds alone.

You can really build quite a reputation for yourself if you combine some of these fancy items with the simple dessert to which a two-burner stove limits you. It is a lot of fun, too, almost like getting your first chemistry set as a kid.

(Each recipe serves 4.)

302 Apple Snow
Cooking time 12 minutes

Press 1 cup Apple Sauce, either canned or freshly made, through a fine sieve to take out all the lumps. Beat the **Whites of 3 Eggs** until very stiff. Stir the apple sauce slowly into the egg whites, adding 2 **Tablespoons Powdered Sugar**, if you have it. If not, use granulated sugar. Add also ¼ teaspoon **Salt**. Chill in the icebox if possible. This can be served either alone or with a boiled custard sauce (No. 306).

303 Apples Normandy
Cooking time 30 minutes

Peel, core, and cut into thin slices 4 **Eating Apples**. In a large, heavy frying pan melt 4 **Tablespoons Butter or Margarine** (the latter is not as good). Over a low flame or with an asbestos pad between flame and pan, fry the apple pieces evenly until a golden color, soft but not browned, 3 to 6 minutes. Apples must be flat in the pan and cook evenly. As soon as apples are done, make a layer of them in an oven dish, a small frying pan, or a saucepan that can be taken to the table. Sprinkle with 1 teaspoon **Sugar** and a pinch of **Cinnamon**. Then add another layer of apple pieces and repeat with cinnamon and sugar. Continue until all the apple has been put into the new container. Put 1 **Tablespoon Butter** cut into small pieces on the top, cover and keep warm until time to serve dessert. Then warm ½ cup **Applejack, Brandy, or Rum** in a saucepan. Pour over the apples and light. Serve flaming. Very spectacular.

304 Vanilla Blancmange
Cooking time 1 hour

In ½ cup **Milk** mix until smooth 3 **Tablespoons Cornstarch** (Duryea's for some reason or other seems best to us), ¼ teaspoon **Salt,** and 4 **Tablespoons Sugar.** Meanwhile heat **3 cups Fresh or Diluted Evaporated Milk** in a double boiler. **P**our a little of this milk into the cornstarch and sugar mixture and then pour all of the cornstarch mixture into the milk in the double boiler. Stir all the while until it begins to thicken, about 6 minutes. Remove spoon, cover double boiler, and let cook for 25 minutes. Take off fire, cool and add 1 teaspoon **Vanilla Extract** (if you do not have vanilla, use rum or brandy). Turn into a bowl that has been wet with cold water and let cool. As soon as cold, put into the icebox. If you wish individual servings and your galley has small cups or sherbet glasses, wet them instead of the bowl and fill with the mixture. Decorate with any bright-colored jelly, such as apple, or with strawberry or raspberry jam. Boiled custard (No. 306) is sometimes served as a sauce.

This dessert can be the beginning of a whole series of cornstarch desserts, as it can be flavored with chocolate, caramel, cordials, or fruit flavors. A handful of blueberries or raspberries cooked in it give it a really rich and different look. ½ cup **Shredded Coconut** added gives another dessert, while ¾ cup **Crushed Pineapple, Strawberry Jam, or Crushed Macaroons** starts it in a new direction. A box of cornstarch brought aboard to a cook with a good imagination, and the what-will-we-have-for-dessert problem is settled.

305 Blueberry Flummery

Cooking time 1 to 2 hours

Butter 6 slices **White Bread** and sprinkle lightly with **Cinnamon.** Cook 3 cups **Blueberries** and ¾ **cup Sugar** for 12 minutes with ½ **cup Water.** Arrange bread and berries in alternate layers. Top layer should be berries. Put in icebox long enough to chill thoroughly, at least 1 hour. Slice and serve with slightly sweetened cream or with **Hard Sauce** made by combining **3 Tablespoons Butter** with **9 Tablespoons Sugar.**

306 Boiled Custard

Cooking time 40 minutes

In a small saucepan put **2 cups Fresh or Diluted Evaporated Milk** on the fire to heat. Do not boil. In the top of a double boiler off the stove, beat **4 Egg Yolks** lightly with a fork. Add to them ¼ **cup Sugar** and ⅛ **teaspoon Salt.** Add the hot milk mixture, stirring slowly. Put top of double boiler in bottom over boiling water. Water should be about 1 inch deep. It must not touch the bottom of the upper pot. Cook, stirring constantly until custard is thick enough to coat the spoon, about 4 minutes. That is, when the spoon is lifted out, there should be a thin coating of custard remaining on the spoon. Pour custard through a layer of cheesecloth in a strainer. Cool custard and add ½ **teaspoon Vanilla, Coffee Extract, Rum, or Brandy.**

Why it is called "boiled" custard is one of those unsolved mysteries. It shouldn't boil. It is, however, another wonderful dessert that is a "mother" to so many others. For instance, floating island is made as follows:

Cooking time 30 minutes

Beat the **Whites of the Eggs** the yolks came from very, very stiff (stiff enough to support a heavy spoon) and mix them after they are stiff with ½ **cup Sugar,** well beaten in and added gradually. Then cook spoonfuls of this meringue in the hot milk you are preparing for the custard. Let the meringues stay in the hot milk 2 minutes, and then turn over with a fork and let the other side cook for a minute and a half. Longer is too long, as the overcooked meringue will deflate. Remove the cooked meringues to a piece of cheesecloth stretched over a colander to drain. When custard has been cooled, flavored, and poured into the bowl in which it is to be served, arrange the meringues on top of it. If you want to be extra fancy, dot them with tiny bits of bright jelly.

Tipsy pudding can be made from this boiled custard. Arrange some pieces of **Stale Cake** (sponge cake or lady fingers are best) in the bottom of a bowl. Sprinkle the cake well with **Rum**, about 2 Tablespoons. Season the custard with **Brandy, 2 teaspoons**, and pour over the cake. Let cool and serve.

Lady fingers and cut-up candied fruit can be combined in the bottom of a bowl. Pour the rum-flavored custard over it and you have what the boys who sail out of Cowes call a "trifle."

With this as a start you can think up dozens of desserts. Why don't you?

307 Bavarian Cream
Cooking time 1 hour 15 minutes

Soak 1 Tablespoon Gelatin (1 envelope) in 2 Tablespoons Cold Water for 5 minutes. Heat 1¾ cups Fresh or Diluted Evaporated Milk with ½ cup Sugar and ¼ teaspoon Salt. Dissolve gelatin in the hot milk, stirring well. Take off the fire, stirring well until mixture begins to set, about 7 minutes. Then add 1½ teaspoons Vanilla. Beat until stiff 1 cup Heavy Fresh Cream. Fold cream well into the gelatin mixture, that is, stir from the bottom. Pour into a wet mold or bowl. Chill thoroughly, at least 1 hour. When ready to serve, turn out on a large platter or dish and surround with crushed and sweetened berries, stewed fruit, boiled-down maple syrup, or a sauce made as follows:

In a heavy frying pan over a medium flame melt 1 cup Sugar. When sugar has turned a light brown, about 5 minutes, add

¾ cup **Boiling Water.** Cook together until syrup has reached the consistency of good maple syrup, about 6 minutes. Then add 3 **Tablespoons Preserved or Crystallized Ginger** cut up fine. Pour around the Bavarian cream as soon as it cools.

308 Marion's Dessert

Cooking time 1 hour 15 minutes

Better make at breakfast time or the night before. Whip until stiff 1 **pint Fresh Cream.** To it add ½ **cup Sugar,** stirring it in well. Soak ½ **Tablespoon (1 envelope) Gelatin** in 3 **Tablespoons Cold Water** for 5 minutes, and then pour it into 1½ squares **Unsweetened Chocolate** melted in a small saucepan. Stir until gelatin is well dissolved, about 5 minutes. Fold into whipped cream (cut vertically down with a spoon, draw spoon across bottom of bowl, and bring it vertically up. Repeat about 12 times) until cream and chocolate are thoroughly mixed. Put into a wet mold or bowl and put in the icebox to chill completely, at least 1 hour. Turn out of mold or bowl onto a platter or large plate. Serve surrounded by boiled custard (No. 306).

309 Coffee Crème

Cooking time 1 hour 20 minutes

Better make at breakfast time or the night before. Soak 1 **Tablespoon (1 envelope) Gelatin** in 3 **Tablespoons Cold Water** for 5 minutes. In a small saucepan heat together 1½ cups **Fresh or Diluted Evaporated Milk** and 1½ cups **Strong Coffee.** Add the gelatin and stir until it is completely dissolved and begins to thicken. In the top of a double boiler off the stove, beat until lemon yellow the **Yolks of 3 Eggs,** add 3 **Tablespoons Sugar,** and stir in well. Beat the **Whites of Eggs** until stiff. Put top of double boiler over bottom in which

1 inch of water should be boiling. The boiling water must not touch the top pot. Pour milk mixture in on top of egg yolks, stirring well until it begins to thicken, about 7 minutes. Then fold in the beaten whites of the eggs. (Cut vertically down with a spoon, draw spoon across bottom of bowl, and bring it vertically up. Repeat about 12 times.) Add **1 teaspoon Vanilla** and stir in. Pour into a wet mold or bowl and chill, at least 1 hour. Turn out on a large plate or platter.

310 Bar-le-Duc

Preparation time 10 minutes

Mix together until very smooth **2 packages (3 ounces each) Philadelphia Cream Cheese** with **3 Tablespoons Heavy Cream or Undiluted Evaporated Milk**. Into this mixture fold **3 Tablespoons of Canned Gooseberries or Currants**. (Cut vertically down with a spoon, draw spoon across bottom of bowl, and bring it vertically up. Repeat about 12 times.) Put in a wet bowl or mold. It is better thoroughly chilled for 1 hour or so. Serve with crisp crackers, on which the mixture should be spread.

311 C. D. N.'s Favorite

Preparation time 0 minutes

A good easy-to-fix dessert. Give each person an apple and a good portion of Camembert cheese. Each can peel the apple, cut it into slices, spread it with Camembert, and enjoy a delicious flavor combination.

312 Crepes

Cooking time 30 minutes

In crepes, or pancakes, you have another of those "mother" desserts. All sorts of combinations, simple or complex, can be concocted to delight your crew and guests. You can make them with prepared pancake flour, doctored up a little. A correct and authentic recipe is easy, and it really is enough better to warrant the extra trouble.

Sift together ½ cup Flour, ¼ teaspoon Salt, 1 Tablespoon Sugar. Moisten this with 3 Tablespoons Rum or Brandy. Add enough Milk or Cream, or Evaporated Milk Diluted or Undiluted, to make mixture fluid enough to beat. Add 1 Egg. Beat well for a minute or so and add Another Egg. Beat again for a minute and then slowly add Milk or Cream until the batter has the consistency of light cream. Then add 2 Tablespoons Melted Butter. Stir very well and test batter for thickness of crepes. To do this heat a heavy frying pan and in it put ½ teaspoon Butter. When the butter reaches the foamy stage pour in about 2 tablespoons of the batter. Tilting the frying pan in all directions, spread the batter around to make a very thin cake. When bubbles begin to break on the top, about 40 seconds, turn cake over and cook on the other side. It will take some adjustment of the heat to get it so that the crepe will be cooked through without being burned on the bottom. That can be done by turning the flame up or down or by trying combinations of asbestos pads between pan and flame. It will also be necessary to thin batter with milk or thicken it with flour until you have a crepe that is the right thickness. It should be as thin as can be handled without breaking. Fresh butter should be put in for each crepe. When crepes are cooked set aside. It is not essential to keep them very hot, as they will be warmed up in the sauce in which they are to be served.

Crepes can be spread with bitter orange marmalade, sprinkled with sugar and grated orange peel, or with other combinations that your imagination might suggest. Then roll them up and put them in a small frying pan or saucepan or dish that can be heated. When ready to serve heat the pan or dish, pour over crepes ¼ cup of Brandy, Rum, or any Cordial you may have on board. Light liquor, baste crepes in the flaming liquid, and serve.

313 Crepes Suzette
Cooking time 35 minutes

A lot of trouble and worth it only if you want to be very fancy. Make crepes as in recipe for crepes (No. 312). As each crepe is cooked, fold it in half and then in quarters. Set aside. You will need at least 2 for each person. To make the sauce, mix 1 **Tablespoon Grated Orange Rind** and 1 **Tablespoon Grated Lemon Rind** with 3 **Tablespoons Granulated Sugar** on which 4 **Drops Vanilla** has been put. (Most of the recipes suggest that this be kept in a tight can or bottle for 3 or 4 days, but it is not necessary.) In a clean small frying pan melt 6 **Tablespoons Butter**. Stir in it the prepared sugar until it is well melted and mixed. Now add 2 **Tablespoons** of each of the following: **Curaçao, Kirschwasser, and Brandy.** Set mixture afire as soon as it has warmed and put folded crepes in it. Baste crepes thoroughly with the sauce. All this last process should be done at the table so that the crepes can be served very hot.

314 French Toast
Cooking time 30 minutes

The French call this Pain Perdu or Lost Bread, probably because the bread would otherwise be wasted because it was not used up. Remove the crusts from 8 **slices White Bread.** In a small saucepan heat together 1 **cup Fresh or Diluted Evaporated Milk**, 1 **Tablespoon Sugar**, and 1 **teaspoon Vanilla.** Let cool, and then dip the bread in, one slice at a time. Do not let bread get soaked. Drain bread and then dip into 1 **Egg** beaten well. In a heavy frying pan melt 3 **Tablespoons Butter or Margarine.** With an asbestos pad between pan and burner, cook toast until it is a golden brown, about 4 minutes on each side. Sprinkle very generously with **Sugar** and serve. Or you can serve with maple or cane syrup or, for hearty souls, with molasses.

315 Condés

Cooking time 1 hour 30 minutes

A large number of French desserts are built around condés which are rice cooked in milk with egg yolks and butter added in many combinations with cooked fruits. They are easy to prepare, can be done ahead of time for several meals, and are filling.

Put **1 cup Rice** in **8 cups Cold Water.** Bring to a boil for 2 minutes. Pour off water, and in colander run cold water over the rice. Put **2½ cups Fresh or Diluted Evaporated Milk, ½ cup Sugar, ½ teaspoon Salt,** and **a little Grated Orange or Lemon Peel** in a saucepan. Add the rice to it and simmer gently until the rice is soft and the milk has been absorbed, about 22 minutes. Beat up **2 Egg Yolks** with **1 Tablespoon Melted Butter.** Stir this thoroughly into the rice. Form the rice into a nicely shaped mound on a large plate and cool or chill thoroughly in icebox, about 1 hour. Just before serving pour over it some stewed or canned fruits that have been boiled down, with the addition of a little sugar, until their syrup is good and thick. The fruits—apricots, peaches, prunes, pears or whatever you choose—can be cooked until very tender and then made into a purée by beating until they are a fine even pulp. This can be chilled and spread evenly over the rice. Such condés can be flavored with rum, brandy, or any cordial you may happen to have aboard.

316 Norwegian Prune Pudding

Cooking time 1 hour 15 minutes

Pit 1 cup Stewed Prunes, either canned or freshly cooked. Add
¼ cup Juice, 1 cup Sugar, ⅛ teaspoon Salt, 1 cup Water.
Bring to a boil. Dissolve ⅓ cup Cornstarch in ⅓ cup Cold
Water and slowly add to the prune mixture, stirring all the
while. Cook mixture for 5 minutes, stirring constantly. Add
1 Tablespoon Lemon Juice and ½ teaspoon Cinnamon. Pour
mixture into a wet mold or bowl and chill at least 1 hour.
When ready to serve, unmold by turning bowl or mold upside
down over a platter or large plate. Surround with whipped
cream or cold boiled custard (No. 306) if you wish.

317 Pot de Crème Chocolat

Cooking time 1 hour 15 minutes

In 2 cups Very Hot Fresh or Diluted Evaporated Milk in a
double boiler, melt 1 pound Sweet Chocolate broken into
small bits. When chocolate is melted and well stirred in, remove from flame, cool a bit (so it won't cook the egg yolks),
and pour into 6 Egg Yolks that have been lightly beaten with
a fork. Stir mixture until well blended and pour into individual cups or into a wet bowl. Chill well at least 1 hour. If in
bowl, unmold on a platter or large plate. This is very rich,
but you can add whipped cream if you want it for decoration.

318 Pie Crust

Preparation time 30 minutes

For any pie you must first have your crust. A number of good
commercial pie crust mixes are available. Follow the directions on the package and you will have a perfectly adequate
crust. Of the dozens of recipes for pastry we have chosen this
one as the simplest and the easiest to do in a galley. However,
use your own if it seems easier or surer to you. In making any
pastry remember these points: Handle the pastry as little as

possible. Chill it as long as you possibly can: 10 minutes on the ice is almost a minimum, 6 hours is much better. Use as little liquid as possible—too much liquid makes the pastry soggy and heavy; too much shortening makes it dry and so crumbly that it is almost impossible to serve; if you use too much flour, your crust will be tough. It is important, you see, to use the quantities recommended in the recipe.

Put the flour sifter, or a fine strainer if you have no flour sifter, on a large sheet of paper. In it put **2 cups Flour**, carefully measured. Add **1 teaspoon Salt** and sift. Place sifter over a bowl and, picking paper up carefully by the edges, pour flour into sifter. Sift again. Measure out ⅓ cup of the flour and salt mixture and mix with it **¼ cup Cold Water**. With a knife in each hand, cut ⅔ cup **Butter, Margarine, or Lard** (half lard and half butter is best in our estimation) into the flour in the bowl until mixture is the consistency of small peas. With the hands mix into the flour-shortening enough of the flour paste to form the mixture into a ball. Chill for at least 10 minutes. Cut the dough into 2 pieces, one slightly larger than the other for the bottom crust. Spread a piece of wax paper, put pastry on it, and flatten it. Put another piece of wax paper over it, and with a rolling pin or a bottle roll out until it is about ⅛ inch thick. Roll in only one direction. Do not roll back and forth but lift roller at the end of a roll and start again in the same place as before. Bottom crust should be about 1 inch larger than the pan in which pie is to be baked, a 9-inch pan. Fold one half of the pastry over the other and lift over the pie tin. Unfold the pastry in place. Roll out the smaller piece of dough in the same way. After filling is in the pie, put in place and cut gashes in the center of it to let steam escape. Moisten the bottom crust along the edge of the pan to make the two crusts stick together and press top crust down with the tines of a fork. With a knife trim off the excess pastry along the edge of the pan.

319 Apple Pie

Preparation time, crust—30 minutes
Cooking time, pie—1 hour to 1 hour 20 minutes

(For boats with ovens.) Put bottom crust in pan as described in No. 318. Peel, core, and cut into very thin slices **8 Tart Apples**. Mix together ⅔ cup **Sugar**, ¼ teaspoon **Cinnamon**, ¼ teaspoon **Nutmeg**, ½ teaspoon **Salt**, and 1 **Tablespoon Cornstarch** or 2 **Tablespoons Flour**. Put this mixture in a paper bag and shake the apple pieces in it until they are well covered with the mixture. Arrange apple slices one overlapping the other, beginning about ½ inch from the outside edge of the pan and piling a little higher in the center. When slices are all arranged, sprinkle with 1 **Tablespoon Lemon Juice** and any of the sugar and spice mixture that is left in the bag. Dot the apples with 2 **Tablespoons Butter**. Wet edge of bottom crust with cold water. Put top crust in place, press down edges with the tines of a fork, put in the oven at 450°, and bake for 10 minutes. Turn oven down to 350° and bake for 40 to 60 minutes more, or until filling is soft. If crust begins to brown too much, put a piece of brown paper over it. A paper bag does well. Serve with good big hunks of American cheese.

320 Charles Gregory's Poor Man's Apple Pie

Preparation time, crust—30 minutes
Cooking time, pie—1 hour 10 minutes

(For boats with ovens.) Peel, core, and thinly slice **10 Tart Apples** to make a high pile in the middle of a pie tin. Over this place a thin sheet of pie crust (No. 318) slashed in the middle to let the steam escape and fastened to the edges of the pan by moistening the edge of the pan with water. Put into a 450° oven for 10 minutes and then lower the heat to 350° and bake for 40 minutes more. Take pie from oven, take off the crust in *w*ne piece, and invert it in another pie tin. Over apples in the pan shake ⅔ cup **Sugar**, and ¼ teaspoon **Salt** and grate over apples 1½ **Whole Nutmegs**. This is the important step that makes it the genuine Connecticut product (3 teaspoons of nutmeg *might* be substituted, if whole nutmegs could not be found on board). Stir in 4 **Tablespoons Butter** and put apple mixture in the inverted crust. Smooth out nicely and keep hot if possible until you are ready to serve it. Serve with American cheese in big hunks.

321 Hetty's Betty or Crustless Apple Pie

Cooking time—50 minutes

(For boats with ovens.) Peel, core, and slice **8 Tart Apples**. Arrange the slices around a pie tin, each slice overlapping another until the pan is well filled. Sprinkle with ⅔ cup **Sugar**, ¼ teaspoon **Salt**, ¼ teaspoon **Nutmeg**, and 3 **Tablespoons Melted Butter**. Place in a 450° oven and bake until apples are soft and beginning to brown slightly, about 40 minutes. Serve hot or cold.

322 Blueberry Pie

Preparation time, crust—30 minutes
Cooking time, pie—50 minutes

Line deep pie tin with pie crust (No. 318). Sprinkle **3 cups Blueberries** with 2 **Tablespoons Flour** and place in the pie tin. Sprinkle over berries ⅔ cup **Sugar** and ¼ teaspoon **Salt**. Stir berries gently until these ingredients are well mixed in. Put top crust in place after moistening bottom crust along edge of pan. To keep juice from running out into the oven, tie a band of wet cotton cloth like a collar around edge of pan or put two 2-inch pieces of macaroni sticking up through slits in the crust. Place in a 450° oven for 10 minutes and then lower the heat to 350° and bake for 30 minutes more. This same recipe can be followed for blackberry, gooseberry, currant, and strawberry pies. Vary the sugar content with the acidity of the fruit. When canned berries are used, increase the amount of flour to 4 tablespoons and decrease the sugar to ½ cup.

323   Rum Omelet

Cooking time 25 minutes

In omelet recipe (No. 260) substitute **6 Tablespoons Jamaica or Other Heavy Rum** for 6 tablespoons cream. Add **2 Tablespoons Sugar.** Cook omelet as in No. 260, but have very moist on top. When cooked and turned out on platter, sprinkle with **4 Tablespoons Sugar,** powdered if you have it. Pour over omelet ¼ **cup Warmed Rum** and set afire. Baste omelet by spooning burning rum over sugar on omelet until melted and fire has gone out. Serve at once.

CANDY

Sometimes there comes that craving for candy, and it is almost certain to be at the time that there is no candy on board. It is easy to make candy if a few simple rules are followed, and it is a great satisfaction to be able to produce it when it is really wanted. It is not probable that you will have a candy thermometer on board, so that the "soft ball" method of measuring whether it is ready to come off the stove will have to do. Take a little of the boiling candy in a spoon and drop it into a little cold water in the bottom of a cup. Roll it around by tilting the cup. If it forms into a reasonably compact ball, it is done. Or you can roll it around with the tips of your fingers. It should be fairly firm but not hard.

324   Fudge

Cooking time 30 minutes

Put into a large saucepan **2 cups Brown Sugar** (white may be substituted), **2½ squares Unsweetened Chocolate** (we like Baker's best) cut up in small pieces, **½ teaspoon Salt**, and **¾ cup Milk**. **2 Tablespoons Corn Syrup** may be added, if you have it on board. Bring to a boil over a low flame or with an asbestos pad between flame and pan. Cook until mixture forms a medium stiff ball when put into cold water—about 25 minutes. Take off the fire and beat in **4 Tablespoons Butter**. When mixture is beginning to become stiff beat in **1 teaspoon Vanilla**. Pour out into a small well-buttered pan (a pie tin will serve). When fudge has partially cooled, about 5 minutes after it has been poured out, cut into squares. Let cool thoroughly before removing from pan.

325   Penuche

Cooking time 35 minutes

Melt **2 Tablespoons Butter** in a saucepan and add **2 cups Brown Sugar**, **¼ teaspoon Salt**, and **¾ cup Milk or Cream, Diluted or Undiluted Evaporated Milk** and stir until sugar is well dissolved. Bring to a boil and simmer without stirring until a drop of the candy in a little cold water makes a reasonably firm ball when rolled around by tilting the glass or with the fingers—about 25 minutes. Turn off flame and let candy cool. When it has cooled for about 3 minutes beat it until it is smooth and creamy. Add **1 teaspoon Vanilla** and beat for a minute. Add **¾ cup Chopped Walnuts or Other Nuts**. Beat again. Press into a well-buttered pan and cut into squares. It is ready to eat when it is cold.

COFFEE, TEA, AND CHOCOLATE

There are many ways of cooking coffee, and each of them is just right for the person who likes his coffee that particular way. We honestly think that a little experimentation with the instant coffees will be rewarding. Our particular favorite is Borden's, but we know other people who are better satisfied with Nescafé or Chase and Sanborn's. The only way you can be sure is to try them all and use the one that satisfies you best. The one great advantage of the instant coffees is that there is no waste, and no messy grounds to get rid of. We have found that boiling water is best. Put a spoon of the instant coffee into a cup and fill the cup with the boiling water. Stir it a moment and you have a good drink.

If you want coffee brewed on the spot, we think that the vacuum coffee makers give a better, more even, brand of coffee than any of the other methods. However, each has its champions. Whether you use the French filter method, a percolator, or a plain old boiled-coffee pot, a great deal depends on the coffee itself. It should be freshly ground with the particular grind that is suited to the method to be employed. And once the coffee is ground, the container should be kept tightly closed. We keep our coffee in a tight screw-top jar in the icebox on the theory that the cold keeps the volatile oils in the coffee instead of allowing them to escape into the air. Whatever else you do, keep your pot clean and well aired, if possible. Certainly the oldest and most generally used method in this country is one of the several variations of boiled coffee. Ours, made over campfires as well as over stoves, is as follows:

326 Boiled Coffee

Cooking time 16 minutes

For 4 people, 2 cups apiece, pour into the coffeepot **9 Heaping Tablespoons Coffee** and **a pinch of Salt** and **1 cup Cold Water.**

Stir coffee until well wet with the water, then add **7 cups Cold Water** and the **Shells of 3 Eggs** crushed (optional). Put on the fire and let come to a boil slowly. The instant the pot boils, take it off the flame. Cool for a minute and then bring to a boil again. Set off the stove and add ¼ **cup Cold Water**, washing down the grounds from the sides of the pot. Let stand 2 minutes and pour. It should be clear, black, and good. If you like your coffee stronger use more coffee, and if weaker, use less.

327 Tea

Cooking time 10 minutes

As with coffee, there are many ways of making tea. We are sure that your Aunt Mary will tell you that tea made in anything but a china pot isn't fit to drink. And she may be right, for a large proportion of the people of the world agree with her. However, good tea can be made in anything. In fact, some of the best tea we have ever drunk was brewed in a lard pail when the temperature of the surrounding country was at 23° below zero. The important thing is to have the water very hot and the tea very good.

We think this is the only way to make tea. First *heat the pot with hot water.* For 4 people, 2 cups apiece, put into the pot **6 heaping teaspoons Tea** and add only enough **Boiling Water** to cover the tea leaves. Let steep 3 or 4 minutes. Fill up pot with **Boiling Water.** Pour into cups through a strainer (or dispense with strainer if you don't mind tea leaves in your cup). Have additional boiling water to dilute tea if desired.

If you are serving more than 4 people, do *not* increase quantity of tea. Simply steep the tea 10 minutes. This will give you very strong tea. Then all you need to do is keep on diluting with boiling water to produce as many as 15 cups.

With tea bags each can steep his own in his own individual cup, or all can be put into the pot and made in the usual way.

The difficulty with steeping in the cups is that the tea cools too much before it is strong enough to drink. We do not believe tea bags make as good tea as the loose variety. However, with the bags it is much easier to get rid of the tea leaves, and perhaps that is worth having the poorer-tasting tea. On a cold day try serving warmed rum in the tea. We have seen sailors that really didn't care much for tea really go for it when served this way.

328 Hot Chocolate

Cooking time 15 minutes

Put into a saucepan 2 squares **Baker's Unsweetened Chocolate** or 4 ounces **Sweet Chocolate**. If the bitter chocolate is used, add ½ cup **Sugar**. If the sweet chocolate is used add **4 Tablespoons Sugar**. In either case add ¼ teaspoon **Salt**. Melt the chocolate in the saucepan over hot water. Then add **6 cups Milk**. Bring to a boil—about 10 minutes. With a rotary beater beat the hot chocolate hard for about 4 minutes. Take off the stove. Add 1 teaspoon **Vanilla** and beat again for a minute. A variation of this chocolate is to add **3 Tablespoons of Rum** instead of the vanilla.

DRINKS

"As he brews, so shall he drink"—
at least so said Ben Jonson.

COCKTAILS

You probably have your own particular specialty, but in case your misguided guests don't like your specialty we are including a few standard recipes, if "standard" can apply to concoctions that are improperly compounded and impiously confounded. We have a friend who conscientiously measures out each of the ingredients into the shaker. When done he sniffs the shaker, reaches for a gin or whiskey bottle and pours in an indeterminable amount. We might add that he makes almost the worst cocktail we know. However, you have all the right in the world to use any proportions and combinations you prefer, but for Pete's sake don't call them by the standard names. Cocktails are certainly subject to change. In the original *Bar Tender's Guide* by the redoubtable Jerry Thomas, the Manhattan had as much vermouth in it as it did whiskey. There was no Martini in the book but there was a Martinez, which may have been a misspelling. It had equal parts vermouth and gin and was further complicated by the addition of dashes of Boker's Bitters and maraschino! The Martini of today has really taken on at least four different guises. They are the Martini, the Dry Martini, the Gibson, and the Perfect. This is how they are made; that is, in some places: in other places they are made differently.

329 The Martini

Place ice in each of the glasses in which a cocktail is to be served. Chill the shaker by putting ice in it. Pour the water melted from the ice out of the shaker and put in, for each cocktail to be served, 1 cocktail glassful of Gin and ⅓ glassful of Good French Vermouth. Shake well. Dump ice out of cocktail glasses and fill glasses. Over each squeeze a small piece of Lemon Skin on which there is no bitter white and drop it in the glass. Pour the "dividend" left in the shaker just as soon as you can so it will not get too diluted by the melting ice. Mix only enough for one round. Make a new batch each time.

330 The Dry Martini

A Dry Martini is made in the same way as a Martini except that the ratio of gin to French vermouth is 4 to 1 instead of 3 to 1.

331 A Gibson

A Gibson is made in the same way as a Martini except that the ratio of gin to vermouth is changed to 5 of gin to 1 of French vermouth and a small pickled onion is put into the glass instead of the bit of lemon peel.

332 The Perfect

The Perfect is made like a Dry Martini except that the vermouth content is made up of half French vermouth and half Italian vermouth. A twist of orange skin without any of the white on it is substituted for the bit of lemon peel.

333 The Manhattan

A Manhattan is made like a Martini except that rye whiskey is used instead of gin and Italian vermouth is used instead of French vermouth. This can be made with bourbon or Scotch. A cherry is substituted for the bit of lemon peel.

334 The Dry Manhattan

The Dry Manhattan is made like the Manhattan except that the proportions are changed to 1 of French vermouth to 4 of rye whiskey.

335 The Daiquiri

For each cocktail to be served put into a chilled shaker the Juice of ½ Lime, 1 teaspoon Sugar, and 2 jiggers (6 Table, spoons) White Rum (Bacardi is best). Add plenty of **Finely Cracked Ice,** shake very hard, and serve in chilled glasses.

336   The Old-fashioned

Put 1 lump or 1 level teaspoon **Sugar** in the bottom of an Old-fashioned glass. Drop on it as much **Angostura Bitters** as it will absorb, no more. Add 1 **Tablespoon Water** and "muddle" —that is, crush the sugar until it is all dissolved in the water. Add 1 jigger (3 **Tablespoons or** ¼ cup) **Rye Whiskey.** Fill glass with **Finely Cracked Ice.** Decorate with a slice of lemon, a stick of pineapple, a section of orange, and a cherry, or some or none of them.

We have not included the hundreds of fancy cocktails such as the Alexander, the Sidecar, and the Stinger. They and most of the others require fluids not usually found on small boats. Ask for them at the club bar. The foregoing require that you have on board only rye whiskey, gin, Bacardi rum, Italian and French vermouths, Angostura bitters, small pickled onions, cherries, limes, lemons, and oranges, which last two you probably have anyway.

LONG DRINKS

Again their names are legion. They include a wide variety of fizzes, highballs, Collinses, and punches. We will list only the few that we think you will get calls for. Most popular of these are:

337   The Tom Collins

Into a shaker over a few lumps of ice put the **Juice of** ½ **Lemon,** ½ **Tablespoon Powdered Sugar** and 1 **jigger or** ¼ **cup Gin.** Shake well. Pour into a large highball glass (10 or 12 ounces). Add a couple of good-sized lumps of ice and fill up glass with **Club Soda.** Stir only enough to mix.

338   The Rum Collins

This is made the same as the Tom Collins except that rum, usually white rum of the Bacardi type, is substituted.

339   The Whiskey Collins

This is made the same way as the Tom Collins except that whiskey is substituted. Any of the ryes, bourbons or Scotches will do.

340   The Gin Rickey

The Gin Rickey is made the same way as the Tom Collins except that the juice of 1 lime is substituted for the lemon juice.

FIZZES

The fizzes are a proud group. They usually include the white of an egg.

341   The Silver Fizz

This is sometimes called a Gin Fizz. In a shaker with a little ice put the Juice of ½ Lemon, ½ Tablespoon Sugar, 1 jigger or ¼ cup Gin and the White of 1 Egg and shake well. Pour into a large highball glass and fill up with Club Soda. This is usually decorated with a slice of lemon.

342   The Golden Fizz

This is like the Gin Fizz except that the yolk of the egg is usually substituted for the white. (It is more economical if you can get half of the party to drink Silver Fizzes and the other half to drink Golden Fizzes. We have never been able to do it!)

JULEPS, TODDIES, AND PUNCHES

343 The Mint Julep

Any propounder or prescriber really sticks his neck out here. Every colonel in each part of the country has his own particular ideas on what the perfect julep is; and with most of them it is a fighting matter, suh, if you don't agree with them. We can do only our simple best. This one we do know has pleased a lot of folks, but it is really a darn nuisance. Perhaps you had better not suggest it.

First wash your mint carefully, removing bruised or wilted leaves and trimming off any stems that seem discolored. Then take a lot of ice and pound it into fine snow. You can do this in a small canvas bag or in a husky dish towel. Dry the ice. This is the real secret if you want the glasses to frost. Put about 2 inches of the ice in the glass and sprinkle on it 1 teaspoon **Powdered Sugar.** Add another inch of ice and ½ **teaspoon Sugar.** Fill glass almost to the top with cracked ice and put on it another ½ teaspoon **Powdered Sugar.** Next stick at least **4 stems of Fresh Mint** down the sides of the glass. Pour in **2 jiggers (about ½ cup) Bourbon Whiskey,** the best that you can come by. Push a long-handled spoon down to the bottom of the glass and jiggle it up and down rapidly until the glass frosts thick on the outside. The time depends somewhat on the humidity, but 2 minutes of jiggling will usually do it. This also gently bruises the mint so that its delicate flavor permeates the whole lovely drink. As it takes some time to prepare each drink, don't let yourself in for it if you have a large crowd. There are lots of fake juleps, but this one is the real McCoy.

344 Gin and Bitters

Said to be wonderful as a seasick preventive. Sometimes called a Crystal Chandelier by the younger set. Put 2 dashes (about

⅛ teaspoon) **Angostura Bitters** in an Old-fashioned glass and twist glass around so that inside is well coated with the bitters. Pour in **2 jiggers (about ½ cup) Gin.** Fill glass up with ice. If there is no ice, add a little cold water. Not quite so good, but there have been times when it tasted better than champagne.

345 Hot Buttered Rum

Mash together until well blended **4 Tablespoons Butter, ½ cup Brown Sugar, ½ teaspoon Nutmeg,** and **¼ teaspoon Cinnamon.** Preheat a large heavy cup with boiling water, empty, and put in a heaping teaspoon of the butter-sugar mixture. Add **1 jigger (¼ cup) Heavy Dark Rum.** We like Myer's best. Fill up glass with very **Hot Water or Cider.** Stir and serve.

346 Hot Irish Toddy

Into an Old-fashioned glass put **1 teaspoon Sugar, 3 Cloves, a Slice of Lemon,** and **1 jigger (¼ cup) Irish Whiskey.** Fill glass with **Boiling Water.** Stir until the sugar is melted and serve at once. Drink hot and reach for another. Rye or Scotch whiskey or rum can be substituted for Irish, but it doesn't seem to have quite the same tang.

347 Rum Flip

For each drink to be served break **1 Egg** into the shaker. Add **2 teaspoons Sugar** (powdered is better) and **2 jiggers (½ cup) Good Jamaica Rum.** Shake very hard with large lumps of ice and pour into glasses. Sprinkle with **Nutmeg** and serve.

348   Sherry Flip

Make the same way as Rum Flip but use 3 jiggers (about ¾ cup) of good sherry in place of the rum.

349   Milk Punch

Into the shaker put 1 **jigger (about 3 Tablespoons) Jamaica or Other Dark Rum, ½ jigger (about 1½ Tablespoons) Brandy, 1 teaspoon Sugar, 1 cup Milk and a few lumps of Ice.** Shake until chilled, pour into a tall glass, sprinkle nutmeg on top, and serve.

Excellent milk punches can also be made with 1 **jigger (or ¼ cup) Scotch, Rye, or Bourbon Whiskey.**

350   Hot Milk Punch

Make this with same proportions as Milk Punch but use very hot milk and leave out the ice.

351   Planter's Punch

The rhyme goes, "one of sour, two of sweet, three of strong, and four of weak." That is, 1 **jigger (about 3 Tablespoons) Lime Juice, 2 teaspoons Sugar, 3 jiggers Good Jamaica Rum, and 4 jiggers Ice or Water.** That is the traditional one. It usually has a **dash of Angostura Bitters** in it and is decorated with the available fruits (not necessary).

352   For a Bad Cough

Pour into a heavy cup 1 **teaspoon Molasses, 1 teaspoon Honey, 1 jigger (about 3 Tablespoons) of Rum.** Fill with **almost Boiling Milk,** stir, and sip. You can get a bad cough several times a day.

10A Fish Chowder

Cooking time 45 minutes

Skin, bone, and fillet 2 lbs. white-fleshed fish (Nos. 11–14). Put skin, bones and head in pot, cover with water; boil for 20 minutes. Discard all but the liquid (see No. 20 Court Bouillon). Cut the fish fillets into bite-size portions. Put into Court Bouillon (water in which bones, etc. were cooked) with **4 Potatoes** peeled and cut into ½-inch cubes. Add **2 Sliced Onions**. Boil until potatoes are soft and fish will flake on a fork. Add **1 quart heated Fresh or Evaporated Milk, 1 teaspoon Salt** and ½ **teaspoon Pepper**. Serve very hot with pilot biscuits.

10B Persian Soup

Preparation time 10 minutes

This is a low-calorie delicious summer soup for four people. Peel and quarter the long way **2 Cucumbers** and remove the seeds. Dice Cucumbers in small pieces. Shake over them a **Teaspoon Cinnamon** and ½ **Teaspoon Salt**. Pour over Cucumbers **1 quart Buttermilk**. Put into refrigerator to chill. Serve with **chopped Fresh Mint** or a **pinch of Dry Mint** on top of each bowl.

10C Greek Lemon Soup

Cooking time 12 minutes

This is a favorite soup in the Middle East. For four, beat up **yolk of 1 Egg** with a fork and add **strained juice of 1 Lemon**. Heat **4 cups Chicken Broth** (we like College Inn best). Pour a little of the broth into the egg mixture and stir. Slowly add the rest of the broth, stirring all the while.

10D French Peasant Soup

Cooking time 30 minutes

Bring 1½ **quarts water** to a boil. Add 1 **Teaspoon Salt**. Meanwhile peel and cut into small dice 4 **Potatoes**. Cut roots and tops off 4 **Leeks** which should be cut into small dice. Take ½ **head of Cabbage** (Savoy Cabbage is best), core it and dice it. As soon as the water is boiling, put these three ingredients in and let them cook until the potatoes are soft, about 15 minutes. Add 1 **Cup Heavy Cream** and 2 **Tablespoons Butter** cut into small pieces, and add bit by bit, stirring all the while. This is a wonderful luncheon soup, particularly if served with Garlic Bread.

142A Green Beans in the Chinese Manner

Cooking time 7 minutes

Cut across in small pieces 2 **pounds String Beans** or 2 **packages of frozen** (not frenched) **String Beans (Green Beans)**, put into a saucepan 2 **Tablespoons Butter**, 1 **teaspoon Salt**. Fry beans, turning over constantly in butter for two or three minutes until each is covered with butter and salt. Then, for unfrozen beans, add ½ **Cup Boiling Water**. Thawing of frozen beans provides water enough. For about seven minutes the beans should be constantly turned. They should be cooked until all the liquid is absorbed and should be crisp and a beautiful green.

259A Eggs Marlou (Courtesy Mrs. Gordon Hyde)

Cooking time 10 minutes

This is a good luncheon dish. Into a frying pan with 2 **Tablespoons Butter** in it, carefully place 4 **Eggs**. Break yolks

289

when eggs are beginning to harden. Place on each a **Buttered Slice of Bread,** butter-side up. Cook until eggs are firm. Turn over and fry bread until it is nicely browned. Salt and pepper eggs and serve.

Index

INDEX

INDEX

INDEX

INDEX

298

INDEX

INDEX

NOTES AND RECIPES

NOTES AND RECIPES

NOTES AND RECIPES

NOTES AND RECIPES

NOTES AND RECIPES

NOTES AND RECIPES

NOTES AND RECIPES